# ANTIDUMPING LAWS and the U.S. ECONOMY

## GREG MASTEL

## ECONOMIC STRATEGY INSTITUTE

*M.E. Sharpe*
Armonk, New York
London, England

**Library of Congress Cataloging-in-Publication Data**

Mastel, Greg, 1963–
Antidumping laws and the U.S. economy / Greg Mastel.
p. cm.
Includes bibliographical references and index.
ISBN 0–7656–0325–X (hardcover : alk. paper). —
ISBN 0–7656–0326–8 (paperback : alk. paper)
1. Antidumping duties—Law and legislation—
Economic aspects—United States. I. Title.
HF1425.M37    1998
330.973—dc21          97–51248
CIP

Printed in the United States of America

The paper used in this publication meets the minimum requirements of
American National Standard for Information Sciences—
Permanence of Paper for Printed Library Materials,
ANSI Z 39.48-1984.

♾

BM (c)  10   9   8   7   6   5   4   3   2   1
BM (p)  10   9   8   7   6   5   4   3   2

To Andrew J. Dougherty,
my dear departed colleague and friend,
and
Alexander J. Mastel, my son

# Contents

# List of Tables and Charts

## Tables

# Acknowledgments

The author wishes to gratefully acknowledge the assistance of Lawrence Chimerine and Andrew Szamosszegi in preparing the economic simulations in this volume and for assistance throughout. Lois Hayes and Andrew Harig provided enormous research and editorial assistance; their efforts are deeply appreciated. Clyde Prestowitz, the entire staff of the Economic Strategy Institute, and a number of outside readers provided invaluable insights into the topic and comments on early drafts of this volume.

The author wishes to particularly thank Dataquest, Inc., and Gene Norrett, vice president of Dataquest, for assistance and advice in preparing the economic simulations of the semiconductor industry.

Any oversights, shortcomings, or errors, however, are entirely the responsibility of the author.

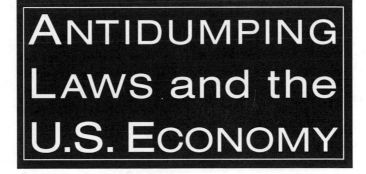

# ANTIDUMPING LAWS and the U.S. ECONOMY

# Introduction

# Antidumping and
# the World Economy

Antidumping laws are a widely accepted element of national trade policies. They aim to counter mercantilistic trade strategy by imposing offsetting duties on dumped imports: imports priced at less than their price in the home market or less than their cost of production. The first national antidumping law was adopted in Canada in 1904. A long list of other Western countries, including Australia, New Zealand, and Great Britain, adopted similar laws over the following two decades. The United States adopted its first antidumping law in 1916, and the current basic formulation for U.S. antidumping law was adopted in 1921.

In more recent years, many other countries have adopted antidumping laws. India, Poland, China, and Mexico—to name but a few examples—have all joined the antidumping club in the last fifteen years, and more countries draft their own antidumping laws each year.[1] (See also Appendix B.)

Provided they operate within prescribed limits, these laws are fully endorsed by the international trading system. In fact, antidumping laws and the world trading system, which was created after World War II to promote open markets and expand trade, have coexisted comfortably since the inception of the trading system. From the beginning, there was a consensus among the framers of the system, then known as the General Agreement on Tariffs and Trade (GATT), that antidumping laws were appropriate.[2] In later agreements, the GATT and its successor, the World Trade Organization (WTO), spelled out the operation of these laws in great detail.

It is fair to say, in fact, that antidumping laws helped to support the creation and continued operation of the world trading system. It is not an accident that most of the frequent users of antidumping laws—the United States, Western Europe, Canada, Australia, and so on—historically have been supporters of open trade and the world trading system. The connection is simple. Countries that practice protectionism do not need antidumping laws; barriers that keep out all imports, by definition, also keep out dumped imports. It is only those countries that open their market that find the need for some recourse against unfairly traded imports. In addition, assurances that imports are fairly traded support a domestic political consensus in favor of open markets.

As might be expected given their wide international acceptance, anti-dumping laws have strong intellectual underpinnings. The case for anti-dumping laws was first made authoritatively in 1923 by Jacob Viner, who argued that dumping did occur, that it was an economic threat, and that national laws to counter dumping were appropriate and desirable.[3]

Much recent U.S. literature on antidumping laws, however, has been critical, often unreasonably so. A book on antidumping laws published by the World Bank began with the jacket comment: "Antidumping is a threat to the liberal trading system that post–World War II Western leadership struggled courageously and effectively to create. It offers a GATT-legal means to destroy the GATT system."[4] The editor and primary author of the World Bank study, J. Michael Finger, later argued, "The most appealing option is to get rid of antidumping laws and to put nothing in their place. Then all the evils of such policy—its power politics, its bad economics, and its corrupted law—would be eliminated."[5]

The U.S. Congressional Budget Office (CBO) has accused U.S. anti-dumping law of coming "untethered from its rationale."[6] Other critics have variously criticized antidumping laws as "stack[ing] the deck in favor of local producers against their foreign competition,"[7] "fraud," "hypocrisy," and "inflict[ing] infinite amounts of unfairness in the name of fair trade."[8] Though there have been several balanced and reasoned analyses of anti-dumping laws in recent years, they have been far less frequent and have engaged in far less purple prose than the critics of the antidumping laws.[9]

Have, as the Congressional Budget Office contended, antidumping laws come untethered from their rationale?

No, and in fact the case for antidumping laws is now stronger than it has been at any time since they were created. Thanks to the most recent round of global trade negotiations, the WTO has an enormously detailed set of rules to police antidumping regimes and ensure that they are not turned into tools of protection. Further, as traditional trade barriers are lowered and international trade expands to include a larger and more diverse group of countries, dumping becomes more feasible and the list of countries that engage in dumping grows. In the United States and other countries enforc-ing antidumping laws, the focus of these laws has increasingly shifted to new players in the world economy, particularly China and Russia.

A widely respected trade scholar, John Jackson, described antidumping laws as an interface device to allow trade between differing national eco-nomic systems.[10] With the end of the Cold War, more diverse economic systems—namely, reforming Communist countries—have entered the world marketplace. Just as antidumping laws have blunted the most negative impacts of the mercantilist trade policies of the previous wave of entrants into global commerce, they can again serve this function with the latest group of entrants to the global marketplace. Far from being a tool of trade protection, antidumping laws remain a mechanism to allow trade between Western market-oriented economies and countries with different economic philosophies without undermining the economies or the industries in the open-market countries.

Further, as this volume will demonstrate through numerous case studies, antidumping laws also work to deter mercantilistic government trade strategies. In so doing, they help to restore the function of the market and prevent misallocation of resources in both the country in which dumping takes place and the country that sponsors the dumping.

Finally, the original economic rationale for antidumping laws articulated by Jacob Viner nearly seventy-five years ago remains just as valid today. Antidumping laws continue as the first and best line of defense for the U.S. economy against companies and countries that resort to predatory and mercantilist tactics to make trade gains. This volume makes the case that continued use of U.S. antidumping laws ensures that international trade works to the benefit of the U.S. economy. To advance the now tired debate on antidumping, it also considers in great detail criticisms of antidumping regimes. Finally, the changes in antidumping laws mandated by the Uruguay Round and current proposals for amendments to U.S. antidumping laws are considered.

A noted critic of antidumping laws, J. Michael Finger, argues that antidumping laws are merely protectionism with good public relations.[11] Actually, the public relations campaign in support of antidumping laws is quite poor; as is demonstrated in the pages that follow, insupportable criticisms of antidumping policy have frequently gone unanswered. More important, this volume will attempt to demonstrate that, far from being the tools of protectionists, U.S. antidumping laws have been and remain based upon sound economics and are an indispensable element of U.S. trade policy.

## Notes

1. General Accounting Office, *A Comparison of U.S. and Foreign Antidumping Practices* (Washington, DC: GAO, 1994).
2. For a good discussion, see John H. Jackson, *The World Trading System: Law and Policy of International Economic Relations* (Cambridge: MIT Press, 1994), pp. 225–229.
3. Jacob Viner, *Dumping: A Problem in International Trade* (Chicago: University of Chicago Press, 1923).

4. J. Michael Finger, ed., *Antidumping: How It Works and Who Gets Hurt* (Ann Arbor: University of Michigan Press, 1992), jacket quote.

5. Ibid., p. 57.

6. Congressional Budget Office, *A Review of U.S. Antidumping and Countervailing Duty Law and Policy* (Washington, DC: CBO, May 1994).

7. Claude Barfield, "Dumping Know-Nothingism," *Journal of Commerce,* March 18, 1993.

8. James Bovard, "Commerce's Latest Fair Trade Fraud," *Wall Street Journal,* January 28, 1993.

9. Examples of the balanced analyses are Thomas R. Howell, "Dumping: Still a Problem in International Trade," in *International Friction and Cooperation in High-Technology Development and Trade,* Charles W. Wessner, ed. (Washington, DC: National Academy Press, 1997), pp. 325–377; Laura D'Andrea Tyson, *Who's Bashing Whom? Trade Conflict in High-Technology Industries* (Washington, DC: Institute for International Economics, 1992), pp. 267–273; Clarisse Morgan, "Competition Policy and Antidumping: Is It Time for a Reality Check?" *Journal of World Trade* 30, no. 5 (1996).

10. Jackson, *World Trading System,* pp. 218–220.

11. This argument is made and restated in a number of ways by the author. See Finger, *Antidumping,* pp. 13–77.

# 1

# Antidumping Laws: Operation and History

Antidumping laws now have a history that stretches back nearly a century. The first step in any rational discussion of antidumping laws must begin with a careful look at that history. This chapter begins that process by analyzing three key questions: (1) How do antidumping laws function? (2) Why were antidumping laws created? (3) How do these laws relate to the international trading system?

## The Operation of Antidumping Laws

The World Trade Organization (WTO) and modern antidumping laws require national authorities to make two separate findings before antidumping duties can be imposed on imported products. First, national authorities must determine that dumping is taking place or that imports are being sold at less than fair value (LTFV). Second, national authorities must also determine that imports are causing "material injury" to the domestic industry that produces a product similar to the imported product in question.

### Less-than-fair-value Determinations

For imports to be sold at LTFV, one of three situations must be demonstrated to exist: (1) imports are priced at less than their price in the home market, (2) imports are priced at less than their price in a third market, or (3) if the above cannot be determined, imports are priced at less than their cost of production. In the United States, the U.S. Commerce Department's International Trade Administration (ITA) is charged with making LTFV determinations.[1]

In recent years, U.S. antidumping cases increasingly have been cases in which imported goods are found to have been sold at less than their cost of production; these are often referred to as "cost" cases. In some instances this is due to a lack of a significant domestic market for a product. Most of the increases, however, are due to new antidumping complaints involving non-market economies that frequently have no reliable domestic price. As a result, an increasing percentage of LTFV determinations are made on a cost basis instead of a price basis.

There are a number of controversies concerning "price" cases, mostly focusing upon whether an accurate apples-to-apples comparison of export sales and home market sales is being made. For example, is it appropriate to compare a single import sale (aka export sales price) with an average of home market prices, and what adjustments can be made to the home market price and the export sales price to exclude certain sales thought not to be representative for one reason or another (prices on special sales, etc.), distinguish wholesale from retail, and assess sales between related parties (i.e., foreign subsidiaries)? These issues are quite complex, and the definitive "right" answer on a specific issue can be difficult to determine. The most recent round of global trade negotiations, which is discussed later in this chapter, set credible standards on most of these difficult issues, and these standards are likely to form the basis of a consensus solution that will last for a number of years.

Cost cases, however, are substantially more controversial than price cases. The most potentially telling criticism leveled at cost cases—that selling below the cost of production is a rational business strategy—is addressed in great detail in Chapter 5. Two other critiques deserve a brief discussion. First, the U.S. methodology in cost cases is criticized for including arbitrary cost factors, such as a standard factor for profit. Of course, determinations on issues such as this are inherently arbitrary, but the determinations made by U.S. authorities have a rational basis drawn from actual experiences and are no more arbitrary than any other profit factor that could be chosen. Further, not including any factor for profit, as some critics have suggested, is certainly not in keeping with normal business practice and thus is far more unrealistic than including a reasonable factor for profit.

Critics have also focused upon the U.S. practice of using surrogate-market costs to determine the true cost in certain countries in which a true market does not exist and thus true market costs are elusive. For instance, in many cases this involves relying on costs in India as a surrogate for costs in China. Not surprisingly, a choice of a surrogate will always be a debatable choice, and the costs in the surrogate are not likely to be precisely the same as the costs in the country accused of dumping. Surrogates are used, however, only in those cases in which the alleged dumping country does not have an established market that would allow costs to be determined. Further, though they are only a rough approximation, as long as the surrogate chosen is reasonably similar to the alleged dumper, using a surrogate providcs a reasonably close estimate of cost,[2] and this approach is the only real alternative to having U.S. authorities simply throw up their hands and allow nonmarket economies to dump.[3] (European and Australian officials employ similar procedures; although both are seeking to refine their procedures.)

The evolution of current nonmarket economy dumping procedures, the controversy surrounding them, and their likely future application are considered in detail in Chapters 3 and 4.

Another sometimes controversial practice of the ITA in developing cost and price information is that of using the best information available (BIA) to set cost figures. If the respondent company does not participate in the investigation, this often means that the cost data will be drawn from that presented by the petitioner. A number of foreign commentators have called this process unfair. Critics, however, seem to ignore the reality that there is no practical alternative, since if the respondent refuses to participate, there is no alternative source of information.

The same commentators often complain that it is costly and difficult for foreign respondents to provide this information—the business confidentiality of which is protected by U.S. law. It is certainly true that gathering such data is a burden, but it does not seem a greater burden than that required to comply with various regulations or to respond to discovery proceedings on other matters, such as discrimination or environmental litigation. Most important, however, is that there is simply no alternative; critics would hardly be more satisfied if the ITA simply made up data, and the knowledge that BIA will be used if they do not cooperate is a powerful incentive for respondents to fully participate in proceedings.

### Material-Injury Determinations

From the outset, U.S. antidumping laws have incorporated the concept that for antidumping duties to be applied, it must be demonstrated not only that imports are being sold at LTFV but also that those dumped imports are causing injury or threaten to cause injury to the domestic industry that is in competition with the dumped imports. As a result, an antidumping law is always, at best, a partial remedy; it offsets only future injury after injury has already taken place. The theory behind this linkage is simple: If the dumped imports are not causing injury, there is no need to incur the administrative expense or the potential trade costs of imposing duties. When antidumping laws were endorsed by the world trading system, the notion that both dumping and injury must be present before duties can be imposed was incorporated.[4]

In the United States, the material-injury determination is made by the U.S. International Trade Commission (ITC). The ITC is an unusual administrative body. It is an independent agency led by three Republican and three Democratic commissioners. Every two years, the chairmanship of the ITC rotates between the Republicans and Democrats. ITC commissioners are appointed by the president and confirmed by the U.S. Senate for a nine-year term. In addition to making material-injury determinations in anti-dumping and countervailing-duty cases, the ITC also performs various analytical tasks, such as assessing the potential impact of trade agreements.

The definition of what constitutes material injury is a matter of some debate. The statute itself is not of much help. It defines material injury as "harm that is not inconsequential, immaterial or unimportant."[5] From the outset, under both U.S. law and the world trading system, material injury included not only actual material injury but also the threat of material injury in the imminent future; threat was judged by examining factors such as the size of the dumping margin, economic trends in the industry, and the past behavior of the alleged dumper(s).[6]

Also, material injury was understood to be a lesser test than the serious-injury test, which was required for relief under the safeguards provisions of the GATT, and now the WTO, as well as under the U.S. Section 201 statute. A number of factors, including import market share, the rate at which imports are increasing, the impact of imports on domestic prices, the financial strength of the domestic industry, and the level of dumping found by the Commerce Department, are all considered in making material-injury determinations. The result is that there are no hard-and-fast rules as to when injury occurs and when it does not. Beyond the established minimum levels of imports in U.S. law and the WTO guidelines, there is no set level at which injury is certainly occurring or certainly not occurring.[7]

In practice, each ITC commissioner has his or her own personal standard for determining injury. One personal standard often is not the same as that of another commissioner and some commissioners vote that injury is occurring far more often than others. As the makeup of the commission shifts, the effective standard for injury shifts. Commissioners' discretion does have some limits, however, since decisions of the ITC can be reviewed by U.S. courts and dispute settlement panels under both the North American Free Trade Agreement (NAFTA) and the WTO.

Further, if the U.S. Congress feels that U.S. laws are not being properly implemented, they can be changed, and if necessary the U.S. ITC can be changed (or not funded) by act of Congress. Various members of Congress have even suggested the possibility of eliminating the ITC and allowing the Commerce Department to make both the LTFV determination and the injury determination; in many other countries, including those of the European Union, a single administering authority makes both determinations. In short, the discretion of ITC commissioners in making injury determinations is wide but not unlimited. Inevitably, however, administering authorities will have considerable discretion in applying particular sets of facts to a general standard set by the WTO or U.S. law. The alternative of trying to specify in agreements or statutes all possible situations in which material injury may occur is unlikely to be preferable or even possible.

## *The Timetable for U.S. Laws*

In the United States, the U.S. Commerce Department and the U.S. ITC function simultaneously in making LTFV and injury determinations. After a case is filed by a domestic industry, the Department of Commerce has 20 days to determine whether the petition meets the basic requirements for an antidumping petition. (It should be noted that, if it chooses, the Commerce Department can self-initiate an antidumping investigation without receiving a petition, but this power is rarely used.) If so, four separate administrative determinations must be made before duties are finally put in place. Within 45 days after the petition is filed, the U.S. ITC makes its preliminary determination of injury (see Table 1.1). At this point, the ITC is generally less rigorous in imposing the injury test, on the theory that this is only a preliminary determination and full rigor will be applied in the final determination, when more complete information is available. Nonetheless, as is noted in the next chapter, a number of petitions do fail this initial injury test and are terminated.

The next step is the Commerce Department's preliminary LTFV finding, which must occur within 115 days of the preliminary injury finding or within 160 days after the petition was filed. A negative finding (a finding of no duty or a duty below the de minimis level of 2 percent) does not, however, terminate the case at this point. After the preliminary determination, the Commerce Department takes further information and comment on its preliminary finding and completes its final LTFV injury determination, which comes no more than 75 days after the preliminary LTFV determination or 235 days after the petition was filed. If the final LTFV determination is negative (zero duty or a duty less than the de minimis level), the case is terminated. If the finding is affirmative (a duty above de minimis) at the preliminary level, the importer is subject to a "suspension of liquidation," which normally requires the importer to post a bond or otherwise guarantee payment of the duty from this point on, pending completion of the litigation. After a final LTFV affirmative, the suspension of liquidation is continued pending the final ITC injury determination.[8]

The ITC's final determination is made within 45 days of the Commerce

## Table 1.1 **Summary of U.S. Dumping Determination Procedures**

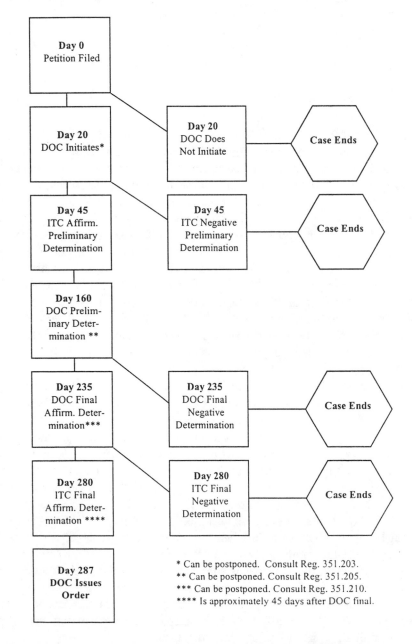

* Can be postponed.  Consult Reg. 351.203.
** Can be postponed. Consult Reg. 351.205.
*** Can be postponed. Consult Reg. 351.210.
**** Is approximately 45 days after DOC final.

*Source: FR* Doc. 97-12201, vol. 62, no. 96, May 19, 1997, p. 27424.

Department's final determination or within 280 days after the filing of the petition. For an affirmative injury finding, at least half of the commission must decide that there has been some injury. U.S. law is sometimes criticized for designating a tie vote an affirmative decision. It is difficult to understand how making a tie vote a negative decision would be any less arbitrary or why a bias against imposing duties in cases in which dumping has already been identified (the Commerce Department's final decision has already been made by this point) would be a preferable outcome. If the ITC's final determination is negative, the case is terminated, the bond requirement is vacated, and imports continue to enter the United States without an antidumping duty. If the ITC decision is affirmative, the duty determined by the Commerce Department is imposed back to the date of the suspension of liquidation. The total length of an antidumping investigation from filing to the ITC's final determination is normally limited by law to 280 days, with the order issued on the 287th day, but in complex cases the deadlines can be extended and in "critical circumstances" they can be shortened.[9]

Under changes in U.S. law passed as a result of the new WTO requirements, all antidumping orders are subject to a sunset review after five years. At this point the duty is terminated unless the Commerce Department and the ITC determine that such action "would be likely to lead to continuations or recurrence of dumping and injury."[10] The application of this sunset provision is discussed in detail in Chapter 6. Once the duty is in place, the administering authorities can be petitioned to undertake a "changed circumstances" review if conditions have substantially changed; for instance, a common change is revising duty levels in light of new information. Periodic administrative reviews also attempt to take into account changes in circumstances.

### Suspension Agreements

It is also important to note that cases do not always end in either the case being rejected or duties being imposed. The U.S. government sometimes negotiates a suspension agreement with the foreign country or countries involved in the antidumping dispute to address the problem identified in the petition. Suspension agreements normally take the form of negotiated volume restrictions on imports or an agreed minimum price.

Due to the stringent requirements of U.S. law, suspension agreements are rarely struck with market economies. Administering authorities have more leeway in cases involving nonmarket economies, however, and suspension agreements are more frequently struck with these countries.[11] (See Chapter 6 for a complete discussion.)

If the suspension agreement breaks down for some reason, the case would restart at the point in the process that it had reached before the suspension agreement was reached; it does not normally automatically result in the imposition of duties (except in those cases in which the ITC had already made a final determination).

Normally, these agreements are negotiated in cases where the economic effect of a duty is potentially large, the trading partner(s) involved is large or faces special problems, or the problem is unusual in some respect. For example, the United States recently negotiated a suspension agreement with three important countries—Russia, Ukraine, and China—on carbon steel plate. Under the agreement, the three countries agreed to restrain their exports to the United States to certain levels and charge a minimum price for their steel.[12] If the alleged dumper violates the terms of the suspension agreement or a final agreement cannot be concluded, the original antidumping investigation continues and the United States can impose or reimpose appropriate antidumping duties.

Typically, the alleged dumper agrees to the suspension agreement because such an agreement grants some market access, which a high duty might block entirely. Also, raising prices is generally preferable to allowing the United States to collect a duty; with a voluntary restraint agreement in place, the respondent country can also sometimes extract economic rents by auctioning the rights to aspiring exporters. The petitioning company agrees because they get certainty of relief from dumping, often at an earlier date. Suspension agreements are often entered into before final determinations. The United States government enters into the negotiations because the suspension agreement allows more flexibility to respond to economic or diplomatic concerns than imposition of a duty. A statistical breakdown of antidumping cases resolved with suspension agreements is included in the next chapter.

Some critics of antidumping laws have asserted that suspension agreements unnecessarily politicize the process of antidumping investigations and work against the interests of countries without political power.[13] This criticism seems misplaced for three reasons. First, the alleged dumpers always have the option of rejecting the agreement and continuing with the antidumping investigation. In effect, suspension agreements under antidumping laws parallel out-of-court settlements in a civil lawsuit. Second, as mentioned, the suspension agreement typically gives the alleged dumper more access, or at least more certainty of access, to the U.S. market than a final antidumping duty would; in cases where this is not true, the alleged dumper presumably refuses to negotiate the suspension agreement. Third, although most commonly negotiated with nonmarket economies, suspension agreements have been negotiated with a range of countries, including developed and developing, rich and poor.[14] This criticism may have more merit in connection with European Union antidumping laws, which employ suspension agreements, also known as undertakings (as they are referred to under the World Trade Organization), more widely than the United States. Administrative authorities in Europe also have more leeway in crafting undertakings than U.S. authorities.

## Rationale for Antidumping Laws

The concept behind antidumping laws can be traced back to the writings of Adam Smith, the author of *The Wealth of Nations,* who wrote of concern for predatory tactics by mercantilist powers.[15] Alexander Hamilton voiced similar concerns in his *Report on Manufactures* in 1791, though he argued for tariffs and not antidumping laws as the solution.[16]

A number of other historical references also point to a fear of predatory dumping, but the first comprehensive exploration was carried out by Jacob Viner, who in 1923 wrote *Dumping: A Problem in International Trade,* which for years stood as the definitive work on the topic. To Viner and others in his time, antidumping laws were to a large extent an extension of antitrust laws, although Viner did recognize the role that protected home markets and differing economic systems played in spawning dumping. In part, antidumping laws were an attempt to combat practices across borders, most notably segment or discriminatory pricing, that were addressed domestically through antitrust legislation.

Modern antidumping laws, however, are rooted primarily in concepts that, although they parallel antitrust laws in some respects, are substantially different. As many who advocated antidumping laws around the world took note of in debates on the topic, antitrust laws targeted practices that were almost exclusively private-sector actions, while antidumping laws were targeted at problems linked to the actions of foreign governments, such as maintaining protected home markets and subsidies. Also, U.S. antitrust laws are focused on promoting consumer interests, while antidumping laws look to producers as the injured parties. As a result of these different problems and objectives, antitrust laws and antidumping laws have evolved along separate paths for almost eight decades.[17]

Because of their long-term need to make a profit, companies can carry out dumping over an extended period of time only if they are supported by government policies, usually in the form of trade barriers, subsidies, and/or lax enforcement of their own antitrust laws, or as a result of using high profits on other products or in other markets to cross-subsidize dumped sales. It is no accident that those sectors in which antidumping actions are common are the very same ones in which trade protection and subsidies abound. The profits gained in restricted markets or from government subsidies allow companies to slash prices even below cost in order to gain market share.

In a very real sense, dumping transfers part of the cost of protectionism from the closed markets to open markets. Since consumers in open markets benefit from lower prices—at least for a time—this cost may not seem obvious. For this reason, some argue against employing antidumping duties.[18]

The case for imposing antidumping duties when confronted with this practice, and thus having antidumping laws, becomes clear when the larger impact of allowing dumping into an open-market country is considered. If antidumping laws did not exist, investment in industries in the open market that were confronted by dumping would decline sharply. After all, investments would be much less attractive in these markets because they would not have secure access to closed foreign markets and would face continued dumping at home, which would sharply cut into profitability. All things being equal, investing in similar facilities in closed markets would be a much more attractive investment.

In the open-market economy, there would always be the constant threat of dumping. Dumping would obviously be a threat in sectors in which dumping had occurred in the past, but there would also be the prospect of dumping in sectors where dumping had not occurred but was possible. This would encourage industries in open markets to be more conservative and more sensitive to the possibility of economic downturns leading to global excess capacity, which would in turn encourage dumping. The investment deterrent effect could thus be widespread and likely to exacerbate economic downturns.

Over time, companies in a market continuously exposed to foreign dumping would effectively become residual suppliers—able to sell in their home market or other open markets only after dumpers from closed markets had gained the market share they sought and then only at something approaching the dumped price. Or, at least, a price that may at any time drop to dumped levels. The combined effect is that under such conditions, industries in the open market would be permanently downsized or driven from the business, and moving resources to other manufacturing sectors would be a very tenuous proposition since they would also be vulnerable to foreign dumping.[19] It is important to note that dumping to dispose of surplus supply or as a result of government policies that encourage surplus production as a matter of national policy are not predatory, as the term is normally used in the context of antitrust laws. Nonetheless, they result in significant economic problems that can best be remedied through antidumping laws.

The negative impacts of uncountered dumping are discussed in more detail in later chapters, but it was these concerns over exposing the domestic economy to the costs of foreign protectionism through dumping that led many countries to adopt and retain antidumping laws.[20]

In recent years, the emergence of reforming nonmarket economies, which often employ both protected markets and subsidies as well as some state-set pricing, has intensified concern over dumping. This also is discussed in more detail in later chapters.

The central rationale for antidumping laws, countering foreign trade practices to ensure a free and competitive marketplace, remains sound today. In fact, recent developments in the world economy make antidumping laws an economic and political necessity for countries that seek to maintain an open-trade policy. After all, it is difficult to imagine that voters and politicians in the United States or elsewhere would continue to support maintaining a market open to trade if that openness exposed them to continued job loss and economic instability due not to the operation of the market but to the operation of foreign governments' mercantilistic policies. If free trade is not perceived as at least generally fair and reciprocal, it is unlikely to survive. Thus, antidumping laws have gone beyond their original function of providing an international extension of antitrust laws. Antidumping laws remedy one of the negative impacts of foreign protectionism; as such, they respond to a critical economic need while helping to preserve political support for free trade.

## History of Antidumping Laws and the World Trading System

Some modern scholars point to the debate on the earliest U.S. antitrust law—the Sherman Antitrust Act (1890)—as the beginning of the dumping discussion in the American political context.[21] As noted, there is a conceptual parallel between antidumping and antitrust, but these early U.S. trustbusters did not propose an antidumping law as a further trust-busting initiative. In fact, dumping was less on the mind of early American trustbusters than some modern scholars suggest. Actually, at the time that the United States began the debate on antitrust protection, U.S. tariffs were so high—often 40 to 50 percent—as to make it virtually impossible for a foreign company to actually engage in predatory pricing. Moreover, early trustbusters were of two minds regarding imports, and many argued that import competition was actually another useful check against the formation of trusts in the United States.[22]

The first national antidumping law was passed nearly a decade later, by Canada in 1904. Once again, modern critics of antidumping laws, in an apparent effort to discredit those laws at their very root, have called into question the Canadian motives in passing this antidumping law. Perhaps the antidumping laws' most outspoken and tireless critic, J. Michael Finger of the World Bank, argues that Canada's law was a Machiavellian attempt by Canada's government to raise tariffs without offending farmers. From Finger's perspective, this is one in a series of innovative Canadian strategies aimed at raising new trade barriers.[23]

Of course, almost a century later it is very difficult to know what was in the minds of Canadian policy makers, and Finger provides little in the way of documentation to support his reading of Canadian history. Thus, it is impossible and unnecessary to defend long-dead Canadian officials. The whole issue also has little to do with the merits of antidumping laws under present conditions. Nonetheless, it is worth noting that W.S. Fielding, Canada's minister of finance, gave a rationale for the Canadian law that greatly resembles that advanced today:

> We find the high tariff countries have adopted that method of trade which has now come to be known as slaughtering, or perhaps the word more frequently used is dumping; that is to say, that the trust or combine having obtained command and control of its own market and finding that it will have a surplus of goods, sets out to obtain command of a neighboring market, and for the purpose of obtaining control of a neighboring market will put aside all reasonable considerations with regard to the cost or fair price of the goods; the only principle recognized is that the goods must be sold and the market obtained.[24]

New Zealand adopted an antidumping law in 1905 and Australia followed suit in 1906, both countries stating a rationale similar to that advanced by Canada.[25]

The United States joined the antidumping club in 1916. As noted, the first U.S. antidumping act, the Antidumping Act of 1916, is often associated with the Sherman Act, the Clayton Act, and the Robinson-Putnam Act—the three major U.S. antitrust statutes. The 1916 act does draw upon some concepts from antitrust legislation, including requiring proof of predatory intent and relying on criminal penalties and treble civil damages as an enforcement tool, all of which were different from the Canadian law.[26]

The requirement for proving predatory intent proved unworkable. Given that the dumpers were in other countries largely beyond the reach of U.S. law, it was virtually impossible to establish predatory intent. Further, predatory intent was found an inappropriate standard. Injurious dumping occurs in many circumstances that do not qualify as predatory, as the term is understood in the context of antitrust laws, but which nonetheless demand remedy. The U.S. Tariff Commission in 1919 reviewed the 1916 law and concluded:

> [The 1916 act] apparently fails, where the Canadian law succeeds, in not contemplating in reasonable cases the prohibition of sporadic dumping, since its penalties apply only to persons who "commonly and systematically import" foreign articles, and in providing that such importation must be made with intent to injure, destroy, or prevent the establishment of an industry in this country, or to monopolize trade or commerce in the imported articles.[27]

A member of the commission, William Culbertson, expanded on this point in his later writing, noting that other types of dumping existed and required remedy:

> (1) the sporadic selling of goods in order to relieve a surplus, that is, the offering of bargain sales in international trade; (2) a permanent policy of foreign industries selling in order to keep their factories running full time; and (3) unfair price cutting, the object of which is to injure, destroy, or prevent the establishment of an American industry. The American legislation of 1916 was directed only against the third type of dumping. It made no provision for preventing the injury to American industries by the first two. . . . [T]he intent of the foreign competitors is of secondary importance so far as national policy is concerned. The result is the thing that is to be prevented.[28]

The report of the Tariff Commission and the shortcomings of the U.S. 1916 law led the Congress to adopt a new law in 1921. The Antidumping Act of 1921 was more closely modeled on the Canadian act; it established antidumping laws as separate from antitrust laws and laid the groundwork for U.S. antidumping laws that continues to the present day. The 1921 act amended the antidumping law in three important ways: (1) antidumping duties based on the extent of dumping replaced civil damages as the enforcement tool; (2) the administration of the act was made an administrative matter rather than a judicial one, with the U.S. Treasury Department (which included the Customs Service) replacing the U.S. courts as the chief decision maker; and, (3) the standard for injury was broadened and no longer required a demonstration of predatory intent.[29] This third major change was probably the most important because it broadened the focus of antidumping laws beyond the narrowly defined category of predatory behavior that is the exclusive focus of antitrust laws.

In the following several years, through the passage of the Fordney-McCumber Tariff Act of 1922 and the Tariff Act of 1930, U.S. antidumping laws were further refined to allow the Treasury Department to make determinations of dumping and injury and impose duties. Judicial review was also limited to matters of law, relieving the courts of administrative decisions.

At about this time, a number of European powers also adopted antidumping laws on the Canadian model. Britain's decision to join the antidumping club in 1921 was particularly notable because Britain had previously been an advocate of unilateral free trade. Through the end of the nineteenth century and the beginning of the twentieth, the British market remained open, with low tariffs and no antidumping laws. At the same time, Britain's industrial competitors—chiefly the United States and Germany—maintained protected markets with high tariffs. German and American steel producers, in particular, took advantage of this situation to dump in the British market to dispose of excess supply and to gain market share. Since German and American markets were closed, British producers could not return the favor. As a result, the British steel makers were unwilling to invest in additional steel capacity in the British market, and the British industry went into decline. Soon dumping spread to other downstream industries and began to have a widely felt impact upon the British economy.[30]

A British commission convened to consider the problem summarized it as follows:

> [I]t is the control of the home market which their tariffs give to foreign countries, combined with the facilities for exportation which they secure through their trust and kartells, and the free access to the British market, which is the condition of their rapid progress relative to the United Kingdom. These tariffs were, in many instances, deliberately adopted to shut out British products which came into competition with home manufacturers. Their adoption has been followed by (i.) the extinction or diminution of British competition in the foreign protected markets; (ii.) the closing of British works or of departments of British works which depended on these markets; (iii.) the rapid growth of the foreign competing industry; (iv.) the appearance in the British market of the products of that industry at prices which the British manufacturer cannot touch. Thus, the positions of the United Kingdom and its most powerful competitors have been reversed.[31]

The impact of the foreign dumping on the British economy was not limited to the economic arena. When World War I broke out in 1914, Britain found that its industrial base was so depleted that it had considerable difficulty sustaining a war effort. Thus, dumping was a national-security issue as well as an economic issue.[32]

After its experience with allowing competitors with closed markets to dump, Britain adopted an antidumping law, which is still enforced today, although the administrative authority has moved from London to Brussels with the advent of the European Union (EU).

Table 1.2

**Legislative History of Antidumping Laws**

| Antidumping Law | Description |
| --- | --- |
| Antidumping Act of 1916 | Similar to antitrust laws of the time, this act established penalties (private damages through court action) for the sale of goods at less than actual market value or wholesale value with the intent to destroy the U.S. industry. Intent to destroy U.S. industry proved difficult to establish. |
| Antidumping Act of 1921 | Passed to strengthen the 1916 act, this act initiated the use of duties based on dumping margins, and gave power to the U.S. Treasury Department to make dumping determinations, rather than going through the courts, because of concern raised by foreign companies gaining market dominance. A looser standard of injury was set with the likelihood of injury as an acceptable complaint. |
| Fordney/McCumber Act of 1922 (Section 316) | Refined both the definition of dumping and the concept of injury. Established the role of the Tariff Commission as the agency making injury determinations and limited courts to reviewing matters of law. |
| Tariff Act of 1930 | Streamlined the collection of antidumping duties once the Treasury Department had established that goods were being sold in the U.S. market at less than fair value and were injurious to the U.S. industry. |
| Trade Act of 1974 | Changed the administrative determination of less than fair value to ensure that products are not sold below cost, rather than just at less than home-market price. It also established time limits for dumping determinations. |
| Trade Agreements Act of 1979 | Implemented the Tokyo Round Agreement (included in which was the Antidumping Code of the GATT). This act repealed the 1921 act, amended the Tariff Act of 1930 to comply with the new GATT code (procedures to apply antidumping duties), and switched the administrative jurisdiction from Treasury to Commerce. |
| Trade and Tariff Act of 1984 | This included changes for determining fair market price, comparing averages in the home market with the price in the U.S. market. |

*(continued)*

Table 1.2 *(continued)*

| | |
|---|---|
| Omnibus Trade and Competitiveness Act of 1988 | Among other provisions, the 1988 act widened the allowable products subject to an antidumping order (i.e., parts, slightly altered products). It also allowed the U.S. trade representative to request that a foreign government take action against third-country dumping if such is found to be injurious to the U.S. industry. |
| The Uruguay Round Agreements Act of 1994 | Implemented the changes mandated by the Uruguay Round agreement. This act amended U.S. dumping law to comply with revised Article VI of the General Agreement on Tariffs and Trade, amended how fair market value is determined, enacted guidelines to evaluate start-up costs, and provided for the review of dumping duties after five years. |

Antidumping laws stayed in place in most of the major powers largely unchanged (the U.S. amendments listed on Table 1.2 are minor administrative refinements and not a wholesale rewrite) through World War II. By the time the world trading system was formed at the Bretton Woods Conference and other events after the war, most of the world's economic powers had established antidumping regimes (see Table 5.1).

During the 1930s, the United States negotiated a number of bilateral agreements under the reciprocal trade agreements program, which acknowledged the problem of dumping and endorsed the operation of antidumping laws. This precedent was followed when the GATT came into existence in 1949. As United Nations (UN) documents noted: "There was general consent among the majority of countries in the discussion on Antidumping and Countervailing Duties, that circumstances might arise in which such duties might properly be applied."[33]

This consensus led to the creation of Article VI of the GATT, which explicitly endorsed the operation of antidumping laws: "[D]umping, by which products of one country are introduced into the commerce of another country at less than the normal value of the products, is to be condemned if it causes or threatens material injury to an established industry in the territory of a contracting party or materially retards the establishment of a domestic industry."[34] The GATT took the approach of allowing existing national antidumping statutes to police dumping instead of leaving the matter to be policed directly by the GATT.

By the 1960s, antidumping laws were in use worldwide and a new set of concerns began to arise. A number of countries viewed the injudicious or unjust application of antidumping duties as a potential threat to free trade. In the Kennedy Round of the GATT (1962–1967), a new antidumping code was negotiated. This code focused on more clearly defining the appropriate procedures for the application of antidumping laws. In 1979, as part of the Tokyo Round GATT agreement, the application of antidumping laws was further defined. The refinements focused on three issues: (1) defining appropriate rules for LTFV determinations of dumping, (2) detailing rules on material injury, and (3) carefully defining administrative procedures for the application of antidumping duties.[35]

In conjunction with the changes just noted, the United States made another important administrative change in its application of antidumping laws in 1979. There was a widespread feeling in the private sector and the Congress that the U.S. Treasury Department, for a variety of institutional and political reasons, was not predisposed to enforce U.S. antidumping laws aggressively. To remedy this, the Congress removed responsibility for enforcement of antidumping laws from the Treasury Department and transferred the authority to the Commerce Department's International Trade Administration. Earlier, the U.S. Tariff Commission had been renamed the U.S. International Trade Commission.

In the Uruguay Round (1986–1994), the global system undertook by far the most extensive rewriting of the GATT—now the World Trade Organization (WTO)—rules against dumping. The Uruguay Round transformed the GATT rules on antidumping from general guidelines to what is now essentially a fully detailed international system to control dumping. Even minute details of injury determinations and LTFV determinations are now specified in the WTO provisions. The major changes in antidumping laws dictated by the WTO are listed in Table 1.3, but a complete list is virtually impossible to make given that there are literally hundreds of changes.

One worthy of particular note, however, is Article 17, which effectively directs the WTO dispute settlement body to give deference to national bodies on the specific determinations on dumping and injury, adopting a standard of review analogous to that applied by U.S. courts in reviews of administrative decisions.[36]

Some have argued that it is not accurate to say that the world trading system is truly compatible with antidumping laws. As noted in the introduction, critics have argued that antidumping laws are a "GATT-legal means to destroy the GATT system."[37] Other scholars have noted that the trading system has never condemned dumping per se, only dumping that causes injury.[38] In large part, this second point amounts to a distinction without much of a difference. Certainly, the trading system has consistently set rules

Table 1.3

**Major Innovations of the Uruguay Round**

*Sunset.* The Uruguay Round Agreement required dumping orders to sunset after five years unless the appropriate administrative authority determined that lifting the duty "would be likely to lead to continuation or recurrence of dumping and injury." This was a substantial change from the previous U.S. practice, which was to leave the dumping order in place until the party subject to the dumping order could demonstrate that the dumping and/or injury would not recur. (Article 11.3.)

*Start-up Costs.* One argument that has been used against antidumping laws has been that the costs of products are naturally higher at the outset, when there is a smaller volume of production over which to distribute fixed costs, and at this point it is normal business practice to sell below full cost. The Uruguay Round sought to address this by requiring antidumping laws "appropriately" to make allowances for start-up costs. (Article 2.3.1.1.)

*Anticircumvention.* Perhaps the most significant issue ignored in the Uruguay Round text was that of anticircumvention. There has been concern for years in the United States that antidumping orders were sometimes circumvented by the respondent companies' making minor changes in the dumped product or a change in the country of origin. U.S. law includes provisions to address this problem, applying antidumping duties on the product subject to the dumping order and also to "like products"—usually interpreted quite narrowly. After a heated dispute in the negotiations, all reference to the concept of anticircumvention was dropped in the text, although it is referenced in the Ministerial Statement accompanying the Uruguay Round.

*Standing.* It has been argued that dumping cases have sometimes been brought by a small portion of the domestic industry involved in a dumping case, while the majority did not support the action. The Uruguay Round agreement requires national authorities to confirm support of the majority of an industry that expresses an opinion before initiating action. In no case can action be taken unless 25 percent of an industry expressly supports the action (often many industry groups express no position on a dumping action). The Uruguay Round does allow certified trade unions to initiate antidumping cases. (Article 5.4.)

*Dispute Resolution and Dispute Settlement.* In implementing the antidumping provisions of the U.S.-Canada FTA, the dispute settlement procedures ultimately proved far more significant than specific provisions. In the Uruguay Round, more substantive, specific changes have been required, but the dispute settlement procedures may ultimately prove more significant than the specific provisions. In recent GATT decisions (there is not yet a sufficient record to evaluate the WTO's performance), the most significant development has been the tendency of some dispute settlement panels to adopt a *very* restrictive view of antidumping provisions, to declare antidumping duties to be a derogation from GATT principles, and to overturn administrative decisions on what can best be called minor "technicalities."

Table 1.3 *(continued)*

The most important change in the WTO process is that dispute settlement procedures have been strengthened in a number of ways. Most notably, a single country can no longer block the adoption of a dispute settlement panel ruling, as was the case in the GATT.

Partially due to the increased power of dispute settlement panels, the scope of review for panels in antidumping cases was explicitly limited. Panels cannot overturn the decisions of national authorities if they have properly established the facts and evaluated them in an "unbiased and objective" manner. Of course, the U.S.- Canada FTA panels were also given a very narrow mandate, but they have been accused of exceeding it. Only time will tell how closely WTO panels stick to their narrow mandate. (Article 17.5.)

*Duty as Cost or Duty Absorption.* At the behest of the European Union, the Uruguay Round agreement allows duties to be increased beyond the dumping margin in those cases where the importing party is related to the dumper, to ensure that the market price of the dumped good increases to reflect the dumping duty. The United States did not alter its antidumping law to utilize this provision. (Article 9.3.)

*Below-cost Sales.* The Uruguay Round Agreement endorses the U.S. practice of excluding sales made below cost in the home market from the home-market price used to calculate the dumping margin. The agreement sets conditions under which these sales can be disregarded, closely paralleling those established in U.S. law some years ago. (Article 2.2.1.)

*Price Averaging.* The agreement provides that dumping margins will "normally" be calculated by comparing a weighted average normal value with a weighted average of export sales, or comparison of normal values with export prices on a transaction-to-transaction basis, to ensure a meaningful "apples-to-apples" comparison. This provision was aimed at certain U.S. price comparisons but still allows the U.S. practice of selecting specific export prices for comparison if "the authorities find a pattern of export prices which differ significantly among different purchasers, regions or time periods, and if an explanation is provided why such differences cannot be taken into account appropriately by the use of a weighted average–to–weighted average or a transaction-to-transaction comparison." (Article 2.4.)

*De Minimis Margins, Import Volume Levels.* The agreement establishes new thresholds for size of the dumping margin (2 percent) and the volume of imports (3 percent of total imports) that must be met in order for an affirmative antidumping determination. (Article 5.8.)

*Note:* Readers interested in a more exhaustive discussion of the provisions of the Uruguay Round should see: Lynn Kamarack, "Uruguay Round Agreement Makes Substantial Changes to Antidumping Code," *East Asian Executive Reports,* March 1994, 6; Labor/Industry Coalition for International Trade, *Implementing the Uruguay Round: What Was Achieved and How To Enact It Into Law* (Washington, DC: LICIT, 1994); and Congressional Budget Office, *How the GATT Affects U.S. Antidumping and Countervailing-Duty Policy* (Washington, DC: CBO, 1994).

within which antidumping laws must operate, but in so doing it effectively endorses the operation of those laws to counter dumping within the prescribed limits. Clearly, there are members of the trading system—many of whose companies are often accused of dumping—that are not fond of antidumping laws, but their position has not prevailed in global trade negotiations. The distinction between endorsing the operation of antidumping laws and condemning dumping, however, is largely a matter of semantics. Antidumping laws have been from the outset fully consistent with the world trading system and remain so today.

The argument that antidumping laws are slowly destroying the world trading system is even less persuasive. The WTO is the strongest incarnation yet of the world trading system, with wider coverage and stronger dispute settlement procedures than its predecessor, and more countries belong to the world trading system now than at any time in history. At the same time, more countries adopt antidumping laws each year. Quite clearly, widespread use of antidumping laws has not retarded the expansion of the world trading system.

Further, by creating a carefully regulated procedure for evaluating allegations of unfair trade, antidumping laws forestall action on an ad hoc basis. There are numerous examples of this problem through history. Viner cites a number of examples of poorly documented allegations of dumping being employed as an excuse for protectionism.[39] More recently, in 1970–1971, Japan raised the prospect of U.S. dumping as part of the rationale for closing the Japanese semiconductor market with trade restrictions.[40] The dumping allegations were not proven, but Japan's Ministry of International Trade and Industry (MITI) still proposed a cartel to restrict foreign competition.

Unfortunately, allegations of dumping are commonly used as an excuse for protection, but documentation is often not offered. By requiring that such claims be rigorously examined and injury proven before trade restrictions can be put in place, antidumping laws provide an important safety valve for the WTO, a way to separate the wheat of legitimate dumping cases from the chaff of protectionist rhetoric.

In practice, the operation of antidumping laws has made the world trading system stronger. As noted in the introduction, antidumping laws are a sort of circuit breaker or interface mechanism that allows trade to proceed smoothly between countries that have radically different economic systems—such as a Communist economy and a free-market economy. If they did not exist, resentment of job losses and factory closings due to "unfair" trade with countries with radically different economic systems would surely provide political support for drastic action to restrict trade with countries that do not support Western free-market economics. The American populace is unlikely to quietly tolerate massive economic displacement as a result of foreign subsidies or trade barriers. Antidumping laws thus prevent political resentment from building up against free trade and against the world trading system. Without such a political consensus the global trading system would be unlikely to survive for long.

## Notes

1. The U.S. system for administering antidumping laws is unusual in that the two determinations in antidumping cases—LTFV and material injury—are made by separate agencies. The U.S. Commerce Department's International Trade Administration (ITA) makes the LTFV determination, and the U.S. International Trade Commission (ITC) makes the material-injury determination. Both determinations are required by the WTO, but in many countries they are made by the same agency.

2. Sanghan Wang, "U.S.Trade Laws Concerning Nonmarket Economies Revisited for Fairness and Consistency," *Emory International Law Review* 10 (Winter 1996): 593. Wang suggests that it would be fairer if the nonmarket countries involved knew their surrogate market beforehand. This is certainly true, but it is difficult to know how to determine the appropriate surrogate until the investigation is completed. Further, the surrogates employed in past investigations normally give a good indication of the likely choice of surrogates in future investigations.

3. The United States does have another statute on the books—Section 406—that could be used to control imports if they cause "market disruption," but this statute has not been used in recent years. Antidumping laws have been preferred because they have a long-established operating history and clear deadlines. Further action under Section 406 is completely at the administration's discretion. Finally, if the ultimate goal is to encourage a market transformation in former nonmarket economies, a mechanism that emphasizes market prices seems preferable to simple import barriers.

In theory, it might also be possible to employ countervailing-duty laws, which are operationally a virtual mirror image of antidumping laws but focus on countering subsidies instead of dumping. In nonmarket economies, however, subsidies are so pervasive that it proves difficult to accurately identify and value all subsidies. The so-called nonmarket economy (NME) antidumping procedures thus became the preferred alternative. Several transitional economies, including China and Russia, have recently sought to win agreement that NME dumping procedures would not be applied to their exports. Such a step would, however, make those exports once again subject to countervailing-duty actions. Given that most manufacturing facilities were constructed at state expense and subsidies persist in provision of inputs (e.g., state-built power plants), several practitioners have suggested that this could actually result in higher duties on the exports of these countries than the current NME antidumping procedures. For more on this topic, see Chapters 3 and 6.

4. General Agreement on Tariffs and Trade Article VI(1).

5. Tariff Act of 1930, Section 771[7][A].

6. Agreement on Implementation of Article VI of the General Agreement on Tariffs and Trade 1994, Article 3.

7. The minimum size of the dumping margin for antidumping duties to be imposed is 2 percent. To be subject to antidumping duties, imports from the alleged dumper must account for 3 percent of total imports.

8. *Federal Register,* vol. 62, no. 96, "Antidumping and Countervailing Duty Procedures," May 19, 1997, pp. 27383–27405.

9. Ibid., pp. 27385–27386.

10. Quote from WTO Antidumping Code.

11. 19 U.S.C. Section 1673c[1].

12. "Commerce Department Initials Agreements Suspending the Antidumping Investigations on Carbon Steel Plate from the Russian Federation, Ukraine, and the People's Republic of China," U.S. Department of Commerce, press release, September 25, 1997. A second agreement was reached later with South Africa—another subject of the antidumping complaint.

13. J. Michael Finger, ed., *Antidumping: How It Works and Who Gets Hurt* (Ann Arbor: University of Michigan Press, 1993), pp. 241–250.

14. This criticism can be more accurately made of the European Union's antidumping regime, which makes wider use of undertakings (also known as suspension agreements).

15. While Smith never used the term *dumping,* he denounced a number of mercantilist government practices, including bounties for exports at less than their "natural price." He also discussed the linkages between mercantilistic commercial practices and monopolies. See Adam Smith, *The Wealth of Nations* (New York: Modern Library, 1994 [originally published in 1776]).

16. Alexander Hamilton, *Report on Manufactures,* 1791.

17. For a good discussion on this point, see Jorge Miranda, "Should Antidumping Laws Be Dumped?" *Law and Policy in International Business* 28, no. 1 (1996): 255–288.

18. This type of analysis is referred to as a static analysis. For a good example, see U.S. International Trade Commission, *The Economic Effects of Antidumping and Countervailing Duty Orders and Suspension Agreements* (Washington, DC: ITC, 1995), publication 2900.

19. Chapter 4 attempts to quantify the economic impact of these effects.

20. For a discussion of events in Canada, Britain, and the United States, see Jacob Viner, *Dumping: A Problem in International Trade* (Chicago: University of Chicago Press, 1923); for an excellent discussion of the events in Britain, see Thomas R. Howell, "Dumping: Still a Problem in International Trade" from *Trade and Competition Policies* (Boulder, CO: Westview Press, forthcoming).

21. Finger, *Antidumping,* p. 18, and Congressional Budget Office, *A Review of U.S. Antidumping and Countervailing Duty Law and Policy* (Washington, DC: CBO, May 1994), pp. 1–6.

22. Compilation of documents in "Bills and Debates in Congress Relating to Trusts, S. Doc. No. 147" (97th Cong., 2d Sess.), p. 190.

23. Finger, *Antidumping,* pp. 14–16.

24. U.S. Tariff Commission, 1919, p. 22.

25. Viner, *Dumping,* pp. 192–215.

26. A number of scholars have noted that despite some apparent ties to antitrust legislation, even the 1916 Antidumping Act is not properly grouped with antitrust laws. See "Rethinking the 1916 Antidumping Act," *Harvard Law Review* 110 (May 1997): 1555.

27. U.S. Tariff Commission, *Information Concerning Dumping and Unfair Foreign Competition in the United States and Canada's Anti-Dumping Law,* House Ways and Means Committee Print, 66th Cong. 1st Sess. (1919) (Committee Prints H2966), p. 33.

28. William Smith Culbertson, *Commercial Policy in War Time and After* (New York and London: D. Appleton, 1924), p. 153.

29. Viner, *Dumping,* pp. 258–265.

30. Aaron L. Friedberg, *The Weary Titan: Britain and the Experience of Relative Decline, 1895–1905* (Princeton: Princeton University Press, 1988), pp. 45–79.

31. *Report of the Tariff Commission,* vol. 1, par. 58 (London: P.S. King, 1904).

32. As noted above, see Howell, "Dumping," for an excellent and detailed history of these events.

33. U.N. Doc. EPCT/C.II/SY at II (1946), cited in John H. Jackson, *World Trade and the Law of GATT* (Charlottesville, VA: Mitchie, 1969), p. 404n.

34. GATT Article VI(1).

35. John Jackson, *The World Trading System* (Cambridge: MIT Press, 1989), pp. 225–228.

36. *Agreement on Implementation of Article VI of the General Agreement on Tariffs and Trade 1994,* Article 17, paragraph 17.6.

37. Finger, *Antidumping,* cover page.

38. Jackson, *World Trading System,* p. 227.

39. Viner, *Dumping,* pp. 51–74.

40. Kenneth Flamm, *Mismanaged Trade? Strategic Policy and the Semiconductor Industry* (Washington, DC: Brookings Institution, 1997), pp. 73–75.

# 2

# The Record of U.S. Antidumping Laws

This chapter presents a detailed statistical breakdown of the record of U.S. antidumping laws. Although such a statistical overview provides little insight into the merits of individual cases, it does shed some light on the overall effect of antidumping laws on the U.S. economy. More important, the statistical breakdown is quite useful and even conclusive in evaluating claims on matters such as allegations of systematic bias by U.S. administering authorities and concerns over the length of time that antidumping orders remain in effect.

Because U.S. antidumping laws have undergone a number of revisions since their inception in 1916, this statistical analysis focuses only upon relatively recent cases, those petitions filed between January 1980 and June 1997. Many of the most recent cases in this group had not reached a final resolution at the time this volume went to press but were included because they are still useful for some statistical comparisons. In total, 732 cases were considered.

The number of cases filed reached a high of 96 cases in 1992 and hit a low of 14 in 1995 (the number given for 1997 is 6, but that is not a complete-year total). For the period, it is difficult to identify any single factor that explains the year-to-year variation in case volume. In general, the volume of cases seems to be inversely correlated with the strength of the economy in the past year or more. This relationship is probably due to the application of the injury test. As explained in Chapter 1, in difficult economic times it is easier for U.S. petitioners to demonstrate material injury. In down economic times, U.S. companies may also be more anxious to seek government intervention to counter foreign dumping.

## Overall Breakdown

Of the 732 cases considered, 315, or 44 percent of them, resulted in antidumping duties being imposed. In another 17 cases (2.4 percent) a suspension agreement was reached that at least partially addressed the concerns

Chart 2.1 **Antidumping Petitions Filed, January 1, 1980, to June 1, 1997**

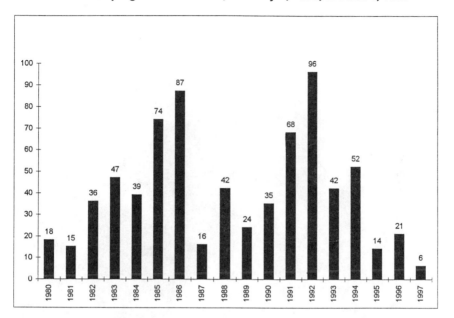

*Source:* Department of Commerce, International Trade Administration.

raised by the petitioning industry. In the remaining 383 cases—53.6 percent of the total—the petition was either rejected or dismissed by U.S. authorities or withdrawn by the petitioner. (An additional 17 cases are yet to be resolved.)

The success rate of cases filed varies from year to year. In 1986, petitioners won relief in almost 70 percent of the cases filed. In 1980, 1984, and 1991, however, the success rate for petitioners was less than 30 percent. In general, the percentage of successful cases rises in those years in which the total number of cases filed falls.[1] This suggests that only strong cases are brought in those years in which the total number of filings is low.

**Failed Cases**

Antidumping petitions fail to result in relief for a number of reasons. The most common reason for failure is that the U.S. International Trade Commission (ITC) or the U.S. Commerce Department finds no evidence of injury or no evidence of dumping, respectively. Over the period, the ITC rejected a total of 243 cases, 99 at the preliminary injury determination and 144 at the final injury determination. The Department of Commerce re-

Chart 2.2 **Antidumping Cases Outcomes, January 1, 1980, to June 1, 1997**

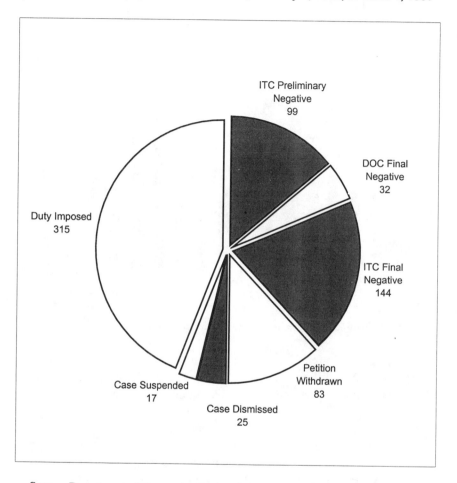

*Source:* Department of Commerce, International Trade Administration.

jected an additional 32 cases because there was no evidence of dumping above the *de minimis* level. Thus, a total of 275 antidumping petitions were rejected by U.S. administrative authorities.

In addition to the petitions that were rejected by either the ITC or the Commerce Department, a number of other cases were resolved without antidumping duties being imposed because the petitions were either dismissed or voluntarily withdrawn by the petitioner. Over the period, 25 cases were dismissed by administrative authorities; dismissal indicates that U.S. authorities believed that the petitioner had not provided sufficient evidence

Chart 2.3 **Successful Antidumping Cases Filed, January 1, 1980, to June 1, 1997**

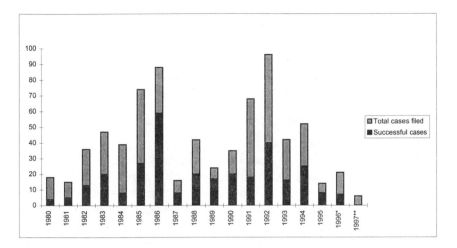

*Source:* Department of Commerce, International Trade Administration.
*11 of 1996's 21 cases remain unfinished.
**All 6 of 1997's cases remain unfinished.

Chart 2.4 **Administrative Rejections of Antidumping Cases, January 1, 1980, to June 1, 1997**

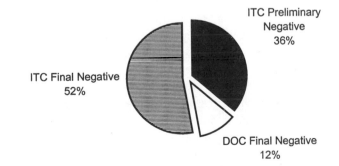

*Source:* Department of Commerce, International Trade Administration.

to proceed with the case. Because of changes in law and practice, most of the dismissals took place before 1985. Administrative authorities no longer typically dismiss cases and instead advise the petitioner to withdraw the petition, or else they rule negatively.

Over the period, another 83 cases ended when the petitioner withdrew the petition. The conditions under which petitions are withdrawn vary, but most commonly it is the result of a change in circumstances or advice from administrative authorities that the petition is unlikely to succeed.

**Suspended Cases**

Over the period examined, 17 cases were suspended. Typically, the suspensions resulted from a suspension agreement being negotiated between the U.S. government and the foreign country or countries involved in the dumping investigation. These cases most often result in some arrangement to end injurious dumping, usually by limiting exports to the United States. As noted in the previous chapter, most suspension agreements involve countries subject to nonmarket antidumping provisions.[2]

Thus, these cases are at least a partial success for the petitioner, but usually result in more exports to the U.S. market than would be likely if antidumping duties were imposed.

The petitions are normally suspended at the point in the process at which the agreement was struck. Thus, some were suspended before preliminary decisions, some before the final Commerce Department determination, some before the final ITC determination, and some after the final ITC determination.

**Revoked Cases**

Of the 315 cases in which antidumping duties were imposed, the duties were subsequently revoked in 54 cases. Normally, the orders were revoked because the circumstances had changed. Common changes that result in revocation include evidence that dumping has ceased, that the domestic industry has ceased to exist, or that there has been other material change in the circumstances that resulted in the imposition of duties.

As would be expected, revocations normally take place after the duties have been in place for a number of years; most of the duties that were revoked stem from cases originally filed before 1986, and none of the duties imposed in cases filed since 1992 have yet been revoked. In many cases, dumping or the threat thereof has persisted for a number of years.

For example, duties from two cases originally filed in 1980 are still in

Chart 2.5 **Antidumping Orders Still in Effect as of June 1, 1997**

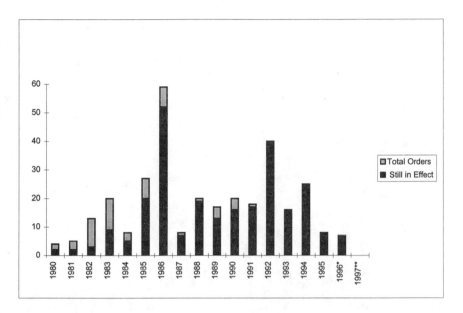

*Source:* Department of Commerce, International Trade Administration.
*1996 has 11 cases unfinished.
**1997 has all 6 cases filed, unfinished.

effect. Both cases are from the chemical sector, in which dumping has been a repeated problem; in short, there might be good reason to leave antidumping orders in effect on these products.

## Listing of Respondent Countries

An examination of the statistics for respondent countries reveals some interesting patterns. In the 1980s and before, antidumping actions were filed against companies from a number of countries, but Japan was by far the most common home country for dumpers. Taiwan, Brazil, and South Korea were also the subjects of a number of antidumping complaints. Canada and West Germany were named in a substantial number of antidumping complaints as well.

If the numbers of dumping complaints per $100 billion in imports are examined, other patterns emerge. As would be expected, the relative ranking of Canada and West Germany appears much lower. Complaints against

Chart 2.6 **Top Twenty Respondent Countries, 1980–1989**

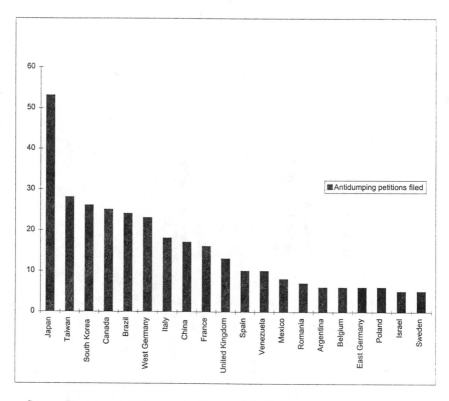

*Source:* Department of Commerce, Bureau of the Census.

Japan also appear moderate given the high import volume involved. China and Brazil have the highest number of antidumping complaints per $100 billion in imports in the 1980s.

In the 1990s, most of the patterns from the 1980s continue. The number of complaints against China, however, dramatically increased. Antidumping complaints also increased against other reforming nonmarket economies, such as Russia and the Ukraine. The combined result has been that the nonmarket-economy antidumping procedures described in Chapter 1 have been frequently used in the 1990s and account for nearly half of all cases in recent years.

When the figures from the 1990s are considered in light of the trade volume involved, China and Brazil again top the list. Overall, the figures from the 1990s correspond fairly closely to those from previous periods.

Chart 2.7 **Top Ten Respondent Countries' Ratio of Antidumping Complaints per Volume of Imports, 1980–1989**

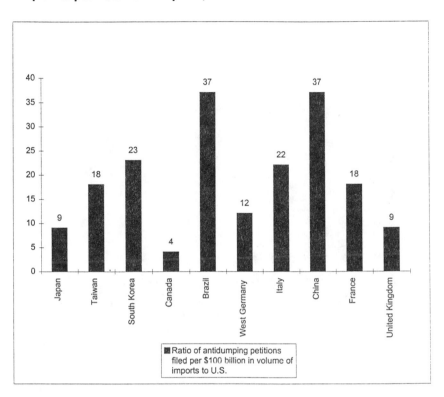

*Source:* Department of Commerce, Bureau of the Census.

## Conclusion

As noted in the beginning of this chapter, statistics give no insight into the merits of individual cases or the specific circumstances surrounding them. Therefore, it is dangerous to assume too much about specific cases from these general, aggregate statistics. For example, as discussed above, though seventeen years is an unusually long period for an antidumping order to remain in place, it cannot necessarily be assumed that antidumping duties have outlived their usefulness in the two cases in which duties have been in place since 1980.

Similarly, success rates in any given year can be influenced by a plethora of factors, including changing economic conditions, the emergence of new

Chart 2.8 **Top Twenty Respondent Countries, 1990–1997**

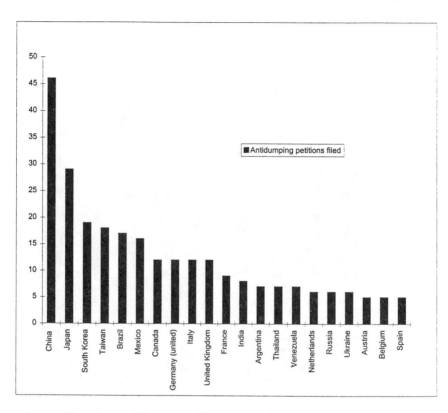

*Source:* Department of Commerce, Bureau of the Census.

foreign producer/exporters, and changes in U.S. law. Potential petitioners often time their filings to correspond with economic conditions or anticipated changes in U.S. law. Thus, it would be simply irresponsible to assume they reflect evidence of systematic bias on the part of administering authorities.

In short, each antidumping investigation is a complex undertaking with its own unique story. Examining cases strictly from a statistical perspective misses all of these special factors. Nonetheless, this statistical analysis should provide the reader with a better grounding in the actual operation of antidumping laws and a sense of the countries most frequently subject to antidumping complaints. As such, statistical analysis is an important part, but only a part, of any serious effort to consider the merits of U.S. anti-dumping laws.

**Chart 2.9 Top Ten Respondent Countries' Ratio of Antidumping Complaints per Volume of Imports, 1990–1997**

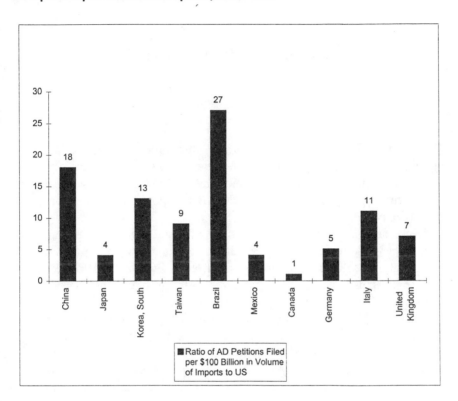

*Source:* Department of Commerce, Bureau of the Census.

## Notes

1. In this regard, 1986 was an anomalous year because both the number of cases and the success rate were high.

2. The requirements for concluding a suspension agreement with a market economy are quite stringent and rarely used. Suspension agreements (undertakings) are more commonly used by the European Union.

# 3

# The Roots of Dumping

To the casual observer, the discussion to this point will raise an obvious question: "Why would a company ever attempt to sell below cost or below the best price it could obtain in the marketplace?" After all, these are profit-driven firms that presumably seek the highest possible price in order to maximize profit.

Those familiar with microeconomics will recall that there are rare circumstances—discussed in detail in Chapter 5—under which a profit-driven firm might price below cost in the short term. But this explanation does little to explain why dumping sometimes persists over a period of many years.

The other instance that may result in firms selling below cost or below normal price levels is when a firm is striving to drive its competitors out of business in order to establish a monopoly. As discussed in more detail in Chapters 1 and 5, predatory pricing in order to establish a monopoly or drive competitors out of business is one of the motivations for dumping. There are only a handful of cases in recent history, however, in which it reasonably can be argued that such a systematic predatory strategy was being followed.

In most real-world cases, dumping is a regular business practice aimed at achieving more limited commercial objectives, such as gaining a commercial advantage through the scale of economy of operations, building market share, or simply disposing of surplus production. In order to understand commercial behavior and the economic rationale for antidumping action in these instances, it is necessary to examine each in some detail.

## Sanctuary Markets and Dumping

As mentioned in Chapter 2, the countries that are most frequently subject to antidumping complaints—China, Japan, Brazil, South Korea—are the same countries that maintain or maintained tightly closed home markets.[1] For many years, the United States has devoted numerous pages of its annual

THE ROOTS OF DUMPING 41

Table 3.1

**Top Respondent Countries to U.S. Section 301 Cases and Final Determinations of Dumping, 1985–1994**

Top respondents to dumping cases, 1985–1994 (final affirmative determination)

| | |
|---|---|
| 1) Japan | 39 |
| 2) China | 23 |
| 3) Brazil | 18 |
| 4) Korea | 18 |
| 5) Taiwan | 14 |
| 6) Germany | 13 |
| 7) India | 9 |

Top respondents to Section 301 cases, 1985–1994 (cases initiated)

| | |
|---|---|
| 1) Japan | 8 |
| 2) Korea | 6 |
| 3) Canada | 5 |
| 4) Brazil | 4 |
| 5) India | 4 |
| 6) China | 3 |
| 7) Taiwan | 3 |
| 8) Thailand | 3 |

*Sources:* Section 301 public case files of the U.S. trade representative's office; U.S. International Trade Commission, *Annual Report 1993, 1994;* U.S. International Trade Commission, *Operation of the Trade Agreements Program, 1985–94.*

*Note:* The European Union is not included in the Section 301 table. As a group of countries, it would be the most frequently cited (nine cases initiated since 1985), but Section 301 cases are brought against the union and not the individual countries. Dumping cases are brought against individual countries, and those have been included in the dumping table.

summary of foreign trade problems to listing these countries' trade barriers.[2] As you will note from Table 3.1, the leading antidumping respondent countries have also been the leading targets of the United States' market-opening trade law—Section 301.[3]

This high correlation between antidumping complaints and closed home markets is more than coincidence. A closed home market allows companies to charge high prices at home because they face no foreign competition. Foreign companies can use the profits from these domestic sales to cross-subsidize export sales at dumped prices.

There are many good examples of this phenomenon in various manufacturing sectors in Japan. Chart 3.1 traces the geographic origin of the profits of Japanese auto companies from 1988 to 1994.[4] Although Japanese auto-

Chart 3.1 **Geographic Source of Profits for Japanese Automakers**

$U.S. billions

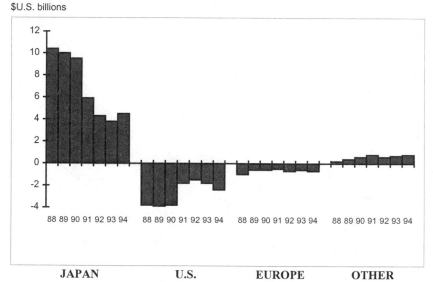

motive companies face some domestic competition, Japanese companies have taken care to avoid entering into sustained price competition among themselves.[5] More important, Japanese auto companies face almost no import competition at home; due to a range of public- and private-sector trade barriers, auto import levels in Japan as a percentage of total Japanese sales have remained in the low single digits throughout the period represented on the chart.[6] As a result, Japanese auto companies have enjoyed strong profits at home, which have offset persistent losses in major foreign markets. Although reliable detailed data has not been collected in other sectors, anecdotal evidence suggests that the same situation exists in many of the manufacturing sectors in which Japan has become a global presence.

Even in cases in which companies are not actively following a dumping strategy, a closed home market can encourage companies to dump. A secure closed home market or sanctuary home market encourages companies to make aggressive production and expansion decisions because they can be certain of selling a percentage of their production at home at good prices. Even if there is a global economic downturn that depresses sales, these companies can depend on secure profits at home and can dispose of surpluses at dumped prices in overseas markets: this encourages aggressive expansion decisions. From a sanctuary market, it is also possible to dump in the markets of foreign competitors to depress the profit margins of those competitors and reduce their funds available for investment in R&D and marketing.

Companies from countries with open markets do not enjoy this luxury. For these companies, there are no sanctuary markets; they face competition in both overseas and domestic markets, and in economic downturns they have no secure markets. As a result, companies with open home markets must be more conservative in making production decisions than those with a sanctuary home market, particularly because they face not only constant fair competition but also the constant risk of dumping from their competitors from sanctuary markets, which further erodes their expected profits. Over time, this puts companies in open-market countries, such as the United States, at a serious disadvantage in competition with companies with sanctuary home markets.

There is a third reason that sanctuary markets contribute to dumping. If a company engages in dumping in foreign markets and its home market is open, the price differential will induce the company's competitors or other resellers to reexport dumped products to the dumper's home market. These reexports would quickly pull the home market price down to the dumped price and erase home market profits. Thus, a closed or restricted home market is also a virtual precondition to a successful dumping strategy.

A pricing competition between two tire companies—Michelin, a European company, and Goodyear, a U.S. company—illustrates the reason dumping strategies are difficult to pursue from an open market. In the 1970s, Michelin, emboldened by strong sales in Europe, attempted to make a major entry into the U.S. market with low-priced tire exports. Goodyear, instead of responding by matching Michelin's price in the United States, chose to cut prices on its tire sales in Europe. In Europe, Goodyear had a small market share and Michelin a large share, and thus Goodyear could cut its prices on a relatively small volume of sales, lower the prevailing market price, and force Michelin to match its price on its much larger volume of European sales. This tactical move—essentially countering dumping with dumping—worked well; Michelin's profits were cut and it was forced to slow its initiative in North America and raise prices. For a variety of reasons, neither company brought an antidumping complaint against the other, but this example illustrates that if markets are open, dumping can often be countered without resorting to an antidumping complaint.[7]

A number of governments have either tacitly or explicitly encouraged their companies to engage in dumping to raise market share by providing a sanctuary home market behind trade barriers. This approach is most often associated with Japan and South Korea, but it has been used by a number of countries. In these cases, dumping has become a de facto element of national industrial policy.

Before beginning a discussion of specific case studies of dumping, it is worth noting that in most real-world examples, dumping is not due just to a sanctuary market, subsidies, or some other single factor. In most cases, more than one of the root causes of dumping are present. The case studies are somewhat artificially grouped under one cause or another for purposes of explanation, but the reality is that two or more factors, such as subsidies, a closed home market, and private-sector collusion, contribute to dumping.

Dumping in the semiconductor sector in the mid-1980s by several Japanese companies is perhaps the classic example of predatory dumping. The semiconductor example has been recounted in a number of sources, but the essential highlights are as follows. The semiconductor was invented in the United States and the semiconductor industry grew up in California's Silicon Valley. In the 1970s, with extensive government support, a number of Japanese companies began to challenge the giants of the U.S. semiconductor industry, such as Texas Instruments, Motorola, and Intel.

For the Japanese companies, the conditions were nearly ideal for dumping. Although they lagged far behind their U.S. competitors in global market share, the Japanese companies benefited from the fact that their home market was largely closed to imports by a series of trade barriers; imported chips held a market share only in the single digits. In the early 1980s, Japanese companies set out to secure a share of the U.S. market by dumping memory chips, known as DRAMs, at a small fraction of their cost of production and often below even their marginal cost of production. U.S. companies filed and won a series of antidumping actions against their Japanese competitors, but technology changes so quickly in the semiconductor market that Japanese companies had begun dumping the next generation of DRAMs before the antidumping order on the last generation had taken effect. The dumping ultimately drove all but two U.S. producers out of the DRAM market.

U.S. companies shifted their focus to manufacturing the more advanced memory chips known as EPROMs. Japanese companies began dumping in the EPROM market, however, and the U.S. semiconductor industry was pushed close to collapse.

The U.S. government responded in the mid-1980s by pursuing both an antidumping complaint against Japanese companies and a Section 301 complaint against the closed Japanese semiconductor market. In 1986, an agreement was negotiated between the governments of the United States and Japan that ended dumping in the United States by setting a minimum sales price and obligated Japan to take a number of steps to open its home market to semiconductor imports, with the ultimate goal of allowing imports at least a 20 percent share of the Japanese market.

Later in 1986, the U.S. government imposed sanctions on Japan for violation of the antidumping provisions of the agreement. The target 20 percent import market share was not actually achieved until the early 1990s but was ultimately met. Some semiconductor consumers, notably the U.S. computer industry, criticized the agreement for raising their input prices. Of course, it was only to be expected that ending dumping would raise semiconductor prices, but the economic implications of the broader argument that antidumping actions raise consumer prices are addressed in the next two chapters.[8]

Despite the initial criticism, the semiconductor agreement is widely considered a success. Japanese dumping was halted, the Japanese market was opened to imports, and the U.S. semiconductor industry has since regained a leading position in the world market.

Although Japanese dumping of semiconductors has not been a problem in recent years, new entrants in the semiconductor market do appear to be dumping. Since 1993, South Korea has been subject to antidumping duties on DRAMs, and the U.S. government recently decided to continue those orders.[9] A primary U.S. maker of the memory chips—Micron Technologies—also brought a new case against Korean and Taiwanese manufacturers of SRAMs, a newer generation of memory chips. The Commerce Department preliminarily imposed duties on both South Korean and Taiwanese producers.[10] As the petitioners note, these countries have built manufacturing capacity in semiconductors with government support and little regard to market signals.[11]

Not all instance of dumping, however, have been so positively resolved. Perhaps the other best-known case of extensive dumping involves the Japanese and U.S. television industries in the late 1950s and 1960s. The facts in this case are quite similar to those in the semiconductor case. U.S. television manufacturers were initially dominant in the industry, but in the late 1950s, Japanese television producers were able to restrict imports with government assistance and formed a cartel to control prices and production. After obtaining licenses for key television technology in the early 1960s, Japan launched a major assault on the U.S. television market through dumping, which was carried out through both below-cost sales and deep rebates to distributors on televisions sold.

Before 1980, U.S. antidumping laws were administered by the U.S. Treasury Department, which was not inclined to take aggressive action to counter television dumping. The Treasury Department did not act on a dumping complaint until 1971, three years after a petition was filed, and it continued to look negatively upon the U.S. television industry's complaints. The actions of Treasury officials in this case led, in part, to the Congress's stripping the Treasury Department of responsibility to implement antidumping laws and transferring it to the Commerce Department.

Persistent dumping largely destroyed the U.S. television industry. Between 1966 and 1970, employment in the U.S. industry dropped 50 percent. By 1975, employment had dropped another 34 percent. In 1968, there were twenty-eight U.S. television manufacturers. By late 1976, only six were still in business.[12]

Japanese electronics manufacturers used their foothold in the U.S. television market and similar pricing strategies to dominate other consumer electronics markets, including VCRs, CD and videodisk players, and stereos. Japanese dominance of some sectors of the consumer electronics industry is now so complete that Japanese manufacturers have been accused of collusion to raise prices in the United States. These allegations eventually resulted in an out-of-court settlement.[13]

Unfortunately, dumping from a sanctuary market remains a problem today. The most recent case of a sanctuary home market supporting dumping involves the supercomputer industry. Again, the supercomputer controversy is a dispute between the United States and Japan, as are the other case studies explored in this section.

The supercomputer sector is one that has been the subject of ongoing wrangling between the United States and Japan. Supercomputers are advanced computers that are employed in a number of tasks, including weather forecasting and weapons design. Supercomputing technology was pioneered by U.S. companies, most notably Cray Research, Inc. Cray has long been the dominant force in the supercomputer industry, with Japanese companies—NEC and Fujitsu, Inc.—entering the field later.[14]

Although Cray has dominated the supercomputer market worldwide, it has a much smaller share of the Japanese market, which is dominated by Japanese vendors. Allegations have been made for years of Japanese dumping of supercomputers in the United States and other markets. Reportedly, Japanese vendors have offered deep price cuts to make sales, sometimes offering the supercomputer at 80 to 90 percent discounts.[15]

When NEC offered to sell a supercomputer to the Massachusetts Institute of Technology (MIT) in 1987 at concessionary terms, the U.S. Commerce Department informed MIT that the sale likely violated U.S. antidumping laws. MIT subsequently dropped plans to buy the NEC supercomputer[16]

The United States also attempted to win more market access for Cray in Japan. Cray had some success selling to the Japanese private sector, holding about 50 percent of that market, but was virtually shut out of the Japanese public sector. A bilateral agreement between the United States and Japan was struck in 1987, but it was a failure. In 1989, access for U.S. supercomputers was made one of the United States' Super 301 priorities with regard to Japan (Super 301 is a U.S. trade law aimed at major trade barriers).[17]

As a result of this pressure, the Japanese government did revise some of its procurement regulations and purchased a few Cray supercomputers. Despite these sales, Cray's market share in Japan, particularly in the public sector, still lags far behind that in other countries. In the first three years of the agreement, the U.S. vendors won 27 percent of the Japanese market. In 1993 and 1994, the U.S. share rose to between 40 and 45 percent, but in 1995 it fell to only 9 percent.[18]

Japanese supercomputer vendors, using profits derived from other computer lines and some profitable supercomputer sales in Japan, have continued to cross-subsidize the dumping of supercomputers. Other segments of the Japanese computer market, such as government procurement of small computers, are heavily dominated by Japanese computer vendors, even though U.S. vendors have a strong presence in the private portion of the market.[19] Profits in these other sectors are available to finance supercomputer operations. Partly as a result of severe price competition from Japanese companies, Cray has also seen its global market share plunge from 75 percent to 55 percent between 1992 and 1996.[20]

The issue of Japanese dumping of supercomputers reared its head again in 1996. In May 1996, the University Corporation for Atmospheric Research (UCAR) of Boulder, Colorado, decided to buy a supercomputer from an NEC affiliate for weather simulations. In July 1996, Cray filed an antidumping petition alleging that NEC's bid indicated that it was preparing to dump supercomputers. In this case, Cray's petition included information on the proposed offer put forward by NEC. Reportedly, NEC offered as many as four supercomputers for the price of one.

After considering the petition, the Commerce Department agreed with Cray that Japanese supercomputer vendors were engaged in dumping. Commerce calculated a 454 percent dumping margin on NEC's supercomputers and a 173 percent dumping margin on Fujitsu supercomputers (Fujitsu had also bid on the UCAR supercomputer). In September 1997, the ITC found that Japan's supercomputer sales posed a substantial threat of injury to the U.S. industry and the duties went into place.[21]

Japanese vendors quickly denounced the Commerce Department's dumping margins but provided little substantive information to counter the allegations of dumping. Price competition appears to be a central and recurrent tactic in the effort of Japanese vendors to gain market share; therefore, dumping is likely to continue to be an ongoing problem.[22]

Each of the case studies used to illustrate the problem of dumping from sanctuary markets to this point has involved Japan, but Japan is hardly the only country that has provided sanctuary markets. Examples of sanctuary markets can be found in Taiwan, South Korea, Brazil, and many other countries.

Often global market access problems can create a number of sanctuary markets around the world and spawn dumping from a number of sources. A good example is the bearing market. Bearings, including ball bearings, roller bearings, and simple bearings, are basic industrial products. In 1986, U.S. bearing producers launched successful cases against Hungary, Italy, Japan, China, Romania, and Yugoslavia. In 1988, another successful round of cases was launched against Germany, France, Italy, Japan, Romania, Singapore, Sweden, Thailand, and the United Kingdom.

Dumping in bearings involves a long list of products and a diverse list of countries. As might be expected, there are also diverse reasons for dumping, including nonmarket economics and subsidies, but most of the countries cited for dumping maintain, through policies ranging from collusion to formal trade barriers, largely closed markets with high domestic prices. The United States, as one of the few relatively open markets and a large market for bearings, thus becomes the most attractive market for disposing of surplus production and building market share.[23]

## Private-Sector Protectionism and Dumping

Sanctuary markets and the profits they create are normally the result of government-erected trade barriers that block competition from imports. Sanctuary markets, however, can sometimes be the result of monopoly or oligopoly control of the home market. In these cases, firms follow classic monopolist (or oligopolist) behavior; they price as high as possible in the domestic market, and in other markets in which they face competition they price at a lower level.[24] Corporate behavior under these monopoly conditions thus parallels quite closely the behavior of firms in government-protected sanctuary markets.[25]

Home market monopolies or oligopolies underlie a number of current antidumping cases. The Japanese film market is a good example of this phenomenon at work. Globally, two companies—Eastman Kodak, a U.S. company, and Fuji Film, a Japanese company—dominate the film market. Kodak holds approximately a 45 percent global market share to Fuji's 35 percent. In the United States, Kodak holds approximately a 70 percent market share and Fuji holds about 12 percent. In Japan, however, Fuji enjoys a 65 percent market share while Kodak holds less than 10 percent.[26]

At first glance, this disparity between the Japanese market and other markets is difficult to explain because most of Japan's formal barriers against film imports have been removed over the years. In the view of Kodak and the U.S. government, however, those formal barriers have been replaced by informal, private-sector barriers.[27] Fuji, often with the cooperation of the Japanese government, has used a number of commercial tactics prohibited by U.S. antitrust laws to restrict foreign access to distribution channels within Japan and otherwise block imports. On behalf of Kodak, the U.S. government challenged the Japanese government's toleration of collusion under the WTO. Despite high expectations on the part of the United States, the WTO dispute settlement panel ignored the problem of collusion and ruled completely in favor of Japan. The panel essentially dismissed U.S. complaints over the Japanese market and, in the words of the *New York Times,* "excused" Japanese protectionism.[28] As a result of this panel decision the WTO has essentially declared that it is not willing to address the problem of private-sector protectionism. As a result, it is likely that in Japan and elsewhere there will be continuing and even increasing efforts to build sanctuary markets surrounded by private-sector, not government trade barriers. Continued dumping is the virtually certain result.[29]

Before its current efforts to open the Japanese film and photographic paper markets, Kodak had successfully pursued an antidumping action against Fuji. In the early 1990s, with the help of profits from its sales in Japan, Fuji began to dump film in other markets, notably the United States, in order to build market share. This dumping cut sharply into Kodak's profits and made it more difficult to invest in research and development and marketing to counter Fuji. Initially, Kodak countered with an antidumping complaint against Fuji regarding photographic paper.[30] Fuji ultimately agreed to end the dumping in the U.S. market in a suspension agreement.[31]

To remedy the problem of antidumping in the longer term, Kodak initiated the just discussed Section 301 action and began looking for alternative methods of distribution in Japan, such as manufacturing film for Japanese retailers under the retailer's in-house brand. For its part, Fuji responded by shifting from exporting film and photographic paper from Japan to increasingly manufacturing in the United States. Film manufactured in the United States is, of course, exempt from antidumping duties.

Unfortunately, the Japanese film market is not unique. Other sectors in the Japanese economy, including flat glass and automotive parts, also appear to be largely closed to imports due to private-sector collusion. In a thorough analysis of Japan's economy, Mark Tilton outlined in considerable detail examples of collusion in the aluminum industry, the steel industry, the petrochemical industry, and the cement industry.[32]

Not coincidentally, the cement sector has been a frequent subject of antidumping complaints. U.S. cement producers filed a series of antidumping petitions beginning in 1976. Much of the allegedly dumped cement originated in Mexico, although Japanese and Venezuelan producers were also involved. In Japan, the dumping seems a typical case of dumping resulting from cartels at home.

In Mexico, the cement case is more complex. Market access barriers, collusion, and an industry-wide overcapacity resulting from protection and collusion all contribute to dumping. Historically, because of tariff and non-tariff trade restrictions and distribution barriers, a few Mexican cement producers—the largest of which is Cemex—enjoyed the benefits of a closed market. These barriers blocked virtually all U.S. exports to Mexico, but before antidumping duties were put in place, Mexican producers exported almost 20 percent of their production to the U.S. market, primarily to southern and southwestern states.

In Mexico, Mexican producers charge market prices for their product. In the U.S. market, however, Mexican cement producers are willing to price at lower levels to secure sales. As a result of this practice, Mexican cement producers were repeatedly found to be dumping, but it was not until 1991 that the ITC found evidence of injury and duties were imposed.

The cement case is complicated by the differential impact on various regions, cross-border investments, and the advent of the North American Free Trade Agreement (NAFTA). If all trade barriers were eliminated by NAFTA, one might assume that Mexican cement producers would lose their sanctuary market advantage and dumping would cease. This is not necessarily the case, however, since the Mexican cement market is highly concentrated and it is possible that, even in the absence of formal trade barriers, Mexican producers could employ their oligopoly power to restrict imports and maintain the sanctuary market.[33]

Unfortunately, there is no internationally accepted standard for antitrust enforcement and a long list of countries, including Japan, Taiwan, and South Korea, are tolerant of what might be called trusts under U.S. law. Even the European Union, which has an economic system close to that of the United States, tolerates a greater degree of private-sector collusion.[34] As a result, cartel-driven dumping will be a continuing problem.

## Subsidies and Dumping

Typically, subsidies and dumping are treated separately under international trade laws and agreements. As should be clear by now, dumped imports are countered by antidumping laws and subsidized imports are generally addressed under countervailing-duty laws. Antidumping and countervailing-duty laws, however, are closely related. In the United States and most other countries, countervailing-duty and antidumping laws are quite similar: both require an injury test; in the United States, both are administered by the Commerce Department's ITA and the U.S. International Trade Commission; and both employ duties to level the competitive playing field.

Dumping and subsidization are also closely related. By lowering the cost of production or the cost of export sale, subsidies result in commercial behavior that can be characterized as dumping—selling below price in the home market or below production cost. Subsidies that lower input costs can lower the marginal cost of production as experienced by the manufacturer or producer. Subsidies that support the construction of plants and equipment can lower fixed costs and radically change cost structures, which can result in dumping over the life of the subsidized facility. As is explored in more detail in the next section, in nonmarket economies there is little distinction between subsidies and dumping.[35] In many sectors, government subsidies are a major underlying cause of dumping.

In the most heavily distorted sector of the global economy, agriculture, large subsidies, and market access barriers result in products and commodities frequently being sold in export markets at prices far below domestic prices and often below the cost of production. The Uruguay Round agreement on agriculture has attempted to lessen the underlying causes of dumping in the agriculture sector by reducing market access barriers, domestic subsidies, and export subsidies.[36] Still, there are certainly problems with dumping in the agriculture sector associated with the trade problems targeted by the Uruguay Round and state-directed marketing efforts. For example, U.S. wheat producers continue to complain that the Canadian Wheat Board dumps wheat in the United States while selling at higher prices in Canada's domestic market.[37]

The role of subsidies as a cause of dumping is probably most obvious in the steel sector. Steel has been a major focus of antidumping actions in the United States and in the rest of the world; about a third of the antidumping actions filed in the United States since 1980 have involved steel and steel products.[38] In the United States and Europe, so many antidumping actions have been filed in the steel sector that antidumping laws are sometimes criticized as "tools of steel protection."

As should be clear from the previous chapters, antidumping laws are hardly the exclusive property of the steel industry. In the United States, antidumping laws are at least as important to high-technology industries, such as semiconductor and supercomputer manufacturing.

There can be no doubt, however, that dumping is a frequent problem in the steel sector. In one country or another, dumping of steel can be linked primarily to trade barriers, private-sector collusion, and state-run steel operations, but the root cause of dumping of steel is consistent global excess capacity in steel production, usually built with state assistance.

For reasons having more to do with national pride than sound economics, countries from China to Germany to South Korea have defined steel mills as an essential element of an industrial economy and as symbols of national prestige. As a result, a long list of governments, including those of Japan, Brazil, South Korea, China, Sweden, Mexico, Germany, Italy, France, and Russia, have pursued aggressive industrial policies to build up steel manufacturing capabilities.[39]

In some of these countries, steel mills are actually owned by the state. In others, they were built with heavy state subsidies and loans. This capacity is almost always built with little or no regard for prevailing conditions in the global steel market. Further, once the mills are built, governments are reluctant to see workers—who are also voters—laid off or permanently unemployed. This often results in the capacity being used to produce steel even during a supply glut. This exacerbates such gluts and encourages import barriers to prevent imports from entering the domestic market; sometimes the state-built or -owned steel companies actually have a measure of control over imports.[40]

These generalizations have not been true of the U.S. market. The United States has a substantial steel industry that has made a competitive resurgence in recent years,[41] but that resurgence is the result of corporate restructuring, the adoption of new production technologies, and the emergence of "minimills," not government subsidies.[42]

During the Reagan and Bush administrations, the United States did negotiate voluntary restraint agreements (VRAs) with steel exporting countries to restrict imports into the United States. In effect, the VRAs functioned as a broad suspension agreement, and countervailing-duty and antidumping cases were less frequently brought against imports from countries subject to VRAs. But the VRA program was terminated in March 1992.[43] In the wake of this termination, some eighty new antidumping cases involving steel were filed by the U.S. steel industry.[44]

Aside from the VRAs, the U.S. market has been generally open to imports, and throughout the last three decades, the United States has imported far more steel than any other market. Even while the VRAs were in place, the United States remained the world's leading importer of steel.[45] This has made the U.S. market particularly vulnerable to dumping in times of global supply gluts. This, in turn, has resulted in numerous antidumping cases brought by the U.S. steel industry.

Several rounds of international negotiations aimed at reducing subsidies and opening steel markets around the world have taken place. The legacy of decades of heavy government subsidies of steel production, however, remains a considerable global excess capacity in steel production, which is likely to result in continuing dumping for many years to come. As one observer of the steel industry noted: "All that steel production has got to go somewhere and the United States is the only market likely to accept it."

**Nonmarket Economies and Dumping**

The so-called nonmarket economy (NME) antidumping laws are among the most widely used and certainly the most controversial provisions of antidumping laws in both the United States and Europe. For decades, nonmarket and reforming nonmarket economies have posed unique challenges to antidumping laws, national trade authorities, and international trade agreements. These problems were greatly complicated by the military standoff between the Communist bloc and the West, but the core problem with building a normal trade relationship is that nonmarket economies do not have a traditional open market.

Of course, NMEs have their own system for directing production and distributing the products to consumers. That system, however, does not rely heavily upon the cornerstone of market economics—the price mechanism. Without a market-determined price, it is difficult to set the terms of trade between the nonmarket world and the market world. Particularly since nonmarket economies traditionally have limited investment and trade contact with market economies and maintain currencies that are not convertible, when they do engage in trade, nonmarket economies often price not to reflect costs but to gain Western currencies to finance other purchases.[46] The problem of appropriate prices on goods traded between market and nonmarket economies seems insoluble even in theory.

Throughout most of the Cold War this problem remained mostly theoretical; there was little trade between the two economic camps, Communism and capitalism. U.S. trade laws, such as export control limitations and the 1974 Trade Act, put severe limits on allowable trade. A statute, known as Section 406, allowed the administration to restrict imports from nonmarket economies if they were responsible for "market disruption," but this statute was never widely employed—probably because it gave the president wide leeway in contrast to the relatively automatic antidumping and countervailing-duty laws.[47]

When imports from nonmarket economies began to cause real injury to sectors of the U.S. economy, U.S. industries looked to antidumping laws as a solution. (As noted in the previous section, within a nonmarket economy it is difficult to decide whether antidumping or countervailing-duty laws are the more appropriate tool to address this problem, because in a true nonmarket economy all inputs are in some sense subsidized by the government. For administrative convenience and because the ITA felt that the actions of nonmarket governments were not reachable under U.S. countervailing-duty law, antidumping laws have come to be the preferred tool in the United States and Europe.)[48] In the 1970s, a few Eastern European countries, notably Poland and Hungary, began some export initiatives to the West. Poland began exporting electric golf carts to the United States in significant numbers. Eventually, U.S. golf cart producers complained that these Polish golf carts were unfairly priced and filed an antidumping complaint.

This antidumping complaint forced U.S. administrative authorities to grapple with the previously largely academic issue of pricing between non-market and market economies. The Polish golf cart case was particularly vexing because Poland did not have a convertible currency and had no usable cost data on inputs, since most were simply provided by the government. Beyond that, there was no domestic Polish market or third market for the golf carts because the carts were exported only to the United States. At the time, golf carts were made by only the United States and Poland. There seemed no way to get a reliable measure of either a market price of Polish golf carts or of the true costs of inputs.

The U.S. authorities were forced to adopt an innovative approach to the problem of pricing Polish golf carts. Officials asked the exporter to provide actual data on the amount of labor, electricity, and other inputs. Surrogate markets were then chosen to set appropriate monetary values for the inputs; the surrogate markets were to be at a similar level of development as Poland's. The input values in these surrogate markets were then tallied, and after standard adjustments, this became the nondumped price for the goods from the nonmarket economy.[49] In 1988, the Congress revised this procedure to require that the surrogate markets chosen must actually produce the product that is the subject of the dumping complaint, the hope being to force a more accurate estimate of the true cost of production.[50]

This procedure will doubtlessly strike many as unusual.[51] Certainly, it is a complex procedure that requires a number of subjective judgments by administering officials, but it is a reasonable approach to solving the problem of setting appropriate prices on goods from nonmarket economies. No better approach to the problem has been suggested, and similar procedures have been adopted by other market countries, as well as the European Union.[52] (As noted in Chapter 6, the European Union is now exploring refining its approach along the lines of the United States' "Bubbles of Capitalism" experiment.)

Of course, there are no purely nonmarket countries. Especially in recent years, to greater and lesser extents, all former nonmarket economies have adopted economic reforms and moved toward market economics. Reforms are under way, market institutions and rules are taking shape, and the price mechanism and the market are increasingly relied upon to make allocation decisions. These changes make the governments of many reforming nonmarket countries resentful of the implication of NME antidumping rules that they are still nonmarket economies.

Nonetheless, many maintain a number of features of nonmarket economics, which makes a normal market-based determination of prices and costs impossible. In many cases, the government still directs the allocation of some inputs, often labor and energy; state planning is still common; and state-owned enterprises receive subsidies and enjoy trade protection, often engage in foreign trade, and are frequent targets of antidumping complaints. As a result, NME antidumping procedures are still widely employed by the United States and Europe. In 1988, the Omnibus Trade Act established six tests to determine whether a country should be judged an NME for the purposes of antidumping laws: (1) convertibility of currency, (2) extent to which wage rates are set by the market, (3) extent to which foreign investment and joint ventures are permitted, (4) extent of government ownership and control of production, (5) extent of government control of resources, and (6) other factors deemed appropriate.[53]

Most nations of the reforming Communist world, including China, Russia, and most of Eastern Europe, are still regarded as NMEs for the purposes of antidumping laws. The Commerce Department has considered the concept that "bubbles of capitalism" or "market-oriented industries" may exist in nonmarket economies.[54] A "bubble of capitalism" or "market-oriented enterprise" would be a company or a sector that is entirely market-based. If such enterprises could be found, it would be appropriate to handle unfair-trade complaints against them as normal countervailing-duty or antidumping cases, depending on the specific nature of the complaint. It is difficult, however, to conceive of any company or sector that would be totally untouched by the operation of a centrally planned economy. After all, even if the company did not receive any direct benefit, it is difficult to believe that all of its primary suppliers would be similarly completely outside the operating centrally planned economy. Thus, the experiment in trying to define isolated examples of market economies within a nonmarket economy seems destined to fail.

In part to address concerns about weaknesses in NME dumping procedures, the Congress has given the president more leeway in striking suspen-

Chart 3.2 **U.S. Imports from China, 1986–1996**

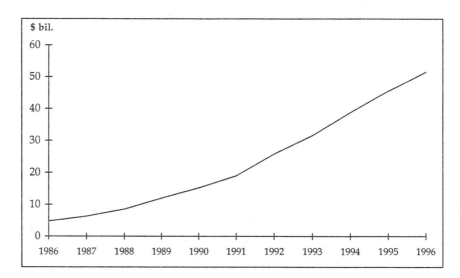

*Source:* Bureau of the Census.

sion agreements with nonmarket economies, the hope being that suspension agreements allow a more flexible solution to unfair-trade problems involving NMEs.[55]

Countries that are deemed NMEs have the opportunity to establish that on both de jure and de facto bases they should not be regarded as nonmarket economies. In a recent case, Poland was able to make such a demonstration but ultimately decided not to take advantage of this designation under U.S. antidumping law.[56] Apparently, Poland decided that the practical result of being designated a market economy could result in higher duties than the NME antidumping procedure.

Both Russia and China have bristled at being classified as NMEs under antidumping laws in the United States and Europe and have tried to raise this issue in their respective WTO accession negotiations. NME antidumping procedures are, however, explicitly permissible under the WTO and, as a World Bank analysis noted, U.S. NME antidumping procedures have not been particularly burdensome on these countries' exports.[57]

Until recently, the NME antidumping procedures were seldom used and little known. In fact, trade between the United States and the NME world was almost negligible into the 1990s. With the end of the Cold War and the subsequent wave of reform in the NME world, however, U.S. imports from NMEs began to increase dramatically.

Chart 3.3 **U.S. Imports from the Former Soviet Union, 1986–1996**

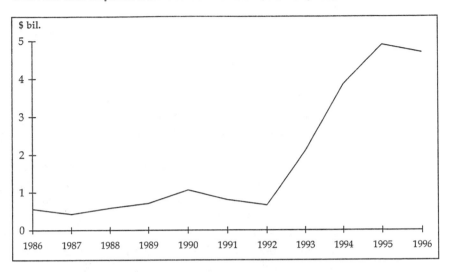

*Source:* Bureau of the Census.

China has become a particularly important force in the U.S. market. U.S. imports from China have grown to over $60 billion annually. China is now the second largest source of the U.S. trade deficit—after only Japan—and, if current trends persist, will soon become the leading source.[58] Globally, China has become one of the world's top ten exporters, and its exports have grown at three times the world average for nearly two decades.[59]

Russian and Eastern European exports to the United States have grown, but not nearly as dramatically as those of China.[60] These European former Communists have, however, become major exporters to the European Union.[61]

Many of these reforming Communists are anxious to gain hard currency from the West, and the officials making export decisions often do not even have a clear idea of production costs. The result is often dumping. Thus, as the volume of trade has increased, so has the number of antidumping cases. As noted in Chapter 2, China has become the leading target of antidumping complaints in the United States. These antidumping investigations involve products ranging from honey to specialty steel products. Russia and some of the former Soviet republics have been the subject of several antidumping investigations on products such as uranium and steel. The European Union has also brought similar cases against both China and Russia as well as several Eastern European economies. As other former and present Communist countries, notably Vietnam, expand their exports to the West, similar antidumping complaints are likely to follow.

As Table 3.2 demonstrates, China's exports of some products that the U.S. Commerce Department defines as high-technology products[62] have increased 1,200 percent between 1990 and 1996. And China has pursued a conscious policy of increasing its presence in advanced manufacturing sectors.[63] Russia, the former Soviet republics, and Eastern Europe have also been working to establish a presence in more advanced manufacturing sectors. To date, these efforts have borne only limited fruit; nevertheless these countries have significant technology and an educated workforce. At some point, they are likely to succeed in exporting a broader range of products.

In sectors where NMEs are not established players, but are attempting to establish a presence, the incentives to dump are even greater. Costs in these new sectors are often high because of lack of experience and other factors and deep price discounts are often used to win over skeptical customers. Therefore, the movement of NMEs into more advanced product categories could well result in more NME dumping.

The fundamental motivations behind NME dumping also remain. Often, exports are produced from facilities built at state expense using some inputs that are provided at below-market costs. There is considerable pressure from the government to build up exports to strengthen the economy. Further, Western hard currency is in great demand because it is in perennially short supply and greatly needed in order to import from the West. The combination of no clear cost structure, pressure to export, and a demand for hard currency creates a powerful incentive to dump exports in foreign markets.

In connection with China, the World Bank made the following comment on this very topic: "China's approach to trade policy so far has been 'mercantilist,' i.e. motivated by achieving export growth for the sake of generating foreign exchange without sufficient regard to its costs."[64] The same could be said for much of the NME world.

The combination of incomplete reform throughout the former NME world and increasing efforts by NME countries to expand exports are almost certain to result in an increased number of antidumping actions against NMEs. If current trends continue, China is quite likely to remain the leading target of antidumping complaints in the United States. If Russia's current economic programs and growth rates continue, it could well join China as a major subject of antidumping actions. Similar developments are likely in the European Union. NME dumping cases seem destined to become even more common in the next decade.

**Conclusion**

This discussion of the underlying causes of dumping would suggest that dumping may become less of a problem if market access barriers are re-

Table 3.2

**U.S. High-Technology Imports from China** (Selected Products)

| Product Category | Value in Dollars | | Percent Change |
|---|---|---|---|
| | 1990 | 1996 | |
| Optical disc (including compact disc) players | 7,851,073 | 343,320,685 | 4,273% |
| Mechano-therapy appliance and massage apparatus | 10,446,574 | 98,231,895 | 840% |
| Printed circuits of plastic/glass, =3 layers | 128,114 | 31,137,974 | 24,205% |
| Certain parts of civil airplanes/helicopters | 17,619,365 | 26,191,156 | 49% |
| Parts of turbojet or turbopropeller aircraft engines | 3,337,443 | 22,850,215 | 585% |
| Certain semiconductor diodes, not photosensitive | 52,180 | 10,858,692 | 20,710% |
| Radio remote control apparatus | 280,629 | 7,660,260 | 2,630% |
| Certain unmounted lenses | 382,215 | 5,317,461 | 1,291% |
| Certain radio transmission apparatus | 149,503 | 2,809,340 | 1,779% |
| Telegraphic switching apparatus | 227,004 | 2,778,586 | 1,124% |
| Certain photosensitive diodes | 2,369 | 1,815,181 | 76,522% |
| Instruments and appliances for use in civil aircraft | 180,432 | 989,226 | 448% |
| Signal generators | 20,904 | 943,185 | 4,412% |
| Video recording or reproducing apparatus, excluding tape | 65,565 | 933,133 | 1,323% |
| Certain medical and surgical instruments and appliances | 468,516 | 892,417 | 90% |
| Certain telephonic and switching apparatus | 148,626 | 586,306 | 294% |
| Parts for diodes, transistors, and similar semiconductors | 30,727 | 551,216 | 1,694% |
| Certain numerically controlled horizontal lathes | 46,448 | 519,490 | 1,018% |
| Certain surveying instruments and appliances, exc. compasses | 83,233 | 485,796 | 484% |
| Electro-surgical instruments, appliances, and parts | 77,120 | 416,271 | 440% |
| Certain numerically controlled horizontal lathes | 159,601 | 390,490 | 45% |
| Certain mounted mirrors | 51,746 | 253,168 | 389% |
| Machine centers with automatic tool changing and other features | 72,938 | 216,379 | 197% |
| Microscopes, exc. optical; diffraction apparatus | 21,350 | 202,311 | 848% |
| Optical direction-finding compasses | 15,750 | 149,651 | 850% |
| Other electrical direction-finding compasses | 6,537 | 139,358 | 2,032% |
| Aromatic lactones used as drugs | 20,173 | 136,497 | 577% |
| Grand Total | 41,946,135 | 560,776,339 | 1,237% |

*Source:* Bureau of the Census.

moved, antitrust procedures are globalized, and NMEs become market economies. Ultimately, this may be true. If market access barriers such as tariffs and nontariff measures are dismantled, it will be more difficult for governments to maintain sanctuary home markets. Negotiations to lower trade barriers have been under way for more than four decades. The global trading system is also increasingly focusing upon subsidy limitation and reduction; this may result in a global reduction of subsidy levels, which in turn will eliminate an important underlying cause of dumping.

There are also discussions on an international antitrust/competition regime, and NMEs are trying to adopt market reforms. If these efforts come to fruition, two other major causes of dumping would be removed. Thus it is possible that developments on other fronts could make antidumping laws less important in the future.

If the prospects for success of these efforts are assessed realistically, however, it appears that the true free, competitive global market is still a long way away. Levels of trade protection have been reduced, but as tariffs and quotas have been reduced and eliminated, new barriers, such as discriminatory standards, have increased. Often, formal trade barriers have been replaced by protection orchestrated by the private sector as is the case in Japan's photographic film market. Protectionism remains a powerful political force in many countries, if not the entire world.

International negotiations to reduce subsidies and establish a global antitrust policy are likely to take decades. There also does not yet seem to be anything approaching a global consensus that all forms of private-sector collusion should be eliminated. In fact, many Asian countries have economic systems that rely upon significant collusion in the private sector that would not be tolerated under U.S. antitrust laws. Even Europe has different standards for antitrust laws than the United States.

The frequent discussion of reform in the NME world may give the impression that economic reform is well under way there. In fact, significant changes have occurred, but many aspects of nonmarket economics are still present in NME countries. Economic planning and state-owned enterprises are still common. More troubling is that many NME countries have made it clear that they do not aspire to become market economies. Chinese leaders speak of a Chinese version of market-socialism, and Russian economic reformers paint a model for the future Russian economy that is far from free-market economics.[65]

In sum, although the causes of dumping may change and may even be reduced somewhat, they are likely to persist for decades, if not permanently remain in place. Therefore, antidumping laws are likely to remain a critical safeguard for the largely open, market-based economy of the United States.

They will also remain an important interface mechanism to allow the United States to trade with NMEs without disrupting its economy. In the short term, given the rapid entry of NMEs into the world economy and the continuing high levels of protection and subsidies in many countries that are leading sources of dumping, it is likely that antidumping complaints could increase over the coming decade. Antidumping laws are likely to remain a critical element of U.S. trade policy for the foreseeable future.

## Notes

1. In recent years, Brazil has taken a number of steps to liberalize its economy. Recently, however, there has been considerable discussion of raising tariffs in conjunction with the formation of the Southern Cone trading area, also known as MERCOSUR.

2. Office of the U.S. Trade Representative, *1997 National Trade Estimate Report on Foreign Trade Barriers* (Washington, DC: GPO, 1997).

3. For an explanation of Section 301, see Greg Mastel, *American Trade Laws After the Uruguay Round* (Armonk, NY: M.E. Sharpe, 1996).

4. The information on this chart is all drawn from public documents. For a detailed explanation of the methodology, contact Woodworth Holdings, Ltd., Automotive Research, Detroit, MI.

5. For a discussion of this phenomenon see Chalmers Johnson, *Japan: Who Governs? The Rise of the Developmental State* (New York: W.W. Norton, 1995).

6. For a discussion of the specific problems in the Japanese market and recent changes, see Office of the U.S. Trade Representative, *1997 National Trade Estimate.*

7. Gary Hamel and C.K. Prahalad, "Do You Really Have a Global Strategy," *Harvard Business Review* July-August 1985: 139.

8. Good discussions of the events surrounding the semiconductor incident can be found in Kenneth Flamm, *Mismanaged Trade: Strategic Policy and the Semiconductor Industry* (Washington, DC: Brookings Institution, 1997); Laura D'Andrea Tyson, *Who's Bashing Whom? Trade Conflict in High Technology Industries* (Washington, DC: Institute for International Economics, 1993); Fred Warshofsky, *The Chip War* (New York: Charles Scribner, 1989); and Clyde Prestowitz, *Trading Places: How We Allowed Japan to Take the Lead* (New York: Basic Books, 1988).

9. Crista Hardie, "Two Korean Memory Makers Challenge," *Electronic News,* May 26, 1997, p. 13.

10. Jack Robertson, Jennifer Baljko, and Mark LaPedus, "Taiwan SRAM Makers Face Severe Dumping Penalties," *Electronic Buyer's News,* September 29, 1997.

11. For a discussion of Korea's strategy, see Seongjae Yu, "Korea's High Technology Strategy," in *The Emerging Technological Trajectory of the Pacific Rim,* Denis Fred Simon, ed. (Armonk, NY: M.E. Sharpe, 1995).

12. For a discussion of these events, see Kozo Yamamura and Jan Van Den Berg, "Japan's Rapid-Growth Policy on Trial: The Television Case," in *Agents of Influence: How Japan Manipulates America's Political and Economic System,* Pat Choate, ed. (New York: Simon and Schuster, 1990), p. 87; Prestowitz, *Trading Places,* p. 201. For a summary of subsequent antidumping investigations, see the U.S. International Trade Commission, *The Economic Effects of Antidumping and Countervailing Duty Orders and Suspension Agreements* (Washington, DC: ITC, 1995), Chapter 10.

13. Paul W. Valentine, "Panasonic to Repay $16 Million to Settle Lawsuit," *Washington Post,* January 19, 1989, p. F1.

14. Tyson, *Who's Bashing Whom?* pp. 76–77.

15. Ibid., pp. 76–84.

16. Ibid.

17. For information on Super 301 and the Cray dispute, see Greg Mastel, *American Trade Laws After the Uruguay Round* (Armonk, NY: M.E. Sharpe, 1996), pp. 33–44.

18. Office of the U.S. Trade Representative, *1997 National Trade Estimate,* pp. 198–199.

19. Ibid., pp. 195–196.

20. Greg Gordon, "Trade Ruling Favors Cray in Rift with Japan Firms; NEC, Others Found Guilty of 'Dumping,' " *Minneapolis Star Tribune,* September 27, 1997, p. 1D.

21. Ibid.

22. An interesting footnote to these events was the issuance of several reports by an institute devoted to the promotion of laissez faire economics—the CATO Institute—criticizing the supercomputer antidumping action. The specifics of these reports are not particularly notable. The reports focus primarily upon generic criticisms of antidumping laws, such as the Commerce Department's being biased, using arbitrary procedures, and imposing heavy information gathering burdens on respondents. Each of these are dealt with specifically in Chapters 2 and 5. The CATO study is also discussed in more detail in Chapter 5. For an example, see Christopher M. Dumler, *Anti-Dumping Laws Trash Supercomputer Competition,* CATO Institute Briefing Paper (Washington, DC: CATO Institute, 1997).

23. U.S. International Trade Commission, *Economic Effects of Antidumping,* Chapter 14.

24. Paul Krugman and Maurice Obstfeld, *International Economics: Theory and Policy* (New York: HarperCollins, 1994), third edition, pp. 116–132.

25. For a discussion of the behavior of such firms, see Gene M. Grossman, ed., *Imperfect Competition and International Trade* (Cambridge: MIT Press, 1994).

26. Dewey, Ballantine, Bushby, and Wood (law firm), *Japanese Barriers on Imported Photographic Film and Paper* (Washington, DC: Dewey Ballantine, 1997), and D.P. Baron, "Integrated Strategy, Trade Policy, and Global Competition," *California Management Review* 39, no. 2 (September 30, 1997): 145–161.

27. Kodak filed a Section 301 petition on this matter May 18, 1995. WTO action was initiated in the summer of 1996.

28. In its arguments before the WTO, the U.S. government has made a number of allegations on the involvement of the Japanese government in restricting access to the Japanese market, some of which involves steps beyond simply tolerating collusion. *New York Times,* December 10, 1997, p. A34.

29. For more information on the U.S. complaint, see Dewey, Ballantine, Bushby, and Wood (law firm) for Eastman Kodak Company, *Privatizing Protection: Japanese Market Barriers in Consumer Photographic Film and Consumer Photographic Paper,* Memorandum in Support of a Petition Filed Pursuant to Section 301 of the Trade Act of 1974, as Amended, May 1975.

30. A more detailed summary of the facts in this case can be found in volume 3 of the prehearing brief in the matter of *Color Negative Photographic Paper from Japan and the Netherlands* before the U.S. International Trade Commission (Investigation #731–TA-661, 662) August 17, 1994.

31. Wendy Bounds, "Fuji Film Signs Accord on U.S. Pricing, Japanese Firm Will Raise Charges on Color Paper; Kodak, Konica Benefit," *Wall Street Journal,* August 22, 1994, p. 41; "Fuji Statement on Signing Suspension Agreement with Department of Commerce," *Business Wire,* August 19, 1994.

32. Mark Tilton, *Restrained Trade: Cartels in Japan's Basic Materials Industries* (Ithaca, NY: Cornell University Press), 1997.

33. For a more detailed examination of the issues of Mexican dumping of cement, see F. Gerard Adams and Andrew R. Wechsler, *Conditions of Competition and the Business Cycle for Gray Portland Cement* (monograph submitted in connection with ITA consideration of the Mexican cement antidumping case), 1990. A brief critical discussion of the cement case can be found in Paul R. Krugman and Maurice Obstfeld, *International Economics: Theory and Policy,* third edition (New York: HarperCollins, 1994), p. 137.

34. For a broader discussion of this issue, see Coalition for Open Trade, *Addressing Private Restraints of Trade: Industries and Governments Search for Answers Regarding Trade-and-Competition Policy* (Washington, DC: COT, 1997).

35. Subsidies and dumping are often so interrelated that it is not unusual to see domestic petitioners file both antidumping and countervailing-duty actions at the same time to address different aspects of the same problem. Both antidumping and countervailing-duty actions have been employed to address trade problems involving Mexican cement, agricultural products, and steel, to name but a few examples.

36. *Final Texts of the GATT Uruguay Round Agreements Including the Agreement Establishing the World Trade Organization,* Agreement on Agriculture, April 15, 1994.

37. Office of the U.S. Trade Representative, *National Trade Estimate,* p. 38.

38. International Trade Administration statistics.

39. For a discussion of these industrial policies, see Thomas R. Howell, William A. Noellert, Jesse G. Kreier, and Alan Wm. Wolff, *Steel and the State: Government Intervention and Steel's Structural Crisis* (Boulder, CO: Westview Press, 1988); William T. Hogan, *Capital Investment in Steel: A World Plan for the 1990s* (Lexington, MA: Lexington Books, 1992).

40. Howell et al., pp. 263–286; Tai-Hwa Chow, *Industrial Policy of Japan: The Steel Industry (1950–1990)* (Pittsburgh: Global Study of the Steel Industry Working Paper Series, University of Pittsburgh and Carnegie-Mellon University, 1993).

41. John H. Grant, Roger S. Ahlbrandt, Frank Giarrantani, and John E. Prescott, *Restructuring for Competitiveness in the Global Steel Industry* (Pittsburgh: University of Pittsburgh and Carnegie-Mellon University, 1993).

42. Roger S. Ahlbrandt, *Involvement of the U.S. Government in the Steel Industry* (Pittsburgh: Global Study of the Steel Industry Working Paper Series, University of Pittsburgh and Carnegie-Mellon University), 1992.

43. For a detailed discussion, see Robert A. Blecker, Thea M. Lee, and Robert E. Scott, *Trade Protection and Industrial Revitalization: American Steel in the 1980s* (Washington, DC: Economic Policy Institute, 1993).

44. International Trade Administration statistics.

45. Blecker et al., *Trade Protection.*

46. World Bank study on China's trade regime. World Bank, *China: Foreign Trade Reform* (Washington, DC: World Bank), 1994.

47. Market disruption is defined as a rapid increase in imports that is a significant cause of material injury to U.S. producers of like or competitive products (P.L. 93–618, 88 Stat. 1978 [1975]). Under the law, the ITC makes a recommendation to the president as to whether market disruption has occurred.

48. For a discussion of efforts to employ countervailing-duty laws to NMEs, see James A. Meszaros, "Application of the United States' Law of Countervailing Duties to Nonmarket Imports: Effects of Recent Foreign Reforms," *ILSA Journal of International and Comparative Law* 2 (Winter 1996): 463.

49. John Jackson, *The World Trading System* (Cambridge, MA: MIT Press), 1994, p. 295.

50. Section 1318 of the Omnibus Trade and Competitiveness Act of 1988; Section 773(b) of the Tariff Act of 1930 (19 U.S.C. Section 1677b).

51. This approach has a number of critics: Sanghan Wang, "U.S. Trade Laws Concerning Nonmarket Economies Revisited for Fairness and Consistency," *Emory International Law Review* 10 (Winter 1996): 593; David A. Codevilla, "Discouraging the Practice of What We Preach: Saarstahl I, Inland Steel and the Implementation of the Uruguay Round Act of GATT 1994," *George Mason Independent Law Review* 3 (Summer 1995): 435.

52. For a good discussion of NME antidumping procedures in both the United States and Europe, see Peter D. Ehrenhaft, Brian Vernon Hindley, Constantine Michalopoulos, and L. Alan Winters, *Policies on Imports from Economies in Transition, Two Case Studies,* World Bank Studies of Economies in Transition Series (Washington, DC: World Bank, 1997).

53. Section 771(18) of the Tariff Act of 1930, as amended.

54. Judith H. Bello et al., "Searching for 'Bubbles of Capitalism': Application of the U.S. Antidumping and Countervailing Duty Laws to Reforming Nonmarket Economies," *George Washington Journal of International Law and Economics* 21 (1992): 665, 673; Richard H. Lantz, "The Search for Consistency: Treatment of Nonmarket Economies in Transition Under United States Antidumping and Countervailing Duty Laws," *The American University Journal of International Law and Policy* 10 (Spring 1995): 993.

55. See Lantz, "Search for Consistency."

56. *Carbon Steel Plate from Poland* (58 Fed. Reg. 37205 [9 July 1993]).

57. Ehrenhaft et al., *Policies on Imports,* p. 32.

58. Greg Mastel, *The Rise of the Chinese Economy: The Middle Kingdom Emerges* (Armonk, NY: M.E. Sharpe, 1997), pp. 20–33.

59. Ibid., pp. 27–28.

60. U.S. Customs Service statistics.

61. European Union Customs statistics.

62. Department of Commerce statistics.

63. Greg Mastel, *The Rise of the Chinese Economy: The Middle Kingdom Emerges* (Armonk, NY: M.E. Sharpe, 1997), pp. 71–75.

64. *China: Foreign Trade Reform,* A World Bank Country Study (Washington, DC: World Bank, 1994), p. 1.

65. Benjamin Kang Lim, "Socialism Right Choice for China-Premier Li Peng," *Reuters World Service,* July 29, 1996.

# 4

# The Economic Case for Antidumping Laws

Many criticize the economic underpinnings of antidumping laws, but these critiques are often unsophisticated. They tend to focus on some microeconomic justifications for below-cost pricing, which are addressed in detail in the next chapter. They also frequently advance the argument—with varying degrees of complexity—that antidumping laws impose new duties, which have a variety of generally acknowledged bad effects, such as higher consumer costs and protection of inefficient domestic producers.

Unquestionably, tariffs or duties do impose economic costs. Many economic thinkers, however, have recognized a number of legitimate rationales for imposing tariffs or otherwise intervening in the market. These include protection of infant industries, preserving national security, and countering foreign protectionism.

Another widely accepted rationale for government intervention is the need to prevent the formation of monopolies or prevent the emergence of other anticompetitive situations. A broad consensus of economists support this objective because trusts can raise prices, stifle innovation, and generally distort economic outcomes.[1] Although as explained in Chapters 1 and 5, antidumping and antitrust laws have diverged in many important respects, antidumping laws still share the objective of combating monopolies and cartels. On the domestic front, antitrust laws attack this problem. On the international front, by guarding against injury from overseas cartels and monopolies, antidumping laws fill part of this function.

In recent years, thinking on international trade problems has evolved to address problems of imperfect competition arising from national monopolies, protected markets, government subsidies, dumping, and related market distortions.[2] Strategic trade theory, which, in the view of some of its leading proponents, supports intervention to influence market outcomes, has evolved from this thinking.

These lines of economic thought, coupled with the traditional arguments for intervening to prevent the formation of monopolies, provide the underlying economic rationale for antidumping laws that is traced in this chapter.

Before going into a detailed explanation of this rationale, however, it is necessary to make a note on the operation of antidumping laws. Antidumping laws can be triggered by all U.S. industries that compete with imported goods, not just a select few. Some of the reasoning advanced below applies only to "strategic" industries or only to manufacturing industries. In the real world, these categories cover the bulk of U.S. antidumping cases. In fact, dumping seems to be concentrated in these industries for a variety of reasons, but there are exceptions. With hundreds of antidumping cases, undoubtedly some can be found that do not smoothly fit the rationales advanced here.

This is not, however, a persuasive reason for limiting the application of antidumping laws to only "strategic" industries. Strategic industries are difficult to define precisely. Most would agree—regardless of the criteria used—that certain high-technology industries are strategic, but even some other "basic" industries invest heavily in research and development and maintain a high-wage workforce—two important criteria often used to define "strategic" industries. In sectors where dumping has been a long-term problem, such as steel or cement, U.S. trading partners seem to have defined the industries as strategic and worthy of extensive efforts to distort the market in order to build a domestic industry.

In addition, there is a basic fairness issue. Based on arbitrary and debatable criteria, it would not be appropriate to take action in cases in which industries are deemed strategic but ignore the same behavior when it affects industries not deemed strategic.

The practical problems of limiting the application of antidumping laws only to strategic industries or only to manufacturing interests would further complicate an already complex administrative process. Ironically, adding the requirement that such a determination be made would likely slow the operation of antidumping laws and make them less able to respond when strategic industries are threatened.

Further, in the case studies section, because of limitations on space and available data, it was necessary to select a few important cases to analyze the economic impact. The examples chosen are typical of other antidumping cases, but they do not necessarily define the entire universe of antidumping cases. The examples have been chosen to demonstrate that antidumping laws can generate significant economic gains, not that they necessarily always do.

## Theoretical Case for Antidumping Laws— Imperfect Competition

Classical economists evaluate the world with models that make a number of simplifying assumptions about how an economy operates. Most models assume that the conditions for perfect competition exist, including low entry and exit barriers, a large number of producers, and an absence of other government-introduced market distortions. If evaluated from the perspective of perfectly competitive conditions, antidumping laws and all other government efforts to influence the market are difficult to justify because they necessarily alter the optimal market outcome.

Unfortunately, this model had great difficulty explaining outcomes in the real international economy, in which trade barriers, subsidies, monopolies, and other market distortions are the rule, not the exception. Most damaging is that these government-introduced market distortions seem to "succeed," at least as the term is defined by the governments that practice the policies.

The standard-bearer for this new economic thinking was Japan, although many have copied the approach in recent years. The history of, and debate over, Japanese economic policies is far too extensive to consider in total here, but interested readers can examine the works mentioned in the notes.[3] As the case studies in the previous chapter demonstrate in detail, Japan has practiced a brand of industrial policy that involved protecting industries in the home market with an eye toward developing industries into export powers. As they begin to enter export markets, Japanese industries almost universally begin to export at prices substantially below the prices charged in the home market—a practice known as dumping. This is a fair summary of Japan's actions in a number of sectors analyzed in this book, including semiconductors, photographic film, bearings, steel, and automobiles.

Classical economic thinking would suggest that Japan's strategy would fail. Japanese consumers would be kept relatively poor because they would be forced to pay excessively high prices for the goods they produce. The trade barriers would encourage inefficiency in the protected industries, eventually rendering them unable to compete in world markets and producing a generally backward economy.

Some of the predictions did come true. The living standard of Japanese citizens has lagged behind the level that would be expected from comparison with Western economies with similar per capita incomes. Such an outcome was acceptable, however, because the primary goal of the economic model was building strong industries, not enriching consumers. Thus, Japanese policy makers were willing to ignore Western economists' protests that Japanese policies resulted in a net loss to the economy due to high consumer costs.

Beyond that, flying in the face of theoretical predictions, Japan's strategy of closing the home market in order to promote exports worked well. The strategy did not turn every industry into a world-class exporter, but it did not produce many laggards either. Quite to the contrary, and due in part to government intervention, Japanese manufacturers plowed the large profits reaped in the domestic market into improving manufacturing techniques, obtaining production technology, and dumping products in export markets. As a result, Japanese firms became leaders in sectors ranging from automobiles to semiconductors.

It seems that many countries around the world were willing to share Japan's judgment that it was wise to sacrifice consumer interests to build production; they closed their home markets and dumped to gain export share. Japan's Asian neighbors, including South Korea, Taiwan, and China, have pursued various permutations of the Japanese strategy.

Some economists and other observers have suggested that the recent economic troubles in Asia are linked in large part to countries following this model.[4] It is difficult to provide a definitive prescription for the economic problems in Asia at this point, but the Japanese economic model does seem to be at least a contributing factor. It would be naive, however, to assume that the Japanese model will be scrapped. From the perspective of its practitioners, the Japanese model has worked for decades and created near economic miracles in Japan, South Korea, and China—to name only a few. The governments of these countries seem to see the Asian economic problems as cause for refining the model, not for scrapping it wholesale. Beyond that, the recent WTO decision to allow Japanese private-sector protectionism in the photographic film market, which is discussed in detail in Chapter 3, has already been read as an endorsement of the Japanese model for international trade.

As Chapter 2 notes, these same Asian countries—Japan, China, and South Korea—have been the most frequent targets of U.S. antidumping actions. But Brazil and several European countries have also been targets of antidumping actions. In most of the sectors where antidumping actions have been brought against these countries, a similar economic situation exists, with industries exporting from behind high external trade barriers. Brazil has not been as successful as some of the Asian countries in pursuing this strategy, but the description of the forces at work in some of the sectors subject to dumping action is still accurate.[5]

Europe exports from behind high trade barriers in the agricultural sector. As noted in the last chapter, in other sectors, such as steel, many European countries have a long history of state ownership and state subsidies. This state support builds excess capacity, which in turn encourages dumping. In this respect, the effect of subsidies is quite similar to the effect of a closed market, which is also present in a number of European countries.

### *Models for Imperfect Competition*

The Japanese success ultimately spurred some rethinking by economists. Concepts of imperfect competition were explored and refined as explanations for Japan's success.[6] Japan's semiconductor industry was the spring-board for several analyses that approached the problem from different angles.

Baldwin and Krugman developed a model for Japan's efforts in the semiconductor industry in its earlier stages when the focus was on 16K memory chips, known as DRAMs.[7] This simulation generated a number of interesting results. First, it found that the free-trade scenario, with semiconductors being freely exported between Japan and the United States, generated the greatest economic gains for both the United States and Japan. Under this scenario, however, Japan never developed a semiconductor industry: If Japan pursued its policy of closing its home markets, it did develop an industry, but actually the Japanese economy as a whole suffered. U.S. gains were also reduced. A third scenario under which both countries closed their markets generated significant losses for both countries.

This simulation seems to fairly closely mirror real-world observations. Given the U.S. lead in technology and production, it seems unlikely that Japanese semiconductor companies could have successfully competed with their U.S. rivals without government assistance. It is also consistent with real-world observations that Japan is willing to sacrifice consumer interests to build production capacity.

A number of other similar analyses point to the same general conclusion.[8] Kenneth Flamm, in particular, completed a detailed update of this modeling exercise, though in general his refinements do not alter the conclusions cited here.[9] In fact, the analysis suggests that dumping is a likely outcome under realistic competitive conditions.

Certainly these results are likely to be repeated in other similar technology-oriented industries, such as supercomputer manufacturing, where similar learning curves, economies of scale, high investments in research and development, and short life cycles are present. This would seem to confirm that the Japanese economic model can succeed—at least in the goal of building industries.

## *The Role of Dumping*

As noted previously, dumping is an integral and, indeed, inevitable result of pursuing the Japanese model. High domestic prices generate large domestic profits, allowing a company to invest in marketing, production capacity, and other functions involved in building an industry. Dumping in foreign markets is also key, because without deep discounts from the home market price, these products would simply not be competitive. This would decrease sales and make it impossible for protected economies to take advantage of economy-of-scale advantages derived from larger production runs. In the case of the Japanese semiconductor industry, without export sales it would have been very difficult for Japanese companies to develop economies of scale in production and become serious players in the global industry, even with a protected home market.[10]

Beyond that, dumping has other competitive effects. Dumping also depresses market prices and takes sales away from competitive companies that do not benefit from a protected home market. If pursued in a concerted manner, dumping can force marginal competitors without secure home markets to exit the industry. If dumping is severe and continuing, even established competitors can be driven from the industry, increasing market share for dumpers and, eventually, the prices they receive. Again, as noted in the previous chapter, these predictions closely mirror actual events in the semiconductor industry. Readers will recall that severe and continued Japanese semiconductor dumping drove all but two U.S. manufacturers from the DRAM business before the U.S. government took action to stop dumping.

If the United States took no action to counter dumping, its impact would be even more dramatic; uncountered dumping would contribute to successful industry building behind trade barriers and reduce competition by forcing competitors to exit the industry.

It is worth noting in this context that there are other reasons why simple simulations would underestimate the ultimate impact of dumping. For example, if dumpers are able to gain a virtual monopoly in a given sector, they can be expected to raise prices to take advantage of monopoly rents—at least to levels that do not spur reentry into the industry. The high fixed costs for entry into many manufacturing industries and the continued threat of dumping would pose substantial reentry barriers.

Given that each generation of technology generally builds upon earlier ones, if a company does not have a presence in manufacturing an early generation of a technology, it can make it difficult to become a manufacturer of later generations. The semiconductor industry again provides a good example. A manufacturing presence in relatively simple memory chips aided a company in establishing the technology, manufacturing know-how, marketing abilities, and related competencies necessary to move into more sophisticated memory chips and, later, logic chips.[11]

In the semiconductor industry, there are examples of companies skipping one generation of chips or stopping production of them early and investing heavily in the next generation. For example, America's most successful semiconductor manufacturer—Intel—completely stopped production of DRAMs to focus only upon logic chips. It is unquestionably harder, however, to reenter an industry after having completely exited it; reentry would require building new production facilities and recruiting a new workforce—among other challenges—instead of simply retooling and focusing engineers and technicians on a new project. This would be particularly true if competitors employing dumping remained in the industry. Again, in the semiconductor industry, Japanese companies dumped in generation after generation of semiconductors. If the U.S. government had not taken aggressive action to counter dumping in EPROMs, another generation of semiconductors, U.S. manufacturers would likely have had great difficulty maintaining a strong position in the EPROM market.[12]

Beyond even that, if an entire *country* was forced to completely exit an industry (that is, all domestic companies exit an industry), it is likely the effects would be larger. A lack of domestic industry would make it more difficult for any domestic company to obtain the technology and know-how to reenter that industry.[13] In this situation, the prospect of renewed dumping would also create a formidable entry barrier.

*Antidumping Duties as a Remedy*

From the perspective of imperfect-competition models, antidumping duties can provide some relief from the detrimental effects of dumping. Several scholars have explored taxes and the concept of an optimal tariff as a partial solution for market distortions.[14]

Taxes and tariffs are often proposed as a second-best alternative to counter a market distortion.[15] From this viewpoint, dumping and the associated closed home market are market distortions. The best approach would be to eliminate the market distortion, but this is often impossible. A second-best solution involves introducing another market distortion to counter the negative effects of the first distortion, such as a tax on the distortion or a subsidy to counter it.

In this case, antidumping duties are not a perfect solution to dumping. They do not force competition in the dumper's closed home market, and they do not prevent dumping in third markets. Antidumping duties also take some time to impose, require sometimes complex calculations, and, under domestic law and the provisions of the WTO, cannot be imposed until the domestic industry involved has experienced injury. In cases involving "critical circumstances," procedures can be accelerated somewhat, but the problems mentioned remain.

Antidumping duties are, however, a second-best solution that minimizes the negative effects of dumping and closed markets on U.S. companies and prevents foreign companies from reaping the benefits of dumping-related longer production runs and, potentially, monopoly rents. The duties also provide a measure of deterrence against countries that would pursue a dumping strategy; the potential limitation on access to the U.S. market makes dumping from a closed market a less attractive strategy that is less likely to succeed in establishing globally competitive industries.[16] Also, efforts have been made through the WTO to counter dumping in third markets through cooperation between national authorities in affected countries.[17]

## Strategic Trade Theory

Another line of economic thinking has sprung up in close association with work on imperfect competition that holds that some industries are of strategic importance and worthy of special attention from national policy makers. This school of thought is defined as strategic trade theory.[18] It bases its thinking on the premise that strategic industries make special contributions to the economy in three ways.

First, many strategic trade theorists endorse the notion that some industries are essential requirements for being involved in other, related sectors.[19] The example advanced in the last section was the semiconductor industry. The semiconductor industry produces critical basic inputs for many other industries. The connection to computers and modern-day consumer electronics is obvious. Less obvious is the connection to automobile manufacturing, civilian aerospace manufacturing, and even production of sophisticated modern weapons.

From a national-security perspective, the semiconductor industry, the aerospace industry, or even the computer software industry could be critical to ensuring that the United States has the wherewithal to produce modern weapons. Semiconductors, for example, might be thought of as the machine tool industry of the computer age,[20] necessary to produce an array of critical products.[21] There is certainly the risk of taking such logic to seemingly absurd extremes (an army marches on its feet, therefore the footwear industry is critical to national security), but few would debate the central premise that some industries have national-security implications and are worthy of government intervention to preserve and promote them.

But strategic trade theory goes far beyond the military side of national security and advances the argument that some industries are similarly critical for economic reasons as well as military ones. Since some industries are essential to the development of others, losing those industries could have economic implications far beyond just the loss of one industry and the employment immediately associated with it. Losing a basic industry could put a country at a competitive disadvantage in a number of related industries. Again, the semiconductor industry is a good example.[22]

The connections between industries often go beyond the obvious one of providing intermediate inputs. For example, there seem to be positive externalities—benefits beyond the obvious—created by high-technology industries. Placing a number of innovative engineers in close proximity may lead to unanticipated new ideas and new technologies that may benefit not just the companies involved directly, but also other companies exposed to the ideas and the localities where these companies operate. Even in an age where ideas can travel easily over the Internet or phone lines, these benefits seem to be focused in the geographic area where the manufacturing and research and development are concentrated. This also explains the tendency of high-tech manufacturing firms to cluster together à la Silicon Valley.[23]

Strategic industries also seem to generate additional benefits through positive externalities. Many strategic industries invest heavily in R&D. Obviously, these investments are made in the hope of generating innovations that contribute directly to the industries doing the R&D, but R&D cannot be precisely focused. Often the resulting new technologies have implications far beyond the industry doing the research, and sometimes researchers stumble upon ideas that, while paying no direct benefits to their own industry, are extremely valuable to society at large. The spin-offs from the space program are good examples of these unforeseen benefits.[24]

There is also strong evidence that wages in some industries, chiefly manufacturing industries, are consistently higher than average wages. Wages in the goods-producing sector of the U.S. economy consistently run ahead of wages in the service sector. Interestingly, some of the highest-wage sectors of the U.S. economy are steel and high-technology manufacturing, the same sectors in which dumping is most common.[25] Some researchers have argued that the high-wage jobs generated by industries such as civilian aerospace manufacturing themselves justify government intervention to promote such industries.[26]

This also raises the long-debated core question: Does it matter what we make? Until recently, conventional economic thinking was that government strategies to dump, subsidize, or otherwise pursue a mercantilist strategy to dominate an industry were of little consequence. After all, if such a strategy were successful, the United States would simply invest in other sectors to create new employment and enjoy the benefits of dumping and subsidies—low consumer prices—in the meantime. Thus, it does not really matter what the United States makes, the argument concluded.

This argument never really held sway with policy makers in most countries, who rejected it as counterintuitive and inconsistent with their experiences. In addition, it ignores the serious adjustment costs of retooling and retraining to enter new industries and the potential entry barriers in new industries. The argument also assumes a full-employment economy, which is historically the exception rather than the rule.

Further, even if the workers and resources idled by dumping are able to find new employment in other sectors, these sectors may not yield the same wages and benefits. Dumping is increasingly a strategy that is pursued broadly in manufacturing sectors, from basic industries to high technology. If the United States simply retreated and allowed dumping strategies to succeed, the composition of the U.S. economy would change dramatically. The U.S. presence in a range of manufacturing industries, from basic to advanced, would shrink. Possibly, employment in the service sector could expand to absorb some or all of these job losses, but these jobs tend to pay less than jobs in the manufacturing sector. As noted above, this would particularly be true with regard to dumping, because U.S. antidumping orders have been concentrated in high-wage sectors.[27] Further, the many economic benefits flowing from strategic industries would be lost.

## *National Strategies*

On the surface, this discussion is focused upon competition between industries in different countries. Antidumping actions are generally brought by private companies against other private-sector competitors. As several scholars have noted, however, competition between industries in different countries is effectively competition between the economic systems of those countries.[28] A full discussion of the economic impact of antidumping laws necessarily returns to competing international economic models.

As noted in Chapter 1, the most vigorous users of antidumping laws have been countries with relatively open markets, such as the United States, Western European nations (and the European Union), and Canada. Those countries following some version of the Japanese model have not found much need for antidumping laws, largely because their markets have generally been closed to imports, particularly in what they deemed to be strategic sectors.

This breakdown is more than just happenstance. Antidumping laws are a critical element of a globally competitive free-market economy. As just discussed, they are a critical defense against the injurious effects of other countries' industrial policies. Without them, a country could find itself driven from key industries and large numbers of workers displaced at the whim of foreign governments.

There are, however, even broader reasons to view antidumping laws as a critical element of U.S. trade and economic policy. In a world in which foreign companies and governments were free to dump at will into the United States, the U.S. economy would be reshaped in important ways.

Investment decisions in the manufacturing sector would be dramatically altered. Not only would companies seeking to invest in the United States have to count on having at best limited access to countries pursuing a Japanese economic strategy due to some combination of public- and private-sector protectionism, but they would also have to plan for the eventuality of dumping into the U.S. market, particularly in times of global oversupply in their industry. These concerns would force U.S. companies to plan production on a smaller scale, with attendant decreased employment, making it much harder to gain economy-of-scale advantages.

More important, the economies following the Japanese model would become much more attractive sites for investment. From these markets it would be possible to gain the advantage of a secure home market and the prospect of gaining additional economy-of-scale advantages through sales (in some cases dumped sales), in open markets such as the United States. All other factors being equal, in the manufacturing sectors where dumping is common, this would make the closed/dumping economies more attractive investment sites. Over time, this would be a significant competitive blow to the U.S. economy, likely to lead to lower wages and a "hollowing out" of the economy as manufacturing sought safer venues for investment.[29]

Certainly, there are a number of offsetting advantages to siting in the United States, such as proximity to a large market and strong infrastructure. Other countries can increasingly offer similar advantages, however, and as a result, the threat of dumping is likely to have an effect on siting decisions in the manufacturing sector.

Antidumping duties provide a partial remedy to this threat. The prospect of offsetting duties being imposed if dumping does occur limits the potential damage from dumping. This allows the U.S. free-market competition model to maintain the economic benefits of competition and the ability to respond quickly to economic changes while insulating itself from a measure of the risk of dumping from countries with other economic models. Thus, antidumping laws are an important adjunct to a U.S.-style market economy; they make this approach to organizing an economy more competitive compared with other approaches.

**Case Studies of the Economic Effects of Dumping**

The debate over antidumping laws often proceeds with both sides making gross generalizations about the effects of dumping and antidumping orders. The actual impact of antidumping orders in the marketplace, however, is often more subtle. To better understand the market impact of U.S. anti-dumping orders, this section examines three typical and much-discussed U.S. industrial sectors that have been much affected by dumping.

*Semiconductors*

Examples of dumping in the semiconductor industry are one of the central foci of the discussion. They also provide an excellent example of the operation of the sanctuary market–dumping strategy and its competitive impact. The facts of the cases are discussed in some detail in Chapter 3, but, in brief, dumping in the U.S. market emerged as a major issue in the early and mid-1980s. Concerted dumping of basic memory chips, DRAMs, and more advanced memory chips, EPROMS, by Japanese companies had a devastating impact upon the U.S. industry. At one point, all but one U.S. producer of DRAMs had exited the market due to dumping.

New antidumping orders against Japanese-produced DRAMs and EPROMs went into effect in 1986. After the orders were entered, the U.S. and Japan negotiated a bilateral agreement that, after sanctions were imposed, resulted in an end to Japanese dumping both in the U.S. market and in third markets, and, after a time, resulted in increased import access to the Japanese market.

The economic impact of the antidumping orders and the follow-up agreement are displayed in Charts 4.1, 4.2, and 4.3. Within the U.S. market, U.S. producers of DRAMs and EPROMs gained strength, but DRAM production was already devastated and never fully recovered. EPROM production, however, was a much different story. At the time antidumping actions were brought, U.S. companies were still dominant producers of EPROMs, though Japanese companies were making rapid inroads. After dumping was stopped, the U.S. market share recovered and the Japanese share declined sharply.

Charts 4.2 and 4.3 tell an even more interesting story. As explained in detail at several points, dumping is part of a global strategy. The impact of thwarting the sanctuary market–dumping strategy through antidumping orders and the U.S.-Japan Semiconductor Trade Agreement had clear effects in global markets for semiconductors. After dumping was halted, the Japanese global share of both DRAMs and EPROMs declined markedly. In the case of DRAMs, the resulting global market was diversified, with U.S. companies gaining share, as did other third-country companies.[30]

The picture in EPROMs (Chart 4.3) is simpler and more clear-cut for U.S. companies. Japan had managed to displace the United States as the leading producer of EPROMs, but once dumping was halted, U.S. compa-

Chart 4.1 **Market Shares in U.S. EPROM Market, 1983–1989**

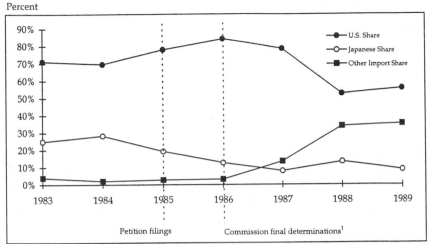

*Source:* International Trade Commission.

[1]Dumping margins ranged from 60 to 188 percent, but no antidumping order was ever issued because the issue was subsumed in the U.S.–Japan Semiconductor Agreement of 1987.

Chart 4.2 **World DRAM Market Shares by Manufacturers' Base Region, 1980–1996**

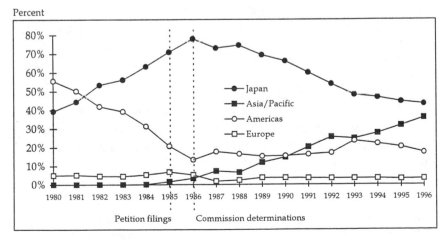

*Source:* Dataquest.

Chart 4.3 **World Nonvolatile Memory Market Shares by Manufacturers'**
**Base Region, 1980–1996[1]**

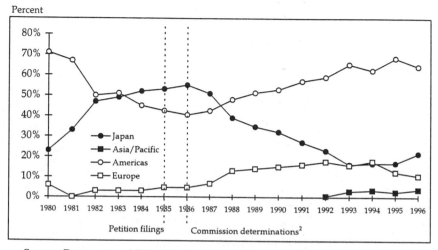

Percent

*Source:* Dataquest and ESI estimates.

[1]Nonvolatile memory refers to EPROMs and "flash" memory.

[2]Dumping margins on Japanese EPROMs ranged from 60 to 180 percent, but no antidumping order was ever issued because the issue was subsumed by the U.S.–Japan Semiconductor Trade Agreement of 1996.

nies regained the dominant position in the market, which they have maintained to the present day.[31]

Putting an end to Japan's sanctuary market and dumping had a number of predictable effects: Japanese share declined, U.S. market share rose, U.S. companies reentered the market, and prices rose (at least for a time).[32] There were, however, other notable effects. With Japanese mercantilism reined in, other companies from Europe and Asia were also able to enter the market. In sum, the global market for both DRAMs and EPROMs became more diverse and competitive, not less so. Unfortunately, semiconductor companies in Korea and Taiwan seem to have followed strategies similar to Japan and have also been subject to antidumping orders and complaints. One U.S. company, Micron Technology, is currently pursuing an antidumping case against producers in Korea and Taiwan. There is also an outstanding antidumping order on DRAMs from South Korea.

### Bearings

Bearing production is another sector in which antidumping complaints have been common. Over the years, antidumping actions have involved a large number of products and an even larger number of companies and countries

Chart 4.4 **Market Shares in U.S. Tapered Roller Bearings and Parts Market, 1983–1993**

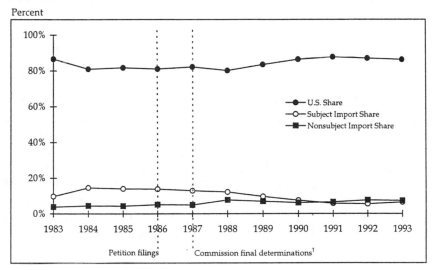

*Source:* International Trade Commission.
[1]Duty order margins, issued in May and June 1987, ranged from 1 to 125 percent.

Chart 4.5 **Market Shares in U.S. Ball Bearings and Parts Market, 1983–1993**

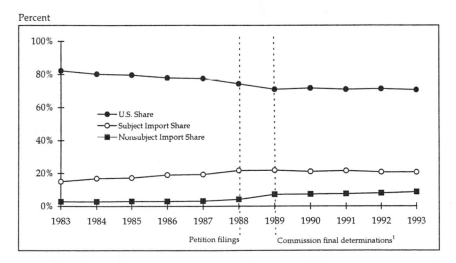

*Source:* International Trade Commission.
[1]Duty order margins, issued in May and June 1987, ranged from 21 to 180 percent.

involved in the dumping. Here again, Japanese companies have usually been the primary—though not the only—focus. Recounting the market effects of all the various antidumping actions would consume much time and space and likely shed little light on larger issues, but it is worthwhile to examine two particular cases. The first involves tapered roller bearings and the second ball bearings; the tapered roller bearing order entered into effect in 1987, the order covering ball bearings in 1989.

It is worth noting that in neither of these cases is there evidence of a dramatic protectionist effect. The market share of U.S. producers rose somewhat, and the market share of the imports covered by the order declined. These aggregate figures do mask some more dramatic changes on the company level. Companies subject to duties at the higher end of the range—125 percent for tapered roller bearings and 180 percent for ball bearings—likely saw their market share decline sharply. In both cases, however, imports that were not subject to the order also increased their market share. The result was a market that was actually more competitive and diverse as opposed to markets from which imports were shut out.

### Steel Pipe and Tube

In the minds of some, steel producers are closely identified with antidumping laws, and many U.S. antidumping cases have involved steel. The impact of steel antidumping orders is difficult to chart for several reasons. First, between 1984 and 1992, the United States negotiated voluntary restraint agreements (VRAs) with many steel-exporting countries. These VRAs limited both fairly traded and unfairly traded steel and thus also limited the impact of dumping. The picture is also complicated because the widespread dumping and subsidization in the sector was the primary reason the U.S. government chose to negotiate restraints. One steel producer, in fact, characterizes the steel VRA program as "one big antidumping case."

Second, during the period of the VRA, the domestic industry pursued antidumping and countervailing-duty actions less frequently. Finally, though they are conceptually distinct, antidumping and countervailing-duty investigations were often pursued in parallel on steel products and it is difficult to distinguish their impacts.

All that said, there are still particular steel products for which interesting case studies can be drawn. Steel pipe and tube is a particularly interesting illustration. Due to concerted dumping, U.S. producers lost their dominant position in the U.S. market between 1983 and 1985. After a series of antidumping orders (illustrated in Chart 4.6), however, U.S. companies had regained a dominant position in the U.S. market, but many of the producers

Chart 4.6 **Market Shares in U.S. Standard Welded Pipe and Tube Market, 1982–1993**

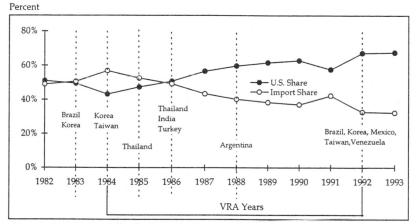

*Source:* International Trade Commission.

[1]Dashed lines represent antidumping and countervailing-duty cases with affirmative commission determinations.

subject to the antidumping measures maintain a significant presence in the U.S. market.

### Estimate of Positive Contribution of Antidumping Laws

The preceding sections of this chapter provide a strong theoretical rationale for antidumping laws, but it is often easier to appreciate economic impacts when they are put in more concrete terms. For that reason, the author, with significant assistance from his colleagues, has completed a simulation to illustrate the positive impact that antidumping laws have had upon the U.S. economy.[33] This is accomplished by examining, in detail, the likely impact that the abolition of antidumping laws would have had upon the U.S. production of memory semiconductors.

Before proceeding with this simulation, a number of possible approaches were considered. The impact of antidumping laws could be considered on an economy-wide basis, but given the dozens of separate cases that must be considered in such a simulation and the additional effect of cases that were threatened yet never filed, this would be an extremely difficult undertaking. Each of the sectors in which antidumping laws have played a role has unique characteristics. Inevitably, general, economy-wide assumptions on economic multipliers, investment, and trade effects would not provide an accurate picture of the individual sectors and would thus be open to criticism.

For this reason, this analysis focuses upon only one portion of one industrial sector. After reviewing the recent history of antidumping laws, production of memory semiconductors, including DRAMs, EPROMs, EEPROMs,
and related memory chips, was selected as the sector to examine.[34] This
sector was chosen for several reasons. First, as already explored in some
detail, repeated dumping of memory semiconductors, primarily by Japanese
companies, is well documented. Second, the semiconductor sector provides
high-wage employment and generates significant R&D spending. Third,
semiconductor production is a sector in which, absent dumping, the competitive strength of U.S. industry is generally conceded and documented
(see the charts in the preceding section).

In analyzing the impact of a hypothetical abolition of U.S. antidumping
laws, extremely conservative assumptions were made. Most important, this
simulation limits its estimate of the negative impact of the abolition of
antidumping laws strictly to the memory semiconductor sector. The potential negative impact of a weakening of the memory sector on production of
more-advanced logic semiconductors and microprocessors, sectors in which
U.S. companies now hold an unchallenged competitive lead and which
generate a larger positive impact upon the U.S. economy than the memory-
chip sector alone does, was not considered.

As explained earlier in this chapter, in all probability, any weakening of
the memory-chip sector would have impacted the logic-chip and microproc-
cessor sectors. Many of the same U.S. companies are involved in the production of both memory and more-advanced chips; all of the companies
now producing logic chips and microprocessors either are or were involved
in production of memory chips at one time. Memory-chip production allowed these companies to build facilities, attract a workforce, generate profits, and develop competitive competencies that contributed to their later
efforts to develop more-advanced semiconductors.[35] The argument can
even be made (and has been made) that a complete or widespread loss of
the memory-chip sector would have made it impossible for U.S. companies
to establish their dominant position in logic chips and microprocessors.
Beyond that, significant weakening of the memory-chip industry could have
impacted the United States' ability to compete in a whole series of high-
technology industries to which semiconductor technology contributes directly and indirectly.[36]

A second conservative assumption made was the range of possible impacts upon the U.S. memory-chip industry projected from the abolition of
antidumping laws. The most conservative scenarios considered anticipate
only a 10 percent to 25 percent reduction in the rate of growth in U.S.
production levels. (It is important to emphasize that no scenario contem-

plates an absolute reduction in production levels. Only the rate of growth is decreased.) Given that before antidumping action was initiated, all but one U.S. producer of DRAMs had been driven from the business and dumping in EPROMs had become nearly as serious a problem, there is every possibility that without antidumping laws, U.S. companies would have been completely driven out of the memory-chip business—and perhaps out of business entirely. Mere reductions in the rate of growth thus seem entirely reasonable—indeed conservative—scenarios to examine.

In this regard, a number of industry observers have indicated that there are economies of scale for both companies and countries in the production of semiconductors.[37] If growth in production levels are substantially reduced, the failure to capture economies of scale may force marginal producers and perhaps marginal countries completely out of business.

At the very least, companies would have sought to produce in markets in which they were not faced with the constant threat of dumping. Thus, even if U.S.-owned companies would have stayed in the market, they would have moved production and most of the associated benefits to another market. So a realistic estimate of the negative impact of eliminating antidumping laws is probably something in the range of a 75 percent to 100 percent reduction in growth of memory-chip production. Reentry into or expansion in the market by U.S. companies would also be unlikely because the threat of dumping would be an enormous market entry barrier, particularly once U.S. companies had fallen behind in production technology and lost their competitive base in the industry.

Third, this simulation does not attempt to incorporate many of the other strategic trade benefits of production in the memory-chip sector, such as R&D spillover benefits and clustering benefits for other high-technology industries. As discussed earlier in this chapter, there is good reason to think that these benefits are real, but in keeping with the effort to apply only very conservative assumptions, it is ignored in this simulation.

Fourth, this simulation does not attempt to capture some of the indirect impacts of Japan's sanctuary market–dumping strategy, such as higher prices for Japanese consumers and other potential negative impacts of a possible Japanese monopoly or near monopoly in this sector.

Finally, in calculating the direct and indirect impact of dumping in memory semiconductors, as Charts 4.8 and 4.9 illustrate, this simulation assumes that the market price for imported memory chips would have been 10 percent lower over the period of the simulation if U.S. antidumping laws were not operating. This would generate attendant consumer benefits, which are balanced against production and investment losses in the calculations. (It is also worth noting that a 10 percent reduction in the price of imported chips would almost certainly result in far more than a 10 percent reduction in domestic production growth because lower-priced imported chips would win large shares of the market from domestic chips. A 10 percent reduction in import prices would likely correspond to at least a 25–30 percent reduction in the growth of domestic production.)

This assumption is also quite conservative because the likely long-term effect on prices would be considerably smaller and might even be a price increase. It is true that the dumping margin on Japanese semiconductors was frequently above 10 percent, but this means only that the Japanese prices are that much below prices in the Japanese market or the cost of production, not necessarily that they are that much below the market price in the U.S. market. The U.S. market price is different from the Japanese market price. In the United States, the market price is derived from competition among many dumping foreign manufacturers, nondumping foreign manufacturers, and domestic manufacturers; at the time of the petition, this was considerably lower than the price in Japan. As the case studies in the previous section demonstrate, the application of antidumping orders, which presumably end dumping, does not usually have a dramatic impact upon price and certainly does not leave domestic producers in a position to capture monopoly profits. During periods of severe dumping, prices may be depressed by more than 10 percent, but prices are unlikely to remain that far depressed below normal market levels for an extended period.

Also, as noted, the dumped price is a suboptimal price resulting from Japan's sanctuary market–dumping strategy and is not a true reflection of the market equilibrium price. Finally, examinations of commercial behavior would suggest that once dumping companies establish a dominant or monopoly position in the market, they are likely to raise prices above competitive market levels. Therefore, over the long term, if dumping succeeded in putting Japanese companies in a dominant position and forcing competitors to exit the industry, price levels may actually rise above market levels and have an additional negative impact upon consumers.[38]

Collectively, if these legitimate additional factors had been added in to this analysis, the likely negative impact from repealing antidumping laws would be substantially increased.

### Simulation Results

To demonstrate the potential negative impact of eliminating antidumping laws, a range of possible negative impacts upon U.S. production of metal-oxide-semiconductor (MOS) memory chips are considered. The range of reductions in the growth rate of U.S. memory-chip production is between 10

Chart 4.7 **Simulated Memory Shipments[1] and Four Scenarios of Slower Growth, 1984–1996**

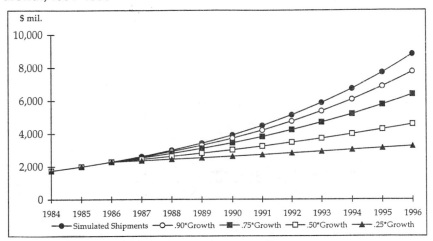

*Source:* ESI estimates using Bureau of Census data.

[1] The growth rate for the simulation was estimated using the slope coefficient of a logarithmic regression of actual shipments against a time variable.

percent and 75 percent.[39] The period examined is between 1984, the first year that reports of substantial dumping in the U.S. market were made, to 1996, the latest year for which data are available.

The simulations attempt to measure the lost economic activity that would have resulted after 1986 if the U.S. government had not taken any action to stop the dumping of memory chips.

As Chart 4.7 demonstrates, the impact of lost memory sales is significant. By 1996, simulated memory sales totaled $8.8 billion. (Actual U.S. memory shipments in 1996 were above trend and exceeded $10 billion.) Even a 10 percent reduction in the growth rate of shipments (i.e., the ".90 * growth" scenario) between 1986 and 1996 would have shaved off $1.1 billion of U.S. memory production in 1996 alone. A 75 percent reduction (i.e., the ".25 * growth" scenario) would have resulted in shipments $5.7 billion below trend.

The economy-wide losses associated with declining activity in the semiconductor industry are even larger. In addition to direct losses of memory production are foregone output from input industries, such as chemicals, plastics, and steel, and foregone investment in plant and semiconductor manufacturing equipment. These adverse impacts in part are offset by the lower memory prices that could result from dumping. Chart 4.8, which takes into account all of these ripple effects, illustrates the net losses to the

Chart 4.8 **Direct and Indirect Impact on U.S. Output of "Lost" Semiconductor Sales, 1987–1996**

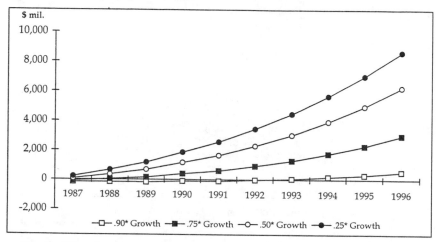

*Source:* ESI estimates.

U.S. economy associated with each scenario. By 1996, economic losses range from $500 million to $8.6 billion.

The ".90 * growth" scenario is actually less than zero from 1987 to 1992 (no antidumping actions were taken until 1986), while the ".75 * growth" scenario is negative in 1987 and 1988. These outcomes demonstrate that in the early years of dumping, the gains from lower-priced memory outweigh the direct and indirect losses as long as the deterioration of the growth rate of U.S. production is not too large. However, competitive losses quickly mount and soon eclipse the transient benefits of lower chip prices. Even the ".90 * growth" scenario, which assumes that dumping results in both larger than realistic consumer benefits and small impacts upon growth in chip production, produces economic losses after 1992.

To give the reader an appreciation for the total impact of unrestrained dumping on the economy over the period, Chart 4.9 provides the cumulative impacts of dumping. By 1996, the cumulative negative impact of dumping of semiconductors on the U.S. economy—even after the potential positive impact of lower chip prices is considered—would range between $323 million and $35.6 billion, depending upon how much U.S. production was replaced by dumped imports.

## Conclusion

As noted in Chapter 5, the study done by the International Trade Commission estimated a collective annual negative impact upon the economy from

Chart 4.9 **Cumulative Direct and Indirect Impact on U.S. Output of "Lost" Semiconductor Sales, 1987–1996**

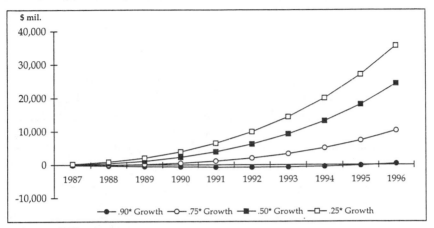

*Source:* ESI estimates.

all antidumping and countervailing-duty orders analyzed of $1.59 billion in 1991. This analysis, however, does not consider the long-term competitive impact upon the domestic industries in terms of lost production and decreased investment. Nor does it consider the large volume of literature on strategic trade theory and imperfect competition that is clearly relevant to the discussion.

As this simulation demonstrates, when the larger competitive impact of dumping is considered in just one important sector, the negative impact of dumping, even under this very conservative estimate, far outweighs the $1.59 billion annual price tag that the ITC places upon antidumping and countervailing-duty laws.

Critics will likely level two criticisms at this simulation of the impact of dumping in memory semiconductor production that are worthy of some discussion. First, the argument will doubtlessly be advanced that semiconductors are unique. It is true that the U.S. semiconductor market does provide a particularly compelling example of the sanctuary market–dumping strategy at work. Unfortunately, it is far from unique.

Japanese dumping of televisions was just as persistent over an extended period of time and was actually as successful in driving U.S. producers out of the industry as the dumping of semiconductors was. Television production, again like semiconductor production, is also a sector that had a significant impact upon related sectors. Without a foothold in television production, U.S. producers lost presence in many other consumer-electronics sectors and was never able to establish production of next-generation consumer electronics, such as VCRs. Similar comparisons can be made with regard to photographic film, supercomputers, and a number of other sectors.

Even in basic production industries, such as steel, the story is likely to be similar. In the face of continued dumping, U.S. producers would have been likely to make very conservative investment and production decisions and, in many cases, would likely have chosen to move all or substantial amounts of production out of the United States, if they chose to stay in the industry at all.

Beyond that, if the U.S. market were entirely open to mercantilistic strategies, such as sanctuary market–dumping, a range of other manufacturing industries that have not been seriously threatened would likely become targets of dumping. Dumping could have an impact in virtually all manufacturing sectors. In sum, the semiconductor industry is far from being a unique case.

Second, many would suggest that, at least over time, under the conditions of the simulation, U.S. investment would shift away from semiconductor production to other productive sectors, which would decrease the negative impact of dumping. To a certain degree, such a shift is very likely to occur. As already noted, one possible and indeed likely shift under the circumstances would be for U.S. semiconductor companies to shift production overseas to escape dumping.[40] Such a shift might preserve some market share for U.S. companies, but it would deny the U.S. economy almost all of the benefits of semiconductor production.

If the entire U.S. economy were open to dumping, much of the manufacturing sector would be unattractive sites for investment, since manufactured products ranging from automobiles to semiconductors are vulnerable to dumping strategies. Thus, within the United States, the shift would likely be away from manufacturing and toward service sectors. As discussed earlier, this would deprive the U.S. economy of many of the ripple benefits of investment in high-technology manufacturing firms and would trade high-wage employment for low-wage employment.

Finally, many will rightly point out that the assumption of large out-year losses is probably not entirely politically realistic. In a sense, this is true. If the abolition of antidumping laws resulted in large out-year losses, as envisioned here, policy makers would almost certainly react to minimize losses. The most likely reaction would simply be to reinstate antidumping laws, but there are other possibilities, such as extending subsidies and adjusting interest rates. The purpose of this illustration, however, is to predict the real likely economic consequences of abolishing dumping laws, not the likely political response. Such a prediction would be more an exercise in political fortune-telling than an economic estimate. This simulation simply provides the economic costs of a decision to eliminate antidumping laws, without considering other possible related policy actions, to illustrate the importance of antidumping laws to the economy. Further, many of the macroeconomic policy tools that might be employed to minimize effects could have other unforeseen negative effects, such as decreasing the value of the dollar, lowering real income, or sparking inflation.

As this chapter illustrates, there is a compelling economic case for anti-dumping laws. Without such a law, the U.S. manufacturing sector would be devastated by foreign mercantilist strategies and the U.S. economy would become a very unattractive place to invest. Just the impact upon one relatively small sector of the U.S. economy, semiconductor production, would be quite serious. The impact on an economy-wide basis would likely be staggering.

Critics have frequently made the case that antidumping laws provide a sop to inefficient domestic industries that cannot compete and inflict serious costs upon U.S. consumers. Any reasonable reading of the facts simply does not bear out this conclusion. Antidumping laws are simply a conservative response to foreign mercantilist strategies; they strive to reestablish some competitive balance and allow market forces and not foreign government policies to determine outcomes. There is considerable economic theory to support this approach to restoring the function of the market.

When the actual impact of antidumping orders is considered, a picture very different from that painted by critics emerges. Almost without exception, after antidumping orders are imposed the market remains competitive, with a number of domestic and foreign firms competing for market share. The prospects for a serious negative impact upon consumers under these conditions is quite small.

On the whole, these data lead to one inescapable conclusion: Antidumping law is a vital safeguard for the U.S. economy. In fact, in a globally competitive marketplace with countries pursuing a variety of national economic and trade strategies, the U.S. open-market strategy is simply not viable without the operation of antidumping laws.

## Notes

1. There are numerous sources on the issue, but here are a few relevant examples: James R. Melvin and Robert D. Warne, "Monopoly and the Theory of International Trade," *Journal of International Economics* 3 (1973): 117–134; Homi Katrak, "Multinational Monopolies and Commercial Policy," *Oxford Economic Papers* 29 (1977): 283–291; Gene M. Grossman and Elhanan Helpman, *Innovation and Growth in the Global Economy* (Cambridge: MIT Press, 1991); Max Corden, "Monopoly, Tariffs and Subsidies," *Economica* 34 (1967): 50–58.

2. Imperfect competition stands in contrast to perfect competition, a condition in which all producers are price takers with no opportunity to influence the market price. Under conditions of imperfect competition, producers can exercise some influence over market prices.

3. See Chalmers Johnson, *Japan: Who Governs? The Rise of the Developmental State* (New York: W.W. Norton, 1995); Laura D'Andrea Tyson, *Who's Bashing Whom: Trade Conflict in High Technology Industries* (Washington, DC: Institute for International Economics, 1993); Mark Tilton, *Restrained Trade: Cartels in Japan's Basic Materials Industries* (Ithaca: Cornell University Press, 1996); Ben Balassa and Marcus Noland, *Japan in the World Economy* (Washington, DC: Institute for International Economics, 1988).

4. For an example of this argument, see Senator William Roth and C. Fred Bergsten, "The Silver Lining of Asia's Economic Crisis," *Washington Post,* December 27, 1997, p. C8.

5. Office of the U.S. Trade Representative, *The National Trade Estimate* (Washington, DC: GPO, 1997), pp. 23–29.

6. For a broad discussion of these issues from a number of perspectives, see Harry K. Kierzkowski, ed., *Monopolistic Competition in International Trade* (Oxford: Clarendon Press, 1984), and Gene M. Grossman, ed., *Imperfect Competition and International Trade* (Cambridge: MIT Press, 1992).

7. Richard E. Baldwin and Paul R. Krugman, "Market Access and International Competition: A Simulation Study of 16K Random Access Memories," in *Empirical Methods for International Trade,* R. Feenstra, ed. (Cambridge: MIT Press, 1988).

8. Andrew Dick, "Learning-by-doing and Dumping in the Semiconductor Industry," *Journal of Law and Economics* 34 (1991): 133–159.

9. Kenneth Flamm, *Mismanaged Trade? Strategic Policy and the Semiconductor Industry* (Washington, DC: Brookings Institution, 1996), pp. 305–371. Flamm characterizes dumping as a problem but expresses reservations about the application of antidumping laws to the semiconductor industry. Many of his concerns are addressed in Chapter 5 of this book. Nonetheless, he suggests negotiation of global minimum prices for semiconductors. Such an agreement would capture many of the benefits of antidumping laws, but it is far from clear that such an approach is realistic.

10. Tyson, *Who's Bashing Whom,* pp. 85–144.

11. Ibid., pp. 85–105.

12. Ibid.

13. Allen J. Scott and D.P. Angel, "The U.S. Semiconductor Industry: A Locational Analysis," *Environment and Planning* 19, no. 7 (July 1987): 875–912; Michael Porter, *The Competitive Advantage of Nations* (New York: Free Press, 1990).

14. Several examples of this can be found in Grossman, *Imperfect Competition.* See in particular papers by Krishna, Bender and Spencer, Eaton and Grossman, and Dixit.

15. Ibid.

16. Some might argue that the imposition of antidumping duties would push the situation closer to a situation like the trade war scenario in the previously mentioned Baldwin-Krugman model of competition in the semiconductor industry. This analogy is not correct, however, for several reasons. First, Japanese semiconductors would not be barred from the U.S. market; they would merely be forced to sell at a nondumped price. In practice, antidumping actions have raised the price of Japanese semiconductor imports above the dumped level, but the exports have continued. The benefits of a competitive semiconductor market are thus preserved. Second, retaliation by Japanese authorities would be prohibited by the WTO.

It is worth noting also in this connection that the U.S.-Japan Semiconductor Trade

Agreement appears to have created conditions that approximate free trade by eliminating dumping and taking steps to open the Japanese market. Once normal market forces were allowed to operate, new companies entered the industry and Japanese semiconductor companies began to build two-way trade relationships with foreign companies. For further discussion, see Clyde Prestowitz, Naotaka Matsukata, and Andrew Szamosszegi, *Prospects for U.S.-Japanese Semiconductor Trade in the 21st Century* (Washington, DC: Economic Strategy Institute, 1996).

17. WTO Antidumping Agreement, Article 14.

18. Many of the sources cited throughout this chapter are leading advocates of this viewpoint, but see also James Brander and Barbara Spencer, "Export Subsidies and International Market Share Rivalry," *Journal of International Economics* 17 (February 1985): 83–100. For a more recent discussion of these issues, see National Research Council, *Conflict and Cooperation in National Competition for High-Technology Industry* (Washington, DC: National Academy Press, 1996). For a critical view of strategic trade theory, at least as often applied, see Paul Krugman, *Peddling Prosperity* (New York: W.W. Norton, 1994), pp. 239–244 and Chapter 10.

19. See National Research Council, *Conflict and Cooperation;* Tyson, *Who's Bashing Whom,* pp. 29–47; National Advisory Committee on Semiconductors, *Attaining Preeminence in Semiconductors* (Washington, DC: GPO, 1992), p. 9.

20. The machine tool industry, however, is still quite important to manufacturing. It is probably more accurate to characterize semiconductors as *another* machine tool industry in the computer age.

21. For a discussion of these issues, see Wayne Sandholtz, Michael Borrus, and John Zysman, eds., *The Highest Stakes: The Economic Foundations of the Next Security System* (London and New York: Oxford University Press, 1992); Theodore Moran, "The Globalization of America's Defense Industries: Managing the Threat of Foreign Dependence," *International Security* 15 (Summer 1990): 57–100.

22. Harold Gruber, *Learning and Strategic Product Innovation Theory and Evidence for the Semiconductor Industry* (Amsterdam: Elsevier, North Holland, 1994). For a broader discussion of the concept, see National Research Council, *Conflict and Cooperation,* pp. 33–35.

23. Annalee Saxenson, *Regional Advantage: Culture and Competition in Silicon Valley and Rte. 28* (Cambridge: Harvard University Press, 1994); Porter, *The Competitive Advantage of Nations.*

24. Zvi Griliches, *The Search for R&D Spillovers* (Cambridge: Harvard University Press, 1990); National Research Council, *Conflict and Cooperation.*

25. U.S. Department of Labor, Bureau of Labor Statistics.

26. William Dickens and Kevin Lang, "Why It Matters What We Make: A Case for Active Trade Policy," in William Dickens, Laura D'Andrea Tyson, and John Zysman, eds. *The Dynamics of Trade and Employment* (Cambridge, MA: Ballinger Press, 1988), pp. 83–112; Lawrence F. Katz and Lawrence H. Sumners, "Industry Rents: Evidence and Implications," *Brookings Papers on Economic Activity: Microeconomics,* 1989, pp. 209–275.

27. Bureau of Labor Statistics.

28. National Research Council, *Conflict and Cooperation;* Tyson, *Who's Bashing Whom;* Lester Thurow, *Head to Head: The Coming Economic Battle Among Japan, Europe, and America* (New York: Morrow, 1992); and Jeffrey Garten, *A Cold Peace: America, Japan, Germany, and the Struggle for Supremacy* (New York: Twentieth Century Fund, 1992).

29. Similar arguments can be found in Thomas Howell, "Dumping: Still a Problem in International Trade," *Trade and Competition Policies* (Boulder, CO: Westview Press, forthcoming).

30. U.S. companies are included as American companies on Charts 4.2 and 4.3. This also includes other North American production, but U.S. companies are the dominant force.

31. It is also worth noting that the countries that have posted dramatic gains in semiconductor production are Korea and Taiwan. Both Korea and Taiwan have, to a greater or lesser degree, followed a strategy similar to that of Japan. Predictably, Korean and Taiwanese companies have also been the subject of antidumping complaints in the United States.

32. In each of the case studies no specific information on prices is included. In a similar analysis, the ITC does attempt to trace price changes related to antidumping orders. Such calculations are very difficult, however. In almost all cases, after an anti-dumping order is imposed, markets remain quite competitive, with a number of foreign and domestic firms in the market and no potential for extracting monopoly rents. Most of the commodities and products examined here, however, are traded on a global market, and swings in price related to many factors are not unusual. Of course, it is predictable that stopping dumping will cause prices to rise, but it is difficult to trace these effects on prices that are affected by literally hundreds of other factors.

33. Lawrence Chimerine, chief economist at Economic Strategy Institute, and Andrew Szamosszegi, research associate at Economic Strategy Institute, made invaluable contributions to these simulations. Any mistake, errors, or oversights, however, are the responsibility of the author.

34. These memory chips, produced with metal-oxide-semiconductor technology, are as a class typically referred to as MOS semiconductors.

35. A number of sources cited previously, including Tyson, *Who's Bashing Whom,* and National Advisory Committee on Semiconductors, *Attaining Preeminence,* make this case.

36. This comment is supported by the previously cited research indicating the geographic benefits of high-technology firms on other high technology firms.

37. See Tyson, *Who's Bashing Whom,* and Flamm, *Mismanaged Trade?*

38. Taking into account these and other concerns, the ITC study assumed a typical price change due to dumping was less than 4 percent while dumping was taking place. U.S. International Trade Commission, *Economic Effects of Antidumping and Counter-vailing Duty Orders and Suspension Agreements* (Washington, DC: USITC, June 1995).

39. The base growth rate for the simulation was estimated using the slope coefficient of a logarithmic regression of actual shipments against a time variable. This methodology yields an annual growth rate of 13.5 percent.

40. It could be argued that many of the firms that design semiconductors in the United States but do production in offshore markets are examples of companies pursuing such a strategy under present conditions. See, for example, Saxenson, *Regional Advantage,* and Porter, *The Competitive Advantage of Nations.*

# Technical Appendix to Chapter 4

## *Greg Mastel, Andrew Z. Szamosszegi, and Lawrence Chimerine*

This appendix presents the methodology and data used in the simulations discussed in Chapter 4. These simulations were an attempt to illustrate the annual economic losses that could have occurred if unmitigated dumping over several years reduced U.S. output in a given industry. In other words, this analysis attempts to address a major shortcoming of traditional analysis: its inability to capture the cumulative effects on output and investment of prolonged dumping.

We chose to examine the semiconductor industry. In particular, this exercise focused on memory chips, known as MOS memories, produced using the Metal Oxide Silicon process. These include dynamic random access memories (DRAMs), static random access memories (SRAMs), erasable programmable read only memories (EPROMs), electrically erasable programmable read only memories (EEPROMs), and flash memory. This segment of the U.S. semiconductor industry was chosen because its survival was clearly endangered by dumping. U.S. DRAM producers were nearly wiped out by Japanese dumping during the 1980s, and U.S. EPROM producers have also been victimized by dumping. Timely antidumping measures preserved U.S. production of DRAMs and EPROMs, and U.S. manufacture of these and other MOS memories has increased strongly.

In these simulations, it is assumed that absent the antidumping cases filed during the 1980s against Japan, and in subsequent years against Korea, the growth rate of memory production in the United States would have been slower than the observed growth rate. In other words, U.S. memory production continues to rise, but rises at a slower rate.

To estimate impact of less memory production, annual data for memory shipments from 1984 to 1996 were collected from the Bureau of the Census. (See Table 4.1A.) The growth rate of memory shipments (13.54 percent) was estimated by using the slope coefficient of a logarithmic regression of actual memory shipments against a time trend. This growth rate was used to construct a smoothed data set for the years 1984 to 1996, and this trend line was the basis for subsequent calculations.

Table 4.1A

**U.S. Shipments, Trade, and Apparent Consumption of MOS Memory**
(millions of dollars)

|      | Shipments | Exports | Imports | Apparent Consumption |
| ---- | --------- | ------- | ------- | -------------------- |
| 1984 | 2,862     | 278     | 2,147   | 4,731                |
| 1985 | 1,973     | 206     | 1,424   | 3,192                |
| 1986 | 1,716     | 123     | 1,233   | 2,826                |
| 1987 | 2,262     | 199     | 1,639   | 3,701                |
| 1988 | 3,255     | 416     | 3,077   | 5,917                |
| 1989 | 3,495     | 723     | 4,160   | 6,932                |
| 1990 | 3,495     | 735     | 3,518   | 6,278                |
| 1991 | 3,539     | 976     | 4,409   | 6,972                |
| 1992 | 4,163     | 1,110   | 5,197   | 8,250                |
| 1993 | 5,027     | 1,503   | 6,519   | 10,043               |
| 1994 | 7,423     | 1,921   | 9,938   | 15,440               |
| 1995 | 10,996    | 2,827   | 16,222  | 24,391               |
| 1996 | 9,672     | 2,767   | 12,762  | 19,667               |

*Source:* Bureau of the Census.

Four different scenarios were calculated, assuming different growth rates of U.S. memory output beginning in 1987: .90 * the actual growth rate (growth); .75 * growth; .50 * growth; and .25 * growth. (See Table 4.2A.)

"Lost" sales (specifically, the domestic production replaced by imports) for each scenario were simply the difference between the trend shipments and the shipments associated with each scenario. The lost shipments for each scenario, which begin accruing in 1987—the first full year that U.S. antidumping orders would have been in place—are presented in Table 4.3A.[1]

The slower growth in memory production would affect growth in the rest of the economy as a result of additional lost economic activity linked to lost semiconductor shipments, such as purchases of input, additional wages, and so forth. After examining a number of macroeconomic multipliers employed in similar simulations, a multiplier of 1.9 was selected to derive the overall economic impact of "lost" purchases of semiconductors.[2]

Completing our estimate required one further adjustment due to lower prices. One argument against antidumping measures is that they remove the price gains to consumers that accrue from dumping. To take this into account, it was assumed that lower prices from higher imports would reduce the average price of memory imports by 10 percent each year.[3] Because lower prices would increase real incomes, and thus generate additional economic activity, this gain in purchasing power was adjusted by a multiplier of 1.1 (see note 2). The annual income effects associated with each scenario, shown in Table 4.5A, are ultimately subtracted from the direct and indirect output losses that were derived above.[4]

Table 4.2A

**Simulated MOS Memory Shipments and Various Growth Rate Scenarios**
(millions of dollars)

|  | Simulated Shipments | 0.90 * Growth | 0.75 * Growth | 0.50 * Growth | 0.25 * Growth |
|---|---|---|---|---|---|
| 1984[1] | 1,737 | 1,737 | 1,737 | 1,737 | 1,737 |
| 1985[1] | 1,989 | 1,989 | 1,989 | 1,989 | 1,989 |
| 1986[1] | 2,278 | 2,278 | 2,278 | 2,278 | 2,278 |
| 1987 | 2,608 | 2,575 | 2,526 | 2,443 | 2,361 |
| 1988 | 2,987 | 2,912 | 2,801 | 2,620 | 2,446 |
| 1989 | 3,420 | 3,292 | 3,105 | 2,810 | 2,535 |
| 1990 | 3,916 | 3,722 | 3,443 | 3,014 | 2,627 |
| 1991 | 4,484 | 4,207 | 3,818 | 3,233 | 2,722 |
| 1992 | 5,135 | 4,757 | 4,233 | 3,467 | 2,821 |
| 1993 | 5,880 | 5,378 | 4,694 | 3,719 | 2,923 |
| 1994 | 6,733 | 6,080 | 5,204 | 3;989 | 3,029 |
| 1995 | 7,709 | 6,874 | 5,771 | 4,278 | 3,139 |
| 1996 | 8,828 | 7,771 | 6,398 | 4,588 | 3,253 |

*Source:* Authors' calculations.

[1] The figures for "Simulated Shipments" and the four scenarios are the same from 1984 to 1986 because there were no antidumping orders issued until 1986.

Table 4.3A

**Lost Shipments Associated with Various Growth Rate Scenarios** (millions of dollars)

|  |  | "Lost" U.S. Memory Sales | | | |
|---|---|---|---|---|---|
|  | Simulated Shipments | 0.90 * Growth | 0.75 * Growth | 0.50 * Growth | 0.25 * Growth |
| 1987 | 2,608 | 33 | 83 | 165 | 248 |
| 1988 | 2,987 | 75 | 186 | 366 | 541 |
| 1989 | 3,420 | 128 | 315 | 610 | 885 |
| 1990 | 3,916 | 195 | 473 | 902 | 1,289 |
| 1991 | 4,484 | 277 | 667 | 1,251 | 1,762 |
| 1992 | 5,135 | 378 | 902 | 1,667 | 2,314 |
| 1993 | 5,880 | 502 | 1,186 | 2,161 | 2,957 |
| 1994 | 6,733 | 653 | 1,528 | 2,744 | 3,704 |
| 1995 | 7,709 | 836 | 1,939 | 3,431 | 4,570 |
| 1996 | 8,828 | 1,057 | 2,429 | 4,239 | 5,575 |

*Source:* Authors' calculations.

The combined direct, multiplier, and price effects associated with each scenario are shown in Table 4.6A. As noted in Chapter 4, the price effects for the ".90 * growth" and ".75 * growth" scenarios during the early years are larger than the direct, indirect, and investment losses due to dumping. This outcome is

Table 4.4A

**Lost Memory Shipments and Multiplier Effects of Various Scenarios**
(millions of dollars)

|      | .90 * Growth | .75 * Growth | .50 * Growth | .25 * Growth |
|------|------|------|------|------|
| 1987 | 63    | 157   | 314   | 471    |
| 1988 | 143   | 354   | 696   | 1,027  |
| 1989 | 244   | 598   | 1,158 | 1,682  |
| 1990 | 370   | 899   | 1,714 | 2,450  |
| 1991 | 526   | 1,266 | 2,378 | 3,348  |
| 1992 | 719   | 1,713 | 3,168 | 4,397  |
| 1993 | 954   | 2,253 | 4,106 | 5,618  |
| 1994 | 1,240 | 2,904 | 5,214 | 7,037  |
| 1995 | 1,588 | 3,684 | 6,520 | 8,684  |
| 1996 | 2,008 | 4,616 | 8,055 | 10,592 |

*Source:* Authors' calculations.

Table 4.5A

**Price Effects of Various Scenarios** (millions of dollars)

|      | .90 * Growth | .75 * Growth | .50 * Growth | .25 * Growth |
|------|------|------|------|------|
| 1987 | 224   | 230   | 239   | 248   |
| 1988 | 312   | 324   | 344   | 363   |
| 1989 | 426   | 446   | 479   | 509   |
| 1990 | 473   | 503   | 551   | 593   |
| 1991 | 628   | 671   | 736   | 792   |
| 1992 | 741   | 798   | 883   | 954   |
| 1993 | 901   | 976   | 1,083 | 1,171 |
| 1994 | 1,056 | 1,152 | 1,286 | 1,392 |
| 1995 | 1,286 | 1,407 | 1,571 | 1,697 |
| 1996 | 1,484 | 1,635 | 1,834 | 1,981 |

*Source:* Authors' calculations.

illustrated by the negative numbers in Table 4.6A. As time passes, however, the effect of lower production and investments leads to losses that exceed the gains resulting from lower prices. In other words, the costs of dumping are contingent on the level of domestic production replaced by imports and the length of time that dumping occurs. Cross and own price elasticities derived from these simulations imply that the damage to the domestic industry would be high, significantly above that embodied in the ".90 * Growth" scenario.[5] The evidence presented here suggests that the continued threat of dumping reduces the growth path of U.S. production and would be a net loss for the U.S. economy over time.

Table 4.6A

**Total Economic Impact of Lost Memory Output—Various Scenarios**
(millions of dollars)

|      | .90 * Growth | .75 * Growth | .50 * Growth | .25 * Growth |
| ---- | ------------ | ------------ | ------------ | ------------ |
| 1987 | −161         | −73          | 75           | 223          |
| 1988 | −169         | 29           | 352          | 664          |
| 1989 | −182         | 152          | 679          | 1,173        |
| 1990 | −103         | 395          | 1,163        | 1,857        |
| 1991 | −102         | 595          | 1,642        | 2,557        |
| 1992 | −22          | 915          | 2,285        | 3,443        |
| 1993 | 53           | 1,277        | 3,022        | 4,447        |
| 1994 | 184          | 1,751        | 3,927        | 5,645        |
| 1995 | 302          | 2,276        | 4,948        | 6,987        |
| 1996 | 524          | 2,981        | 6,221        | 8,612        |

*Source:* Authors' calculations.

## Notes

1. These scenarios assume that U.S. memory exports were not affected by dumping. Realistically, exports would have declined as well, thus magnifying the economic impact presented in Chapter 4.

2. Multipliers such as these are frequently employed to compute the economic impact of additional or lost increments economic activity associated with such changes as additional or decreased government purchases of goods and services. For example, N. Gregory Manikiw, *Macroeconomics* (Worth Publishers: New York) 1992, p. 241, suggests a multiplier of 2.5 in analyzing government spending. In considering the impact of tax cuts (recall that the price reductions discussed in this model are really the result of duties not applied and thus a tax cut), Manikiw suggests a multiplier of 1.5. This difference in multipliers occurs because not all of the additional income from a tax cut is spent on goods and services; thus, a dollar in tax cuts does not generate as much economic activity as a dollar spent purchasing new goods or services. These estimates are typical of textbook macroeconomic multipliers employed in these calculations.

Based upon additional real world data, most consultants and others that carry out analyses employing these multipliers have settled upon lower figures. An informal survey of the multipliers commonly employed in these economic analyses by various consulting firms indicated a range for expenditure multipliers of 1.7 to 2.1. Comparable tax cut multipliers range from 1 to 1.2. For examples of such analyses, contact the WEFA, Inc., or DRI/McGraw-Hill. As would be expected, the results of this simulation vary somewhat depending upon the multipliers selected, but the overall results are robust across the range of multipliers.

3. The 10 percent price effect likely overstates the gain to consumers. An ITC study estimated a 13.4 percent reduction in the U.S. price of electrical and industrial apparatus imports in 1991 if antidumping and countervailing duties were removed. However, prolonged dumping tends to reduce competition. Absent U.S. competitors, foreign producers would have had a strong incentive to raise prices of imported DRAMs. See U.S. International Trade Commission, *The Economic Effects of Antidumping and Countervailing Duty Orders and Suspension Agreements* (Washington, DC: ITC, 1995), 4–11.

4. These calculations assumed an import price elasticity of demand equal to 1.0, meaning that lower prices did not change the value of inputs in a given year.

5. The most recent work providing cross elasticities for semiconductors reports an own price elasticity of demand for imports of −1.7, and a cross price elasticity of demand for the domestic good of 1.47. These refer to short-term elasticities; long-term elasticities would be much higher. See Gary Hufbauer and Kimberly Ann Elliott, *Measuring the Costs of Protection in the United States* (Washington, DC: Institute for International Economics, 1994).

# 5

# Responding to Critics

Over the last two decades, antidumping laws have been the subject of a seemingly endless barrage of criticism from foreign governments, foreign companies, and a number of academics. Much of the analysis already detailed in previous chapters explicitly or implicitly responds to some of their charges, but to ensure that the reader has the opportunity to compare the argument on both sides, this chapter will respond to each of the major criticisms directly and answer several of the prominent recent works that are critical of antidumping regimes.

## Antitrust Versus Antidumping

Many critics of antidumping laws base their position on the claim that antidumping laws are an extension of antitrust laws and thus they should be judged by how well they further antitrust objectives and how closely they conform to procedures of antitrust laws.[1]

This criticism begins from a misreading of history. It is true that antitrust laws and antidumping laws share the same general objective of establishing rules for the competitive marketplace and emerged at roughly the same period in history, but from the very beginning they had quite different specific objectives.[2] Simply put, antitrust laws were consumer protection statutes; they aimed to ensure that consumers were not harmed by private trusts and cartels. Antidumping laws had the broader objective of protecting the U.S. economy from harm from the unfair practices of foreign governments and foreign companies, with an initial focus on the interests of U.S. industries and their workers.

Further, the natures of the problems the laws seek to counter are quite different. Antitrust laws are aimed primarily at attacking collusion, price-fixing, and other anticompetitive practices by private actors within the U.S. economy. Antidumping laws are focused on what is done by actors that are outside U.S. borders and by actors that are either directly supported by or in some cases are foreign governments. This difference explains many of the operational differences between antitrust laws and antidumping laws. Because the actions of foreign principals, particularly foreign governments, are largely beyond the reach of U.S. courts, steps must be taken at an earlier stage to prevent damage. In contrast, antitrust laws can and frequently have been invoked after a trust has already formed, to break up the trust through court orders.

These same orders cannot be easily leveled at foreign actors. For example, if U.S. companies have already exited an industry because prolonged dumping has made operation in particular sectors unprofitable, they may not be interested in reentering under the constant threat of renewed or continued dumping and the prospect of competing with a foreign company that has a protected home market or otherwise enjoys the support of its home government. The nature of the problems they seek to combat forces antidumping laws to be invoked before the competitive marketplace has been irreversibly damaged by dumping. Because U.S. administrative agencies and courts have it within their power to reverse much of the damage done by trusts, antitrust actions can be put off until substantial damage is already apparent in the marketplace.

Finally and probably most important, antitrust laws are aimed at a narrow range of practices that are defined for the purposes of these laws as predatory. Antidumping laws are aimed at a longer list of practices, including (1) consistent but sporadic dumping by foreign companies to dispose of surpluses resulting from government subsidies given to expand their operations, either to create employment or capture economy-of-scale advantages, and (2) export sales at very low prices cross-subsidized by high prices at home, made possible by protected home markets, again with the objective of supporting high production levels to preserve employment or capture economy-of-scale advantages. These practices do not have clear parallels in the domestic realm and are not a focus of antitrust laws, but they are a critical focus of antidumping laws. Unless these practices were countered by antidumping laws, the U.S. economy could face severe disruptions, as analyzed in previous chapters.

Of course, antidumping laws also seek to counter truly predatory behavior that aims to drive competitors from the marketplace. The vast majority of antidumping investigations in the United States seem, however, to come from one of the two categories just described, not "predatory" practices.

The broader scope of antidumping laws is clear from the history of U.S. antidumping laws presented in Chapter 1. There is no need to repeat the entire history, but it is worth noting that the authors of the original U.S. antidumping laws were well aware of the broader scope of coverage of antidumping laws. A member of the Tariff Commission, William Culbertson, who reviewed U.S. antidumping laws in 1919 specifically noted the broader set of problems that antidumping laws attempted to address.[3]

Thus, the critics who point to the differences between antitrust laws and antidumping laws as evidence of the latter's flaws simply misunderstand the purpose of antidumping laws. Antidumping laws and antitrust laws have different purposes and, not surprisingly, different functions and outcomes. Antidumping laws are designed to protect the American economy from the injurious effects of foreign protectionism, subsidies, and the like, while antitrust laws are aimed primarily at preventing the creation of trusts.

Given their different purposes, an international agreement on antitrust enforcement would not, by itself, be sufficient to replace antidumping laws. Given different international attitudes on the desirability of blocking the creation of trusts and combating anticompetitive practices, it is unlikely that an international regime would be as effective in countering these practices as U.S. law. In short, an international agreement may not be a good substitute for antidumping law, although it may be a useful adjunct.

More fundamentally, as explained in previous chapters, dumping results from a range of government practices, including protectionism, subsidies, and government-set pricing. Failure to enforce antitrust laws abroad can also result in closed home markets, which in turn make dumping possible, but this is only one of several causes of dumping. Even if universal international application of antitrust laws were possible, many of the underlying causes of dumping would remain. Given this, an international agreement would be a poor substitute for current antidumping laws.

### Replace Antidumping Laws with Safeguard Laws

A number of critics of antidumping laws have proposed replacing them with safeguard actions.[4] Safeguard actions are legal under the WTO. They are temporary measures to restrict imports in order to allow the competing domestic industry to downsize, become more competitive, or otherwise adapt to import competition. The WTO limits such safeguard actions to eight years (four years with a four-year extension). Before safeguard relief can be granted, "serious injury" to a domestic industry due to import competition must be found.

In some circumstances, safeguard actions can serve a useful purpose. Most commonly, they provide companies and workers in an industry that is no longer competitive the opportunity to retrain for other jobs and reinvest in other sectors. On occasion, however, a safeguard action can provide the critical adjustment time to allow an industry to become more competitive. The example of Harley-Davidson, a U.S. motorcycle company, which received relief through a safeguard action and was able to regain competitiveness and urge termination of import limits ahead of schedule, is often cited to illustrate this point.[5]

Despite occasional success stories, however, safeguard actions were never conceived as a substitute for antidumping laws. The most important distinction between antidumping actions and safeguard actions is that antidumping actions deal with *unfairly* traded imports while safeguard actions deal with *fairly* traded imports. In safeguard actions, the primary issue is whether imports cause serious injury. Thus, the negative competitive impacts of dumping would not be addressed or even considered. After a maximum of eight years, import relief would be withdrawn even if the dumping continued.

A greater practical problem would be the serious-injury standard for relief. As explained in Chapter 1, there is also an injury test that must be employed before antidumping duties can be imposed, but the injury test in this case is material injury. Neither term is precisely defined, but material injury is a substantially lower standard than serious injury. The serious-injury standard is, in fact, so high that no U.S. industry has petitioned for safeguard relief in recent years.[6]

Under U.S. law, replacing antidumping actions with safeguard actions also risks politicizing the process of considering trade problems. As explained in Chapter 1, the president has little discretion in antidumping actions; once material injury and dumping are established, an antidumping order or a suspension agreement is mandatory. But relief in safeguard cases is entirely discretionary. Even if serious injury is established, the president can deny import relief if he believes it is not in the national interest. As a result, even after serious injury is found, the debate over relief sparks a lobbying contest between foreign governments, foreign companies, and a variety of U.S. interests.

In sum, replacing antidumping laws with safeguard action amounts to simply abolishing antidumping laws. One advocate of replacing antidumping laws with safeguard actions actually proposed simply abolishing antidumping laws as his preferred option.[7] Thus, moving to a system that relied exclusively on safeguard actions would have most of the negative economic impacts of abolishing antidumping laws. Most notably, such a change would have the effect of opening the U.S. economy to nearly unlimited foreign dumping.

## U.S. Administering Authorities Are Biased

Probably the most frequent charge leveled at U.S. antidumping laws is that they are biased against foreign respondents and that the administering agents in the United States apply the laws in a way that disadvantages foreign respondents. Various approaches are used to document this claim.

Some criticize specific procedures, such as the Commerce Department's use of best information available, the application of a profit factor in cost cases, and the use of surrogate markets in cost cases. Similarly, the U.S. ITC's practice—which is directed by law—of requiring that a tie vote on injury result in an affirmative decision on injury is also criticized as unfairly biased. Each of these specific criticisms is discussed in Chapter 1, which outlines the relevant administrative procedures.

Beyond that, it is important to note that most of the critiques were written before the Uruguay Round went into force. As noted previously, the new WTO standards on antidumping laws are carefully negotiated, quite specific, and subject to oversight by binding dispute-settlement panels; a number of new protections for respondents' interests, such as new standing requirements, *de minimis* levels of dumping, and negligible import levels below which action cannot be pursued, are included in the WTO antidumping provisions. (For a more complete listing of notable WTO innovations in antidumping regulations, see Chapter 1. The complete WTO antidumping code is also included in Appendix A.)

Undoubtedly, critics will always find fault with specific procedures discussed in isolation, but national antidumping laws are now regulated by an effective international regime through the WTO. Current antidumping procedures have been the subject of painful and detailed negotiations. Each individual procedure is part of a package that is designed to ensure the equitable and effective function of antidumping laws and balance the interests of petitioners and respondents. From time to time, some procedures may have had an unduly negative impact upon respondents' interests, but these are the very procedures the WTO antidumping code seeks to correct. At the very least, the WTO procedures, which will not be fully implemented for several more years, should be given a chance to establish a track record before the same tired old criticisms are trotted out to condemn them.

In the case of U.S. laws, critics are correct in noting that the laws were written by the U.S. Congress and the Congress is probably closer to domestic petitioners than to foreign companies. Nonetheless, foreign interests have been well represented in congressional debates on antidumping laws and have won their share of disputes. For example, despite considerable lobbying by domestic interests, the United States has not adopted a number of antidumping practices used in Europe and permissible under the WTO, such as the so-called duty absorption procedures mentioned in Chapter 1, which would likely result in higher antidumping duties in a number of cases.

Fundamentally, U.S. antidumping laws are applied through a transparent administrative process in which respondents are allowed to make their case at every juncture. The same cannot be said for a number of other countries' antidumping laws; antidumping authorities in Mexico and Europe have often been accused of operating "black box" procedures under which the process for setting dumping duties or negotiating undertakings is closed.[8] In addition, U.S. antidumping laws are subject to judicial oversight to ensure that administrative agencies properly apply the laws. Finally, the WTO and NAFTA provide additional international checks on the operation of U.S. laws. On the whole, the process hardly seems to be hopelessly biased against respondent interests.

To buttress their argument, critics of antidumping laws often turn to statistical arguments to prove that petitioners always win relief. A careful look at the recent record, however, debunks that argument. As the International Trade Commission pointed out in a recent study, *during no year between 1980 and 1993 has the total volume of imports subject to antidumping investigations exceeded one half of 1 percent of total imports into the United States, and in most years the level was far lower.*[9] The total percentage of all imports covered by antidumping duties has remained at these low levels since then. Simply put, antidumping actions simply have not resulted in a wave of protectionism. Considered in the context of total U.S. imports, antidumping orders make barely more than a ripple.

Also, most antidumping cases filed have not resulted in the application of duties.[10] In cases in which a determination was issued, more have been rejected by the Commerce Department or the U.S. ITC than have been granted antidumping relief. In addition, a number of petitions have been voluntarily withdrawn or terminated by administering authorities before a determination was reached. As noted in Chapter 2, from 1980 to 1997, only about 44 percent of the antidumping cases filed have resulted in the imposition of antidumping duties. Beyond that, many cases were simply never filed because petitioners were discouraged by administration officials from proceeding with their cases.

Further, it is not appropriate to look at the percentage of cases filed that result in affirmative determinations as the final determinant of whether or not administrative procedures are biased. As noted, the cases that are actually filed are those that petitioners believe have a strong potential to succeed; otherwise petitioners would not invest large amounts in legal fees to support the cases. Most fundamentally, however, the merits of the cases and the state of the economy—the latter, as discussed, influences the probability of affirmative injury determination—have a direct and obvious impact on case outcomes that is ignored by those who focus too much upon overall statistics.

Table 5.1

**Antidumping Investigations, 1980–1993: Coverage of Subject Imports Relative to Total U.S. Imports and Weighted Average Margins for New Case Filings, by Year**

| Year | Subject Imports ($Million) | Subject Imports as a Share of Total U.S. Imports (%) | Weighted Average Margin (%) |
|------|------|------|------|
| 1980 | 103.7 | 0.04 | 13.2 |
| 1981 | 40.0[1] | .02[1] | 3.9[1] |
| 1982 | 194.8 | .08 | 19.3 |
| 1983 | 566.1 | .21 | 15.5 |
| 1984 | 93.6 | .03 | 21.1 |
| 1985 | 757.7 | .22 | 42.5 |
| 1986 | 1,398.0 | .38 | 14.4 |
| 1987 | 372.2 | .09 | 35.6 |
| 1988 | 980.5 | .22 | 69.8 |
| 1989 | 1,255.0 | .26 | 16.8 |
| 1990 | 694.4 | .14 | 27.2 |
| 1991 | 541.7 | .11 | 41.0 |
| 1992 | 2,158.0 | .40 | 30.4 |
| 1993 | 258.8 | 0.04 | 41.6 |

*Source:* U.S. Customs data and compiled by U.S. International Trade Commission staff; *The Economic Effects of Antidumping and Countervailing Duty Orders and Suspension Agreements*, Investigation No. 332–344 (Washington, DC: ITC, 1995), p. 32.

[1]Excludes data that could not be aggregated without revealing business proprietary information.

A permutation of the above argument holds that the Department of Commerce, in particular, is biased in its LTFV findings. It is unquestionably true that the Department of Commerce issues fewer negative final determinations than the ITC, but the comparison is misplaced. The Department of Commerce and the ITC are focused on entirely different questions; the Commerce Department considers whether imports are priced at less than fair value, while the ITC considers whether the imports have created material injury. The factors that affect one have little or no impact upon the other. It is entirely possible and, in fact, common for imports to be dumped but not cause injury, and vice versa.

Petitioners can more easily self-screen their petitions to predict the outcome of a Commerce Department determination than they can to predict an ITC determination. The Commerce Department's standards in antidumping cases are explained in some detail, and the evidence, or lack thereof, of dumping is usually clear to potential petitioners when they are considering filing a case. In the case of injury, the individual standards employed by

ITC commissioners are less clear and constantly subject to change as the makeup of the commission changes. Further, an important basis for the ITC's final injury determination is the overall strength of the economy almost a year after the period from which the supporting data for an initial petition are drawn. A myriad of unknown and unknowable intervening factors can affect the future economic strength of a given petitioning industry and have an impact upon the ITC's material-injury determination. It is therefore not surprising that petitioners are better able to predict the decisions of the Commerce Department than of the ITC.

Also, many of the weakest cases filed are rejected by the ITC in their preliminary injury finding. Thus, the ITC acts to screen out those cases before the Commerce Department ever has a chance to rule on them.[11]

Another permutation of this argument is that cases are sometimes filed simply to harass foreign companies and browbeat them into exiting the U.S. market or raising their prices. Certainly, antidumping actions do put a burden upon the respondent, but they put at least an equal burden upon the petitioner, and as the above analysis has demonstrated, statistically respondents prevail more often than not. Perhaps most important, on this issue more than others, a prime focus of several new WTO agreement provisions—tightened standing requirements, *de minimis* dumping levels, and minimum levels for dumped imports—is eliminating baseless antidumping cases; it should be given the opportunity to work.

Some baseless cases may have been filed to force concessions from foreign companies, but that has certainly not been a frequent problem and protections are in place to prevent it. Similarly, the Commerce Department and the ITC have undoubtedly occasionally made errors in applying the law or analyzing facts. Keep in mind that literally thousands of administrative decisions have been made in hundreds of antidumping cases in the last two decades. It would be surprising indeed if an occasional mistake were not made.

As the previous analysis in this book demonstrates, however, on the whole, antidumping laws have worked well and eight decades of operational experience and international negotiation have produced sound, workable procedures. Especially in the United States, which, owing to its historical traditions and political institutions, has probably the most transparent and accessible process in the world for reaching administrative decisions under its trade laws, there is simply no evidence of systemic administrative difficulties.

## Use of Average Cost Versus Variable Cost

The criticism of antidumping laws that meets with the most sympathetic response from economists is that antidumping laws focus upon average total cost, referred to as fully allocated cost, instead of average marginal cost. To understand this argument it is first important to revisit the microeconomics of corporate production decisions. Average total cost is made up of two elements: fixed costs and variable costs. Fixed costs, also known as sunk costs, are the expenses incurred regardless of the level of production; fixed costs are costs such as plant and equipment costs. Variable costs are those costs that vary directly with the level of production; variable costs include such items as payments for intermediate inputs, electricity, and hourly wages.

Setting average total costs at the level below which dumping occurs seems to be counter to normal business practices in two ways. First, since fixed costs are sunk costs that already have been incurred regardless of the level of production, it is economically rational for a company to continue production so long as the market price obtained for the goods produced covers variable costs and makes some contribution to fixed costs, even if it does not entirely cover average total costs. Thus, from an individual company's perspective and under these conditions, it is rational for a company to dump. This set of facts is sometimes used to argue that antidumping duties should be scrapped entirely or imposed only if companies are selling below their variable costs, which is taken as evidence of predatory intent. (In the semiconductor industry, some observers have argued that declining variable costs make even this approach difficult.)[12]

Of course, this argument explains dumping only in the short term. In the long term, as any microeconomics text will point out, all costs are variable. If prices failed to cover costs for more than a short period, rational actors will find new sectors to invest in and stop money-losing ventures. Certainly, they would not expand their investments in an industry where costs could not be covered. Particularly in high-technology industries, which have been the focus of many antidumping actions, the distinction between fixed costs and variable costs is questionable. In the high-technology sector, technology evolves so quickly that production facilities become obsolete within a year or two and product life cycles, themselves, may last only a year or two. Thus, before an antidumping case can even be brought, a product life cycle may be over or in sharp decline. Certainly, under these conditions, all costs can be said to be variable.

This microeconomic reality is thus not an adequate explanation for behavior in those companies that have made dumping a common practice for years and even decades. As the case studies demonstrate, long-term dumping is not merely the result of a temporary decision to sell at prices above variable cost but below total cost. Instead, long-term dumping is commercial behavior supported by government policies that allow or provide market protection, collusion, subsidies of production or corporate cross-subsidization from another sector or market in which they enjoy one of these same economic advantages.

Further, although it may be rational economic behavior for an individual company to price below average total cost, that does not necessarily mean that it is desirable for a country to allow it. In light of the economic costs of dumping, explained earlier, it is entirely appropriate for a national government to implement a policy aimed at preventing or combating dumping. This closely parallels a number of other instances in which governments have chosen to prohibit behavior that would otherwise be economically desirable for companies to pursue; for example, both the formation of trusts and polluting are economically rational ways to increase profitability in some instances, but many national governments, including that of the United States, have chosen to prohibit both. The fact that companies might dump in the absence of government intervention in no way necessarily argues against government prohibitions on dumping.

The second case in which cost structure might result in dumping, at least for a short period, is known as forward pricing. This is a more acceptable explanation for short-term dumping. In essence, it holds that when production is beginning, prices are certain to be below average total cost for a time. Consider the first unit to come off a new assembly line. For that unit, the average total cost would include *all* fixed costs because there are no other units to spread the costs over. Of course, companies do not attempt to cover all of their production costs on the first unit. Instead, they plan to spread those costs over a reasonable production run; this process of pricing to distribute costs over a given production run is generally referred to as forward pricing of start-up costs.

Taken to an extreme, forward pricing would make dumping virtually impossible to define, since the total production run supported by a given fixed investment is impossible to define until the end of the production cycle. Nonetheless, forward pricing is a normal business practice. In light of this reality, the new WTO antidumping provisions take note of this and allow for forward pricing. The new WTO provisions include the following direction to national authorities: "[C]osts shall be adjusted appropriately . . . for circumstances in which costs during the period of the investigation are affected by start-up operations."[13] Presumably, this provision will result in reasonable allowances for the spreading of start-up costs in national dumping laws.

## Other Countries Will Copy Antidumping Laws or Retaliate

One argument sometimes used against U.S. antidumping laws is that other countries are likely to follow U.S. antidumping practices. Therefore, since the United States has significant export interests, U.S. authorities should be conservative in their implementation of antidumping laws.

This argument was stronger before the Uruguay Round was implemented. As already pointed out in other contexts, the WTO prescribes a detailed set of rules on the operation of antidumping laws. It is now virtually impossible to use antidumping laws as a blatant tool for protectionism. If a country attempts to implement its antidumping laws in an abusive manner, it can be challenged before the WTO. Given the numerous procedural safeguards on antidumping and the dispute-settlement procedures of the WTO, this would seem a more than adequate remedy to the problem of other countries twisting the concept of antidumping into blatant protectionism.

Another logical flaw in this argument is that most other countries have adopted antidumping laws on their own. As Table 5.2 demonstrates, in recent years, China, Mexico, and India—to name but a few—have adopted antidumping laws. In all likelihood, within a few years, almost all WTO members are likely to adopt antidumping laws or put into place administrative procedures that have the same effect. This is not to say that other countries can retaliate against the United States for its antidumping laws, as long as the United States operates its antidumping regime within the limits prescribed; such retaliation would be a violation of the WTO's principles. But antidumping laws are hardly a new idea and at this point they are likely to come into wider use. The appropriate focus for the United States should be ensuring that other countries operate the laws they adopt in the same transparent and WTO-consistent manner that the United States docs.

Perhaps the greatest flaw in the logic of this argument is the assumption that if the United States does not have or does not use its antidumping laws, other countries will follow suit. The United States was not the first country to adopt antidumping laws, and antidumping laws are now an established part of the international trade policies of most major trading countries. In many respects, the European Union and several other countries are considerably more aggressive than the United States in their application of antidumping laws. A unilateral decision by the United States to abandon antidumping laws is not likely to inspire other countries to follow the U.S. example.

## Notes on Specific Studies

In the last several years, a number of interesting analyses critical of antidumping laws have been written and are worthy of some individual attention. Of course, many of the arguments considered in these works are addressed elsewhere in this book, either above or in previous chapters.

Table 5.2

**Antidumping Laws Around the World**

| Country | First Antidumping Law Enacted | Cases Initiated by Country (1980–1993)[1] | Cases Initiated Against Country (Worldwide, 1981–1993) |
|---|---|---|---|
| Canada | 1904 | 450 | 51 |
| New Zealand | 1905 | 32 | 18 |
| Australia | 1906 | 597 | 6 |
| United States | 1916 | 638 | 175 |
| Japan | 1920, 1991[2] | 3 | 197 |
| Great Britain | 1921 | Included in EU figures | |
| Finland | 1968 | 17 | 12 |
| European Union | 1968 | 411 | 509 (not including European countries listed on chart) |
| Austria | 1985 | 7 | 22 |
| Sweden | 1985[2] | 13 | 25 |
| Mexico | 1986 | 87 | 26 |
| Korea | 1986 | 13 | 117 |
| Brazil | 1988[2] | 18 | 88 |
| Poland | 1991[2] | 24 | 46 |
| Colombia | 1991[2] | 2 | 7 |
| India | 1992[2] | 8 | 31 |

*Sources:* Country embassies; General Accounting Office, *International Trade: A Comparison of U.S. and Foreign Antidumping Practices* (Washington, DC: GAO, Dewey Ballantine, 1994); U.S. International Trade Commission, *The Economic Effects of Antidumping and Countervailing Duty Orders and Suspension Agreements,* Investigation No. 332–334 (Washington, DC: ITC, 1994).

[1] As reported to GATT Committee on Antidumping Practices
[2] Year of first antidumping case

Nonetheless, these works often couch their critiques in a way that requires a more tailored response, and readers may benefit from a direct response to particular studies.

## *The Congressional Budget Office*

In 1994, the Congressional Budget Office (CBO) issued a report titled *U.S. Antidumping and Countervailing Duty Law: A Policy Untethered from Its Rationale.*[14] The report was sharply critical of antidumping laws; it focused heavily upon the differences between antidumping laws and antitrust laws, and it criticized numerous administrative procedures employed in U.S. antidumping investigations as inherently slanted in favor of U.S. industries seeking antidumping relief.

The report was issued before the changes negotiated during the Uruguay Round were implemented. Many of the allegations of administrative bias seem to be addressed in part or in total in the Uruguay Round.

A large number of these allegations of administrative abuse focused on the Commerce Department. Using data drawn from other sources and dealing with the 1980s, the report repeats the claim that the Commerce Department too frequently finds evidence of dumping or subsidies. This argument is answered in detail earlier in this chapter.

As noted, the claim that antidumping laws should be more closely linked to antitrust laws is simply misguided. Although antitrust laws and antidumping laws were created at about the same time and share some objectives, they have from the outset been quite distinct in terms of their focus, implementation, and ultimate objectives. Those who echo this criticism would be well advised to first look carefully at the history of antitrust and antidumping laws and the current objectives of both. To argue that antidumping laws are untethered from the principles of antitrust and therefore for that reason should be eliminated or radically reformed is to display limited knowledge of the legislative history of these issues and no knowledge of their current distinct objectives.

### The World Bank

A World Bank economist, J. Michael Finger, is perhaps the most consistent and vehement critic of antidumping laws. In the numerous publications he has either authored or edited on the topic, Finger has made most of the criticisms of antidumping laws dealt with in this volume. He is fond of repeating the claim that "[a]ntidumping is ordinary trade protection with a grand public relations program."[15]

Most of his writings on the subject are pre–Uruguay Round and many of his soundest specific criticisms are addressed by the Uruguay Round agreement. Finger's critique of antidumping laws, however, is wide-ranging. In one form or another, each of the individual arguments considered in this chapter has been raised by Finger. He also has criticized the origins of antidumping laws as historically rooted in protectionism.[16] This criticism is discussed in Chapter 1.

In one of his largest works on this topic, *Antidumping: How It Works and Who Gets Hurt,* Finger relies heavily upon five case studies of the impact of U.S. trade laws on particular foreign interests. Several of the case studies are written by foreign nationals from the countries subject to the trade action; not surprisingly, the case discussions are less than balanced. For example, a case study by a Swedish economist focusing on the Swedish steel industry fails to mention that the Swedish stainless steel companies subject to antidumping action were also the subject of antitrust action by European officials.[17] In addition, only one of the several antidumping findings against Swedish stainless steel manufacturers was ultimately overturned on GATT review, and that decision to overturn was on the basis of the standing of the petitioner, not the facts of the case.[18] The case studies are also pre–Uruguay Round, and thus the effects of recent reforms on the case studies are not considered.

Most important, the case study approach as employed in Finger's volume is not particularly useful. For the most part, these case studies focus on individual cases chosen from hundreds. Most of the criticisms are specific to the facts of these individual cases and have little application beyond them. Even if it could be demonstrated that U.S. antidumping laws were misapplied in five cases, such a small and carefully selected sample would certainly not be sufficient to draw a verdict on the hundreds of times antidumping laws have been used.

## The International Trade Commission

In 1995, the U.S. International Trade Commission issued a major study of U.S. antidumping and countervailing-duty laws. The study included much useful information on the operational history of antidumping laws. Several of the case studies employed also provide useful background on the industries involved.

The most frequently cited conclusion from the study is an economic estimate that for the year 1991, antidumping and countervailing orders imposed a $1.59 billion cost on the U.S. economy, equivalent to .03 percent of U.S. GDP. This calculation is really only a restatement of the nearly universally accepted conclusion that tariffs are almost always a net negative for the economy.[19] The ITC has imposed a simple static analysis—albeit a relatively comprehensive one—of the costs and benefits of tariffs without considering the effects on factors, such as industry investment, analyzed in Chapter 4.

No serious observer would deny that almost any new tariff, including antidumping duties, is likely to have a negative effect on the economy if analyzed from a static perspective without considering the competitive effects of those duties. From the outset, however, antidumping laws have been put in place because they were justified by the adverse competitive effects of dumping. Thus, a simple tariff analysis of the impact of antidumping laws is not terribly meaningful.

As ITC commissioners Rohr and Nuzum noted in their dissent on the report, the ITC analysis does not consider "the long-term competitive implications of injury from unfair trade practices."[20] As the competitive analysis of antidumping laws in Chapter 4 illustrates, if the larger competitive impacts of dumping are considered, antidumping laws are sound economic policy.

## The CATO Institute

A recent antidumping case involving supercomputers inspired the CATO Institute, a Washington think tank, to produce a number of publications that are sharply critical of antidumping laws in general.[21] A much different reading of both the facts and merits of this particular case is included in Chapter 3. Of particular note, the CATO analysis pays scant attention to the long history of trade frictions in the supercomputer sector and the repeated examples of dumping.

In order to evaluate the arguments made in the CATO Institute publications on supercomputer dumping, it is important to first understand its ideological orientation. The CATO Institute is a libertarian/conservative organization devoted to the promotion of a laissez-faire economic policy, of which opposition to antidumping laws is a part. To quote the CATO Institute, it is committed to, among other things, "free markets" and "limited government."[22]

The CATO Institute consistently opposes government intervention in and regulation of the economy. As such, it is a staunch opponent of programs such as environmental regulations, gun control, government involvement in child care or health care, and public broadcasting. CATO has also advocated privatizing the functions of the Food and Drug Administration and the entire Social Security program. On the international trade front, they take the view that dumped products should be viewed as good buys and that Americans should seize the opportunity to purchase them. Scant attention is given to the competitive impacts of dumping that are the focus of this volume and the core of the case for antidumping laws.

Though the focus of the recent CATO writings has been the issuance of an antidumping order on supercomputers, most of the arguments presented are really generic criticisms of antidumping laws. Great weight is given to the argument that the Commerce Department (and apparently other agencies of the U.S. government) is systematically biased against importers and foreign companies.[23] This argument and most of the others advanced by the CATO Institute are addressed in detail earlier in this chapter.

## Conclusion

The debate over antidumping laws has raged for years, and it would be impossible for any volume or even series of volumes to answer all the various criticisms that have been leveled at them. This chapter is intended to demonstrate the flaws in at least the most common critiques of antidumping laws.

It would be difficult to imagine how any laws that have required literally tens of thousands of administrative decisions in countries around the world over a period of eight decades could operate without criticism. In fact, it is difficult to imagine such laws operating without making serious errors. This generalization is surely true of antidumping laws. Over the years, mistakes have been made, and antidumping laws have even been employed intentionally for protectionist effect. At times, procedures may have been cumbersome. A series of agreements under the world trading system has, however, remedied most of these problems. By and large, antidumping laws presently work well as a remedy to a practice that would otherwise ravage industries in open-market countries. The U.S. system for enforcing these laws is undeniably transparent and provides ample opportunities for importers and foreign companies to fully and fairly participate. Undoubtedly, antidumping laws can and will be improved, but they now function smoothly and achieve the purpose of blocking mercantilistic trade strategies.

## Notes

1. See, for example, Congressional Budget Office, *U.S. Antidumping and Countervailing Duty Law: A Policy Untethered from Its Rationale* (Washington, DC: CBO, 1994).

2. Interested readers should review Chapter 1 and see also Jorge Miranda, "Should Antidumping Laws Be Dumped?" *Law and Policy in International Business* 28, no. 1 (1996): 255–288, and "Rethinking the 1916 Antidumping Act," *Harvard Law Review* (May 1997): 1555.

3. William Smith Culbertson, *Commercial Policy in War Time and After* (New York: D. Appleton, 1924), p. 153.

4. J. Michael Finger, *Antidumping: How It Works and Who Gets Hurt* (Ann Arbor: University of Michigan Press, 1993), pp. 58–59.

5. Vaughn L. Beals, "Harley-Davidson's Key Argument for Tariff Protection," *New York Times,* April 20, 1983; "Industry Still Has Anti-Import Tricks up Its Sleeve," *Journal of Commerce,* June 23, 1987.

6. Safeguard actions are used more frequently in some other countries, including the European Union.

7. Finger, *Antidumping,* p. 58.

8. See, for example, Laura D'Andrea Tyson, *Who's Bashing Whom? Trade Conflict in High-Technology Industries* (Washington, DC: Institute for International Economics, 1992), pp. 232–235.

9. U.S. International Trade Commission, *The Economic Effects of Antidumping and Countervailing Duty Orders and Suspension Agreements,* Investigation No. 332–344 (Washington, DC: ITC, 1995).

10. Compilation of statistics from the Department of Commerce's Import Administration Office's database on countervailing duties and antidumping cases.

11. Ibid.

12. Kenneth Flamm, *Mismanaged Trade? Strategic Policy and the Semiconductor Industry* (Washington, DC: Brookings Institution, 1996).

13. Uruguay Round Final Text, *Agreement on Implementation of Article VI of the General Agreement on Tariffs and Trade 1994,* Article 2.2.1. See Appendix A.

14. Congressional Budget Office, *U.S. Antidumping.*

15. See, for example, J. Michael Finger, *The Origins and Evolution of Antidumping Regulation* (Washington, DC: World Bank, 1991).

16. Ibid., pp. 6–8.

17. *EC Commission Decision of July 18, 1990,* Official Journal No. L 220/28 (August 15, 1990).

18. Noted in "Frozen Pipes," *The Economist,* April 6, 1991, p. 69.

19. U.S. International Trade Commission, *Economic Effects.*

20. Ibid., p. VII.

21. Christopher M. Dumler, *Anti-Dumping Laws Trash Supercomputer Competition* (Washington, DC: CATO Institute, 1997).

22. The address for the CATO Institute Web page is www.cato.org./main.

23. Dumler, *Anti-Dumping Laws.*

# 6

# Current Issues

Since they were first passed in 1916, U.S. antidumping laws have been subject to nearly constant amendment in order to reflect new conditions, respond to new problems, and comply with new international agreements. The Uruguay Round provided the most comprehensive revision of anti-dumping laws to date; in response to the Uruguay Round, the United States has implemented and is implementing literally hundreds of separate changes in its antidumping procedures. Still, pressure for change continues as new provisions are implemented, old legislative battles continue, and conditions change.

In the coming years, a number of changes in U.S. antidumping laws are likely to be discussed, and ultimately, some will be implemented. In order to give the reader an appreciation for the issues that are currently on the horizon in this debate, this chapter reviews in some detail four changes in antidumping laws and procedures that are currently being discussed: (1) proposed changes in antidumping procedures regarding nonmarket econo-mies (NMEs), (2) implementation of sunset reviews on antidumping orders mandated by the Uruguay Round, (3) continuing proposals for short-supply exemptions in antidumping orders, and (4) proposals to change U.S. laws to ensure that antidumping duties are not simply absorbed by the exporter without changing the market price of the goods subject to the order.

## Nonmarket Economy Antidumping Procedures

For many years, antidumping procedures directed at NMEs have drawn considerable fire from critics of U.S. antidumping laws. An extensive de-scription of current procedures and their history is included in Chapter 3, but a few essentials must be reviewed for this discussion. NME antidump-ing procedures attempt to address the practical problem that prices and costs—as those concepts are understood in a market economy—do not exist, or are at least very difficult to determine, in a nonmarket economy, which by definition does not rely upon the price mechanism. As a result, authorities in the United States and Europe have relied upon prices and costs in surrogate markets—market economies that are comparable to the subject NME in terms of development, standard of living, and other related factors—to determine costs in NMEs for the purposes of antidumping laws.[1]

From the outset, these procedures have been subject to criticism from a number of perspectives. Unquestionably, administrative authorities have considerable room for subjective judgments in implementing NME antidumping procedures. These procedures, however, are necessitated not by the arbitrariness of national laws or administering authorities, but by the very nature of the problem. It is simply not possible, even in theory, to find comparable price and cost data for NMEs; the choice then is to either give NMEs a free pass on antidumping laws, apply laws other than antidumping laws to the problem, or attempt to make antidumping laws workable in this context.

As is discussed below, an exemption from antidumping laws is not a credible option; it is doubtful that domestic industries or lawmakers would quietly allow plants to be closed and workers laid off because industries in nonmarket economies chose to export to the U.S. market at dumped prices to generate hard currency, to dispose of surpluses, or for some other purpose. As is explained in Chapter 3, other trade laws, such as Section 406 and countervailing-duty laws, have not provided a solution to NME trade problems.

Since other options have not proved feasible, U.S. authorities have had no choice but to make current antidumping laws workable within the context of the relationship between NMEs and market economies. Antidumping procedures have become what some scholars refer to as "the interface" that facilitates trade between market economies and nonmarket economies.[2] Market economies are built around the price mechanism; pure nonmarket economies do not rely upon price. NME antidumping procedures provide the mechanism for establishing comparable prices at which trade can occur.

NME antidumping procedures were not initially the subject of much attention when they were quietly implemented by the United States in the mid-1970s. The European Union adopted similar procedures, and the WTO explicitly allowed national authorities in cases in which market prices could not be determined to determine costs on "such a reasonable basis as the authorities may determine."[3]

In recent years, however, trade with reforming NMEs became a much more intensely debated issue. The primary reason for the increased attention has been the dramatic increase in imports from reforming NMEs. China is the most notable example. U.S. imports have risen at a near exponential rate to more than $60 billion per year. A number of other reforming NMEs, including Russia, Ukraine, and Poland, have also had some success in exporting to the United States, although they do not rival China.[4] Not surprisingly, antidumping complaints under NME procedures have risen dramatically as well. China is now the leading respondent country under U.S. laws, and Russia, Ukraine, Hungary, Latvia, Kazakhstan, and others have also been the subject of antidumping complaints.[5]

For reasons explained in Chapters 1 and 3, a number of the U.S. cases involving NMEs have been formally resolved through suspension agreements. In addition, some problems that would likely have resulted in antidumping actions were forestalled through government-to-government agreements. The most important example of such an agreement is a global market-sharing agreement on aluminum that was aimed at heading off a major market disruption resulting from Russian entry into the world aluminum market.[6]

In those cases not addressed through suspension agreements, duties tend to be higher than duties in other antidumping cases—often approaching or even exceeding 100 percent.[7] Several factors account for these higher-than-normal duties, including the failure of some respondents to participate in the investigation or provide information to defend their actions, as well as the fact (discussed below) that many NME exports are priced with little regard to costs of production.

In Europe, a similar pattern has been apparent. The European Union (EU) does have substantial and growing imports from NMEs, although they have not risen as quickly as U.S. imports from NMEs.[8] Europe has also employed NME procedures in nearly fifty cases since 1989. These cases have involved a number of respondent countries, including China, Russia, Belarus, Hungary, and Poland. Probably because of their proximity, the European Union has initiated relatively more actions against Russia, the former Soviet republics, and Eastern Europe than has the United States. By one estimate, nearly one quarter of total European imports from Russia and the former Soviet republics are subject to antidumping duties or undertakings.[9] As is the case in the United States, however, the most frequently cited NME respondent country in Europe is China.[10]

*NME Procedures Under Fire*

Though they have been in place for twenty years, NME procedures have come under intense criticism in recent years. Most of the criticism comes from the primary targets of the procedures, China and Russia. The governments of these countries have complained that the procedures are arbitrary and discourage economic reform in their countries. The heart of their argument seems to be that reforming NMEs need access to major markets in order to finance their reforms. They also take umbrage at being characterized as NMEs and argue that they are not given sufficient credit for implementing significant economic reforms.

These arguments have little merit. The issue of arbitrariness was addressed earlier, and NME exports have grown strongly despite NME procedures.[11] Further, though it would likely create uncertainty, it is ultimately not clear that eliminating NME antidumping provisions would result in lower duties on NME exports, since they would otherwise be subject to countervailing duty and antidumping investigations. As noted in Chapter 3, Poland chose not to graduate from NME status, perhaps for this reason, even though it likely could have met the relevant burdens of proof.

As also explained in Chapter 3, the rationale for continued application of NME antidumping rules remains unchanged: The economies subject to NME antidumping rules are not entirely market economies. Despite considerable economic reforms, China, Russia, and most other transitional economies still maintain many features of nonmarket economics (state ownership, planning, and so on), and true costs and prices often cannot be determined on a market basis.

### The WTO and NME Antidumping Rules

The grumbling by China and Russia has focused on negotiations over these countries joining the WTO. Both countries have frequently raised the issue of their status under U.S. and European antidumping laws in WTO negotiations. In response to Chinese and Russian criticism, the European Union recently changed the name of their procedures to eliminate the term "nonmarket economy" from its antidumping laws. It appears, however, that the EU plans to continue to operate its laws in much the same fashion, except in those cases where Chinese or Russian enterprise functions in a true market. The actual operational details of this European change are not available as this book goes to press; it appears, however, that the EU is adopting a standard much like the "bubbles of capitalism" approach attempted by the U.S. Department of Commerce. Unless European officials are more successful in finding bubbles of capitalism than their U.S. counterparts, this may end up being little more than a name change for European procedures.[12]

The focus of Chinese and Russian negotiators on this issue is, in many respects, difficult to understand.[13] WTO membership certainly does not provide an exemption from antidumping investigations. Many WTO members, such as Japan, South Korea, and Brazil, are frequently the subject of antidumping duties.

Some outside observers have pointed to access to WTO dispute-settlement procedures and oversight as a possible benefit of WTO membership in connection with NME dumping.[14] This point is correct and may be of some importance with regard to the EU. As noted, however, the WTO explicitly allows the application of NME antidumping procedures. Further, as discussed in Chapter 1, WTO panels are also directed to give deference to national authorities on matters of fact in connection with injury and dumping findings.

In bilateral discussions aimed at WTO accession, however, it is possible that China or Russia could convince either the United States or Europe to stop applying NME antidumping rules to their exports. Apparently, such efforts have made headway with the European Union. Such an agreement could be included in a WTO accession agreement or side letter. More likely, it could be a bilateral agreement concluded in parallel with the WTO negotiations or even a simple change in administrative procedure.

### U.S. Legislative Front

Somewhat surprisingly, Russian complaints over U.S. NME antidumping rules seem to have found a sympathetic audience in the Clinton administration. In the closing days of the congressional debate on the legislation to implement the Uruguay Round, the Clinton administration made a proposal—dubbed the "economies in transition" (EIT) proposal—that would have dramatically changed U.S. antidumping laws as they apply to Russia, the former Soviet republics, and the countries of Eastern Europe. Probably because of the volume of antidumping investigations that would have been affected, China was not included in the EIT proposal. (The proposal is said to be the result of Russian complaints over U.S. antidumping laws made in an ongoing bilateral trade forum headed by Vice President Gore and Russian prime minister Chernomyrdin.)

Since the proposal was made with little advance debate and had no legislative history, it is difficult to state precisely what the impact of the proposal would have been, but the proposal had two features that would have made it far less likely that duties would be imposed on products from the participating countries.[15] First, the EIT proposal would have imposed a higher standard for action (injury standard) than current law. Second, the administration would retain discretion on whether or not to act once the standard had been met; this would fundamentally change the nature of antidumping laws by making action entirely discretionary.[16]

This EIT proposal did not do well in Congress. It was overwhelmingly rejected by the House Ways and Means Committee, and once it was clear the proposal was headed for a similar rejection by the Senate Finance Committee, it was withdrawn by the administration. Administration sources have occasionally suggested reviving the proposal in some form, but no action has been taken.[17] It is possible that the concept could eventually be revived in connection with WTO accession negotiations.

One of the reasons that this proposal has probably lost some currency is that the option of negotiating suspension agreements allows the administration to soften the impact of antidumping laws on NMEs. As explained in Chapters 1 and 2, U.S. law gives the administration considerable leeway in concluding suspension agreements with NME dumpers. Often these agreements take the form of restraint agreements, which essentially impose a negotiated quota on NME exports. Under such an arrangement, the domestic petitioner gains a measure of relief from dumping, but the NME also gains some assurance of the ability to sell some of its products in the U.S. market. From the perspective of the NME, this is often preferable to a high duty, which might foreclose exports entirely.

### Future NME Dumping

As discussed previously, there is good reason to think that the problem of NME dumping is likely to become more severe. The exports of NME countries are expanding rapidly. The rate of growth of these exports, undoubtedly, will vary from year to year in response to patterns of economic growth, exchange rates, and other factors, but growth is likely to continue.

Perhaps more significant is that the list of products exported by NMEs has expanded considerably. NME countries are generally thought of as producers of basic manufactures and commodities, such as aluminum and steel. Historically, this has generally been true. China has developed a significant international presence in manufacturing, but its products have generally been low-tech and labor-intensive. Russia and some East European countries have substantial manufacturing capacity, but in most cases these manufacturing facilities were built during the Cold War and are not globally competitive. The exports from these countries to the United States have been dominated by commodities.

As noted in Chapter 3, however, these patterns are already changing. NMEs are already exporting increasingly sophisticated products, and as a result, the range of products covered by antidumping orders has also increased and is very likely to increase further in the future.

## The Need for NME Antidumping Procedures

What are the implications of abandoning NME antidumping procedures? As explained above, the problems that initially resulted in the creation of special antidumping rules remain, and antidumping rules still seem superior to the other alternatives for ensuring fair trade in NME imports. In fact, as noted, if NMEs were simply treated as normal economies, subject to countervailing-duty and antidumping laws, what the ultimate result would be is not entirely clear.

Standard antidumping and countervailing-duty laws are not designed to deal with NMEs, which is why NME antidumping procedures were created in the first place. If forced to handle NME cases under standard antidumping and countervailing-duty laws, administrative authorities would have a number of options; some of these approaches would result in higher duties and some would result in no duties. If all inputs provided at government direction were considered subsidies, duties could be higher than under present law. Alternatively, if these were not considered subsidies and no domestic market or input costs could be determined, no duty might result.

Whatever the ultimate result, in the short term this sudden change in U.S. antidumping procedure is certain to result in ambiguity and in increased legal fees as a new round of trade cases are filed and litigated.

Most who criticize NME procedures, however, worry little about this problem because they take the position—implicitly or explicitly—that NMEs should be exempt from all fair-trade measures. Some hold this position because they oppose antidumping and other trade laws on principle, others because they believe that NMEs deserve special treatment—an exemption from antidumping laws.

In essence, this second viewpoint assumes that trade is another way of extending aid. This position may make sense from the NME perspective, but it is utterly untenable from the perspective of the United States, and probably that of Europe as well. After all, does the United States really have an obligation to close plants and allow workers to become unemployed so that Russia and China can reduce their unemployment and keep their factories open? Of course not.

Any sort of exemption, whether it is negotiated or results from a change in law, would be a serious mistake for other reasons. Most important, it would essentially give NMEs a license to dump. Presently all countries are subject to antidumping laws. There are no exceptions even for countries with which the United States maintains a free-trade agreement. There is simply no good reason to make a special exemption for NMEs.

The potential practical results of such an exemption are also sobering.

Many domestic industries that are presently competing with NME dumping, including steel, aluminum, apparel, and others, would be devastated. As the list of products exported by NMEs expanded, the list of impacted industries would also expand.

Further, far from rewarding economic reform, an exemption from U.S. antidumping law would condone the continuation of mercantilistic strategies aimed at building up hard currency reserves and other similar objectives. This would actually hinder rather than promote true economic reform in present NMEs.

Critics frequently attack NME antidumping procedures, and certainly those procedures have the appearance of an ad hoc solution, but no one has yet proposed a superior approach to finding comparable prices and costs. NME procedures remain the most sensible approach to creating an interface mechanism between market and nonmarket economies through which prices can be established and fair trade can occur. As long as many transitional economies remain nonmarket economies to varying degrees, the interface mechanism is still needed.

Finally, most of the potential weaknesses in current procedures can be, and have been, addressed with skillful use of suspension agreements. The administration was granted more leeway by Congress in negotiating suspension agreements in cases involving NME dumping because there was a recognition that the circumstances were unique. Suspension agreements can be used to ensure some market access for NMEs without disrupting domestic industries. By setting minimum import levels for a respondent country to be subject to an antidumping investigation, the WTO also provides some protection for NMEs that export only small amounts.[18] In sum, current procedures allow flexibility for addressing problems that may arise in connection with NME dumping; eliminating them would do serious damage to the U.S. economy and reward NME mercantilism.

## Sunset Reviews

Perhaps the most significant change mandated by the new WTO antidumping code is the requirement for a sunset review of all antidumping orders after five years. The concept of sunsetting antidumping orders has been discussed for some years. For understandable reasons, there has been concern that antidumping orders should not stay in effect indefinitely because conditions often change; companies enter and exit the market, business practices change, product categories change, technology evolves, and trade patterns shift.

Reflecting potential market changes, all countries that operate antidumping laws, including the United States, incorporate review mechanisms into their antidumping laws. The United States, for example, includes "changed circumstances" reviews and administrative reviews, which are discussed in another context in the next section. As the data from Chapter 2 indicate, most antidumping orders are ultimately terminated through these reviews. There is not, however, in the United States or elsewhere, a universal and systematic process in place for reviewing orders with an eye toward termination of unneeded orders.

After noting that antidumping duties should stay in place only long enough to counter dumping, the WTO set a requirement for a sunset review every five years:

> [A]ny definitive anti-dumping duty shall be terminated on a date not later than five years from its imposition (or from the date of the most recent review under paragraph 2 if that review has covered both dumping and injury, or under this paragraph), unless the authorities determine, in a review initiated before that date on their own initiative or upon a duly substantiated request made by or on behalf of the domestic industry within a reasonable period of time prior to that date, that the expiry of the duty would be likely to lead to a continuance or recurrence of dumping and injury.[19]

In implementing this provision, the United States Congress went into considerable detail in defining the procedures used to determine if injury and/or dumping was likely to recur. U.S. implementing legislation and the accompanying Statement of Administrative Action note that the injury determination in a sunset review is not the same as a normal material-injury finding, but rather is a "counter-factual analysis," in which the commission must decide "the likely impact in the reasonably foreseeable future of an important change in the status quo—the revocation or termination of a proceeding and the elimination of its restraining effects on volumes and prices of imports."[20]

In making this determination, the ITC is instructed to examine a number of factors, including magnitude of dumping, import volume, price effect of imports, and impact on the industry in the period preceding issuance of the antidumping order.[21] In conducting the sunset review, the commission is directed to consider whether the industry is "vulnerable" to injury due to its general economic health.[22] Evidence that the exporter has absorbed the duty and continued to dump is to be taken as strong evidence that injury will recur if the duty is eliminated;[23] the Commerce Department is directed to look for evidence of duty absorption in the administrative reviews of orders undertaken every two years and report to the ITC if evidence of absorption is found.[24] If injury has ceased as a result of the antidumping order or a suspension agreement, this may be taken as evidence that the industry would deteriorate if the order were eliminated.[25]

More broadly, the commission is directed to consider all relevant economic factors in making its determination, including increased production, unused production capacity, or large inventories of the subject product held by the dumper. This allows the commission to consider the existence of the root causes of dumping in determining whether material injury is likely to occur if the order is eliminated.[26]

In making its portion of the sunset determination regarding the likelihood of renewed or continued dumping, the Commerce Department is directed to consider many of the same factors as the ITC. The Statement of Administrative Action terms the existence of continued dumping found in administrative reviews after the antidumping order is in effect as "highly probative of the likelihood of continuation or recurrence of dumping."[27] Even if dumping ceases after the order takes effect, this can be taken as evidence that the exporter cannot succeed in the U.S. market without dumping.[28]

At the time this volume goes to press, the functioning of sunset reviews is still a theoretical matter. All existing orders have been grouped for review according to their age, and cases involving similar products have been combined to facilitate their consideration. The Commerce Department and the ITC are set to begin sunset reviews of the first group of cases in the summer of 1998.

## The Stakes in Sunset Reviews

Sunset reviews may seem to be just another technical issue associated with antidumping. Certainly they are in some sense technical, but they have critical implications for the operation of antidumping laws in the United States and around the world.

Sunset reviews spring from the understandable premise that antidumping orders should not remain in place permanently without review. Of course, in the United States, this was never the case—administrative reviews and changed-circumstances reviews provided opportunities to reconsider and revise antidumping orders. Nonetheless, a comprehensive review of the circumstances surrounding an antidumping order through a sunset review does have appeal. Depending upon how they are carried out, however, sunset reviews pose some risks. For example, simply relitigating each case after five years is unlikely to benefit anyone, except perhaps the lawyers who conduct the litigation.

The central challenge facing administering agencies is to determine what would happen if a given antidumping order were eliminated. In short, the issue is whether eliminating the order would be "likely to lead to a continuation or recurrence of dumping and injury"—as the WTO agreement put it.

Most of the congressional implementing legislation on sunset reviews focused upon defining this phrase from the WTO agreement. Obviously, such a determination requires a crystal-ball judgment by administering authorities on the likely behavior of foreign actors and economic conditions in the United States and around the world.

The implementing legislation directs Commerce and the ITC to consider a large number of factors in deciding these questions. Some of these factors, such as the production capacity and past behavior of the companies and/or countries subject to the antidumping order, are clearly essential to predicting the likely result of removing an antidumping order.

As Chapter 3 explained, however, there are a number of economic conditions that spawn dumping. These include government-maintained sanctuary markets, cartelized home markets, government subsidies that help create surplus capacity, and the operation of nonmarket economic institutions, such as state-owned enterprises and state trading companies. When these conditions exist, dumping is the almost inevitable result.

If a home market is protected by trade barriers, a company is certain to reap premium prices at home and sell at whatever the market will bear in export markets—a textbook example of dumping. The behavior of monopolists is also well known and directly parallels the behavior of companies with protected home markets, reaping monopoly profits in cartelized home markets and selling at lower prices in competitive export markets. Government subsidies drive companies to build excess production capacity without regard for market signals, which in turn encourages dumping to dispose of the excess production. Finally, NME governments continue to have only a weak connection to the free market and a strong desire to raise hard currency, a combination almost certain to result in dumping.

Some progress has been made in addressing the causes of dumping, but the record is mixed. On the one hand, many rounds of international negotiations have lowered formal trade barriers, made it more difficult to maintain sanctuary markets, and begun to limit government subsidies, although much work remains to be done.

On the other hand, in the recent case regarding the U.S. complaint on behalf of Kodak that Japan allowed Fuji film to collude with distributors to block imports to Japan, the United States lost a landmark decision. This WTO decision seems to allow Japan and other countries to close their markets by allowing private-sector collusion. As the *New York Times* editorialized on this topic: "[The panel] could have warned the Japanese that a waiver for past anti-competitive behavior provides no immunity for the future. Instead it absolved all Japanese wrongdoing." The *Times* continued,

"The dispute panel's ruling tells Japan that its protectionist ways are acceptable as long as they are subtle."[29]

The panel ruling is likely to be read by Japan and other countries that closing markets through collusion is acceptable, and those that are not enthusiastic about trade liberalization—a large group of countries—will not miss the lesson. As noted earlier, private collusion has already sparked dumping of cement, film and photographic paper, and a number of other products. More is certain to follow. The underlying causes of dumping may be changing form, but they are not disappearing. Sanctuary markets maintained by trade barriers are simply likely to be replaced by sanctuary markets maintained by collusion, and the potential for dumping will continue.

### Standards for Decisions in Sunset Cases

The standards used by administering authorities in implementing the sunset provision will profoundly affect the impact of antidumping laws. Experience has demonstrated that when underlying problems such as sanctuary markets exist, dumping is a continuing problem. In many of the foreign industrial sectors involved in dumping, such as Japanese electronics, South Korean electronics and steel, Mexican cement, and Russian and Chinese steel—to name only a few—dumping has been demonstrated to continue over a long period in a number of U.S. cases. Beyond that, the same companies are often subject to antidumping orders in other countries.[30] Over time and as conditions change, it is possible that the commercial behavior might change and dumping may cease, but as long as the fundamental conditions that encourage dumping continue to exist, such a change is unlikely.

Thus, removing antidumping orders with the fundamental causes of dumping still in place is likely to simply result in renewed dumping and renewed injury. As the implementing legislation notes, the conditions surrounding each case are unique and should be considered individually, but in cases in which the fundamental causes of dumping are still present, removing the order is only likely to result in more dumping, more injury to domestic industries, and additional injury to the U.S. economy. In these cases, lifting antidumping orders would clearly be a mistake.

In light of this, in implementing the sunset provision of the Uruguay Round antidumping code, U.S. authorities should give great weight to factors such as the relative openness of the dumper's home market to imports, the presence of government-subsidized excess production capacity, and/or the operation of state trading entities in a nonmarket economy. Experience has demonstrated that if these home market conditions continue to exist, there is a great likelihood that removing the antidumping order will result in renewed dumping and injury, and therefore the order should remain in place.

## Short-Supply Exception

In recent years, much debate in the United States Congress regarding antidumping laws has focused upon the concept of a short-supply exception. Various versions of such an exception have been proposed over the years, but all would allow antidumping duties to be suspended for some period if domestic supplies of the product subject to the antidumping order were inadequate.

### History

The concept of a short-supply exception gained popularity in connection with the voluntary restraint agreements (VRAs) on steel imports that the United States employed during the Reagan and Bush administrations. In administering the VRA program, the administration allowed for imports of various classes and grades of steel that were either not produced in the United States or not produced in sufficient quantities outside of the VRA import limits.[31]

Some respondents in antidumping investigations, and their customers, attempted to apply the same concept to antidumping orders. To support their proposal, they argued that for a number of products subject to antidumping orders—ranging from flat-panel displays to bearings—there was not sufficient domestic production available to meet consumer needs.

The facts in many of these cases are debatable, but the issue gained some currency. Since outright repeal of antidumping laws was not seen as practical, opponents of antidumping laws focused their legislative efforts upon a short-supply exception, and several versions were introduced in Congress in the early 1990s.[32]

The proposals, however, met with little success. For the reasons outlined below, supporters of antidumping laws viewed such an amendment as having the potential to seriously weaken antidumping laws. While the legislation to implement the Uruguay Round was being considered in Congress, both the Senate Finance Committee and the House Ways and Means Committee considered and rejected by a large margin versions of short-supply proposals.[33]

Commerce Department officials opposed these proposals when they were presented to Congress, but they did attempt to address some of the concerns of short-supply proponents in the regulations implementing the

Uruguay Round. The Commerce Department made no specific short-supply exception in its regulations but did note in the preamble to its rules that it planned to address the problem through existing mechanisms.[34] Commerce pointed to two areas where legitimate concerns about short supply can be addressed. First, Commerce has said it will endeavor to avoid the unnecessary imposition of antidumping duties on products that are not really causing injury to domestic industries. In preliminary discussions with petitioners, Commerce investigators are directed to ensure that the scope of a petition is an "accurate reflection of the product for which the domestic industry is seeking relief."[35]

Second, in the preamble discussion, Commerce also noted that it could use changed-circumstances reviews to alter antidumping orders if the domestic industry stops producing goods subject to the order or other unique changes occur to create a shortage. Under normal conditions, respondents, customers, and other parties cannot petition for a changed-circumstances review. The Commerce Department noted, however, that it was willing to use its power to self-initiate such a review if circumstances warranted.[36]

### Conceptual Problems with Short-Supply Exceptions

On its face, the short-supply exception seems to be a reasonable concept with some precedent supporting it. A closer examination, however, reveals that any steps beyond those already taken by the Commerce Department could pose a significant risk to the integrity of antidumping laws.

The most obvious problem with the short-supply exception is that the analogy drawn with the steel VRA program is simply not apt. On occasion, it is possible that VRAs can block the importation of certain types of steel. Antidumping orders, however, *never* absolutely block imports of the subject products; they only require that the goods be sold at a nondumped price. If a domestic customer wishes to import a product subject to an antidumping order, they need only ensure that the purchase is made at the nondumped price or, more precisely, that the duty is paid on the product.

Although the average size of antidumping duties in recent years has hovered between 25 and 33 percent, it is true that for some products antidumping duties can be high.[37] Nevertheless, even in these cases the product can be imported. Further, the cases in which duties are high are those in which dumping is most egregious and potentially poses the most serious threat to the U.S. economy. Waiving duties in these cases would seem particularly ill advised.

Beyond that, there are other conceptual problems with the concept of short supply in the context of antidumping laws. The fundamental purpose of dumping is normally to gain market share at the expense of the domestic industry. If dumping continues for some period of time or is severe, domestic producers frequently leave the industry or reduce production capacity; as applied, the material-injury test is often focused on detecting just this type of adjustment of the domestic industry. Thus, successful dumping almost invariably creates a shortage of domestic supply. Barring the imposition of antidumping duties, if there is insufficient domestic production creates a catch-22 situation—antidumping orders cannot be imposed unless there is injury that reduces domestic production, but if there is a reduction in domestic production, an antidumping order would create a shortage and should not be imposed.

Much of the initial debate on short supply was focused upon an antidumping case involving flat-panel displays. Flat-panel displays are the displays used on computer terminals and displays in a variety of other products, including aircraft and weapons.[38] Japanese companies dominate production of flat-panel displays. U.S. companies seeking to enter the industry made a persuasive case that the Japanese companies involved were dumping displays in order to keep the U.S. concerns from entering the field.

In 1990, an antidumping case was filed and approved by both Commerce and the ITC. In 1991, antidumping duties of 62 percent were imposed on five Japanese producers, but two years later the petitioner withdrew the petition after a change in management and a change in perspective on the antidumping case. U.S. computer companies that purchased flat-panel displays for use in assembling computers and related products opposed the duty. They argued that the duty put a undue competitive burden upon them.[39] (In 1994, the Defense Department launched a separate effort to spur the creation of a domestic flat-panel industry for national-security reasons—flat-panel displays are a critical part of many modern weapons.)[40]

The flat-panel case is unique in a number of respects. In fact, it is so unique that it is deceptive to focus too much attention upon it in the context of antidumping laws, and it would be a mistake to draw broad lessons regarding antidumping laws based upon this case. It has, however, been used as the most frequently cited example by proponents of the short-supply proposal. For that reason and because the flat-panel case does focus attention upon one important aspect of antidumping laws, it warrants some discussion.

As the careful reader will note, from the beginning of antidumping laws to the Uruguay Round agreement, the concept of "material retardation" of the establishment of a domestic industry has been discussed as one way in which the material-injury test could be satisfied. Cases focusing upon "material retardation" are quite rare, and it is difficult to find an example in recent history other than the flat-panel case.

Most would, however, agree that material retardation is an important concept for inclusion in antidumping laws. In fact, since it involves efforts by foreign manufacturers to retain monopoly power, the goal of combating material retardation would likely gain wider support—at least in concept—than antidumping laws in general. Few would argue that a foreign monopoly is not a matter of some concern to the U.S. economy. It is worth noting that in these cases there is by definition a domestic short supply—indeed, no supply—in material-retardation cases. Thus, a short-supply exception would effectively bar material-retardation cases.

More generally, as the Commerce Department has argued, a short-supply exception is likely to enormously complicate the administration of anti-dumping laws.[41] In addition to all of the issues that need now be explored in relation to an antidumping investigation, including standing, scope, dumping, and injury, an entirely new round of litigation would be launched to determine if there is adequate domestic supply. This judgment would be made against standards that are yet to be determined, but these additional procedures are likely to greatly complicate antidumping law enforcement.

Most of the proponents of short-supply exceptions are also opponents of antidumping laws. It is thus not terribly surprising that the proposals do great damage to the antidumping laws and run counter to the laws' fundamental purpose. The concept of short supply may make sense in the context of administering a VRA, but, for the reasons just outlined, it makes no sense in the context of antidumping laws. Short supply simply cannot result from the imposition of antidumping duties; it is merely an issue of what price will be paid for the imported good. Most important, a short-supply exception would have the perverse effect of allowing dumping to continue in those instances in which it has been most effective in injuring the domestic industry.

The Commerce Department's efforts to address this problem administratively seem likely to be sufficient in those cases where a legitimate problem exists, such as when the domestic industry has simply gone out of business for other reasons and does not plan to reenter or there are no domestic petitioners interested in a particular product. These cases are likely to be rare, but it is appropriate that administering authorities prepare for such eventualities.

Beyond these limited circumstances, the short-supply concept has little merit and is barely more than an indirect attack on the antidumping laws. Since opponents of antidumping laws are likely to remain active, however, the short-supply issue is likely to resurface.

## Duty Absorption or Duty as a Cost

Since antidumping laws were first created, there has been concern that some of the foreign companies subject to antidumping orders have attempted to circumvent or otherwise frustrate antidumping investigations and orders. Some of the common approaches include making slight or cosmetic changes in a product or setting up assembly and/or packaging operations in another country to avoid antidumping orders. The U.S. Commerce Department continues to address such efforts at circumvention as appropriate.[42]

Probably the most common approach to circumventing an antidumping order is simply absorbing the duty and continuing to dump. In essence, this practice involves dumping at still greater margins in the wake of an antidumping order in order to continue to pursue the commercial objectives of the original dumping. In such circumstances, the price of the dumped good would not rise after the dumping order, although the foreign company engaged in dumping would presumably pay a higher cost to maintain the dumped price.

Duty absorption usually involves transactions between related parties of a multinational company. In a typical case, a foreign company ships to a related party, usually a subsidiary in the United States. Through a variety of accounting operations the cost of the antidumping duty is somehow shared between the U.S. subsidiary and the foreign company—often the foreign parent simply absorbs the duty, but the price of the good as seen by the customer remains unchanged or is only slightly higher.

Allegations of duty absorption have frequently been made in connection with steel, electronics, bearings, and most other products subject to frequent antidumping action.[43] There are a number of reports of contracts in which the dumper agrees not to change its prices even if it subsequently becomes subject to an antidumping order. Most of the specific information on cases, however, is proprietary information kept from public view by a protective order.[44]

Duty absorption, however, is notoriously difficult to prove. The impact that changes in exchange rate and technology as well as other factors may have upon prices charged for goods can obscure instances of duty absorption, particularly when the dumpers—as is almost always the case—seek to cloak their actions. Beyond that, as an accounting matter, it is very difficult to trace the transfers between foreign companies and their U.S. subsidiaries. The issue of transfer pricing has been addressed with regard to international taxation and other accounting matters, but a universally satisfying solution has not been reached. Further, regardless of the transfer price, the foreign company could simply direct its U.S. subsidiary to absorb the loss and keep prices at the dumped level.

Duty absorption has been a topic of discussion for many years in the United States and Europe. In the United States, Commerce officials have committed to monitor implementation of antidumping orders for evidence of duty absorption. As discussed above, in the case of sunset reviews, duty absorption is to be taken as evidence of the continued need for the anti-dumping order. These steps seem amply justified but are not as aggressive an approach to the problem as many have suggested.[45]

The European Union has a more sweeping approach to the problem of duty absorption. The European approach is known as duty as a cost. Under this approach, commercial transactions after an antidumping order is imposed are monitored. If the duty is not being passed on to the customer, the antidumping margin is recalculated with the duty included as a cost. This has the effect of substantially raising antidumping duties in those cases where duty absorption is found.

This European practice of treating absorbed duties as a cost in dumping calculations is explicitly endorsed in the WTO antidumping code. Article 9.3.3 of the code authorizes national authorities to treat absorbed duties as another cost to be calculated in setting dumping margins. An even more direct approach to this problem would involve ensuring that the duty is assessed on the first unrelated-party transaction involving the good, but such an approach did not find favor with WTO negotiators.

Despite considerable debate, the United States chose not to adopt the European duty-as-a-cost practice in administering its antidumping laws. Opponents have emphasized the difficulty of policing transfer pricing and the prospect that a duty-as-a-cost standard would raise antidumping duties. It is, of course, true that a duty absorption provision would raise antidumping duties if dumpers chose to absorb duties. The purpose of the provision, however, would be to deter duty absorption; if successful, this would mean the provision would result in no change in duties.

In any event, duty absorption continues to be a major topic in the U.S. antidumping debate. If Congress considers major changes in U.S. law, this issue is likely to be raised again.

## Notes

1. Judith H. Bello et. al., "Searching for 'Bubbles of Capitalism': Application of the U.S. Antidumping and Countervailing Duty Laws to Reforming Nonmarket Economies," *George Washington Journal of International Law and Economics* 21 (1992): 665, 673.

2. John Jackson, *The World Trading System: Law and Policy of International Economic Relations* (Cambridge: MIT Press, 1989), p. 218.

3. WTO Agreement on Implementation of Article VI of the General Agreement on Tariffs and Trade 1994, Article 2.3.

4. Bureau of the Census statistics.

5. International Trade Administration statistics.

6. Erle Norton and Martin Du Bois, "Foiled Competition: Don't Call It a Cartel, But World Aluminum Has Forged New Order," *Wall Street Journal,* June 9, 1994, p. 1.

7. International Trade Administration statistics.

8. European Union customs statistics.

9. These calculations are drawn from Brian Hindley and Patrick A. Messerlin, *Antidumping Industrial Policy: Legalized Protection in the WTO and What to Do About It* (Washington, DC: AEI Publications, 1997). The authors provide limited methodology for their calculation.

10. Though its policy recommendations are debated below, a good summary of the application of EU NME antidumping procedures can be found in Brian Hindley, "The Regulation of Imports from Transition Economies by the European Union," in *Policies on Imports from Economies in Transition: Two Case Studies,* Peter D. Ehrenhaft et al., eds. (Washington, DC: World Bank, 1997).

11. Ibid., pp. 25–26.

12. James Harding, "China: EU Gesture over Dumping Rules Welcomed," *Financial Times,* December 18, 1997.

13. Bruce Stokes, "A Parley Without a Point?" *The National Journal* 28, no. 42 (October 18, 1997): 2098.

14. Hindley, "Regulation of Imports," p. 58.

15. Peter Behr, "White House Seeks Change in Antidumping Penalties," *Washington Post,* June 25, 1994, B1; John Maggs, "White House Abruptly Seeks Major Dump Law Changes," *The Journal of Commerce,* June 24, 1994, p. 1A.

16. The EIT proposal is discussed in Greg Mastel, *American Trade Laws After the Uruguay Round* (Armonk, NY: M.E. Sharpe, 1996), pp. 97–98, 177.

17. Bill Schmitt, "The Metals Industry Will Help Shape New Trade," *American Metals Market,* January 19, 1995, 17.

18. WTO Antidumping Code, Article 5.8.

19. Ibid., Article 11.3.

20. Uruguay Round Agreements Act, Statement of Administrative Action, p. 214.

21. Ibid., and Section 752(a)(1) of the Tariff Act of 1930 as amended.

22. Uruguay Round Agreement Act, Statement of Administrative Action, pp. 214–215, and Section 752(a)(1)© of the Tariff Act of 1930 as amended.

23. Ibid.

24. Uruguay Round Agreement Act, Statement of Administrative Action, pp. 215–216.

25. Ibid., p. 214.

26. Uruguay Round Agreements Act amendments to the Tariff Act of 1930, Section 752(a)(2)(A-D).

27. Uruguay Round Agreement Act, Statement of Administrative Action, p. 220.

28. Ibid.

29. *New York Times,* December 10, 1997, p. A34.

30. For example, certain Japanese electronic companies have been involved in more than a dozen dumping investigations, dumping margins have consistently been found against some Japanese bearing companies over a period of twenty-five years, and U.S. and European officials have cases against many of the same products involving the same companies.

31. For information on the steel VRA program, see General Accounting Office, *International Trade: The Health of the U.S. Steel Industry* (Washington, DC: GAO, 1989); Robert Blecker, Thea Lee, and Robert Scott, *Trade Protection and Industry Revitalization: American Steel in the 1980s* (Washington, DC: Economic Policy Institute, 1993).

32. Short supply was a primary focus of two days of congressional hearings on antidumping laws. House Committee on Ways and Means, Subcommittee on Trade, April 23 and 24, 1996 (available only in transcript form at press time).

33. Of course, nothing in the Uruguay Round antidumping agreement required the creation of a short-supply exception, but the implementing legislation included a major rewrite of U.S. antidumping laws. Proponents of short-supply exceptions apparently thought this presented a good opportunity to press for consideration of the issue.

34. Department of Commerce, *International Trade Administration, Antidumping Duties; Countervailing Duties;* Final Rule, 19 CFR Part 351 et al.

35. Nancy Kelly, "The New Antidumping Regulations from Commerce," *New Steel* 13, no. 6 (June 1997): 105.

36. Ibid.

37. This is a general figure drawn from review of Federal Register notices of Commerce Department antidumping proceedings.

38. Michael Borrus and Jeffrey A. Hart, "Display's the Thing: The Real Stakes in the Conflict over High-Resolution Displays," *Journal of Policy Analysis and Management* 13, no. 1 (1994).

39. A discussion of the flat-panel case can be found in Hearings of the Trade Subcommittee of the House Ways and Means Committee on Proposed Antidumping Regulations and other Antidumping Issues, April 23 and 24, 1996 (available only in transcript form at press time).

40. Flat Panel Display Task Force, *Building U.S. Capabilities in Flat Panel Displays, Final Report* (Washington, DC: Department of Defense, October 1994).

41. Ibid., testimony of Susan Esserman, assistant secretary of commerce for import administration. Ms. Esserman's testimony also includes a full discussion of Commerce's efforts to address the short-supply problem administratively.

42. After a heated debate, the Uruguay Round antidumping code did little on the topic of circumvention beyond language in the Statement of Ministers indicating that it was a topic upon which little could be agreed, but which would be returned to at a later date.

43. In the bearing case, for example, despite orders being in place, Commerce Department reviews have found some Japanese companies to be dumping consistently over a period of more than twenty years. Federal Register notices provided upon request.

44. For a discussion of this issue, see Terence P. Stewart, "Antidumping and Countervailing Duty Laws: Their Use and Misuse," in the forthcoming book by the Dean Rusk Center for International and Comparative Law, University of Georgia, and the Institute of Social Science, University of Tokyo, 1997, pp. 73–75. Also note Michael Y. Chung, "U.S. Antidumping Laws: A Look at the New Legislation," *North Carolina Journal of International Law and Commercial Regulation* 20 (Summer 1995).

45. In *Antifriction Bearings (Other than Tapered Roller Bearings) from France, et. al.,* 57 Fed. Reg. 28360, 28370–71 (Department of Commerce June 24, 1992) (section 4, comment 1), Commerce held that "evidence of below-cost transfer pricing is not in itself evidence of reimbursement of antidumping duties" and the petitioner must "establish a link between alleged below-cost transfer pricing and the payment of antidumping duties." Obviously, this is a rather difficult standard to meet because in a related-party transaction it is unlikely that the purpose of the reduction in transfer prices will be explicitly identified as for payment of antidumping duties. It is thus fair to say that the U.S. approach on duty absorption is not aggressive.

# 7

# Conclusion

In a recent debate on antidumping laws, the author was challenged to provide "one reason why consumers should be forced to pay higher prices for imported goods." The viewpoint behind this question is similar to that of the unnamed Reagan administration official who some years ago argued that the United States should not take any action to combat dumping of supercomputers. As the official reportedly stated his position, "If the Japanese want to dump supercomputers, I will buy one. . . . We could all buy one."

This statement will strike most as simplistic, but it is at the core of the logic of many antidumping critics. The central premise of these critics is that there is no reason to be suspicious of low-priced imports and that there is certainly no justification for imposing duties to raise their price.

Of course, there are numerous examples in which, for various public-policy reasons, the government raises the price of goods. The most obvious examples are the sales taxes that governments impose to finance their operations. Taxes, fees, and regulations that raise the prices of goods in order to protect the environment or promote consumer safety also provide apt examples.

The complex connection between antidumping and antitrust laws is discussed at length in Chapter 1, but it is worth noting in this context that the efforts of national authorities to curb dumping also parallel enforcement of antitrust laws. If left to their own devices, the predatory action of trusts to drive their competitors out of business or prevent entry into a market would, for a time, result in lower consumer prices. As a matter of policy, however, the United States is willing to forgo these short-term consumer gains for the sake of maintaining a competitive marketplace. Similarly, dumping may lower short-term consumer prices, but its long-term economic impact far outweighs these transient benefits.

But to return to the question that opened this chapter, why *should* consumers be forced to pay higher prices to counter dumping? This is perhaps the core question of the debate over antidumping laws. It is worth noting that, in theory, antidumping laws only aim to return prices to nondumped levels and thus represent an attempt to approximate the natural equilibrium price that the market would generate. Thus, when applied properly, anti-dumping duties do not necessarily raise prices above market equilibrium levels. Nonetheless, if antidumping duties function as intended, consumers are likely to pay higher prices for imported products than they would if they were able to purchase products at dumped prices.

As stated at the beginning of this volume, there are nevertheless a number of legitimate rationales for the continued use of antidumping laws—some legal, some competitive, some economic, and some political. These different rationales are built on two interrelated core arguments—one based on fairness and the other based strictly on economics—for the continued vigorous enforcement of antidumping laws.

**Fairness**

Most of this volume has focused on what can best be described as economic rationales for the use of antidumping laws. The original authors of anti-dumping laws, however, made little reference to charts, graphs, and economic simulations in making the case. In his seminal work on the topic, *Dumping: A Problem in International Trade,* Jacob Viner relied almost entirely upon anecdotal analysis and employed only a few very simple tables for illustrative purposes.[1] The legislative debates on antidumping laws, from the time the laws were established until the present, focus more upon what can broadly be called fairness issues than upon computer simulations and discussions of marginal cost versus average cost.

Given their historical roots, it is appropriate to begin a summation of the case for antidumping laws with a discussion of the reasons why fairness compels their continued application. In the United States, there is a deep and abiding suspicion of commercial practices that are often called "predatory" or "cutthroat." U.S. antitrust laws, however, define "predatory" quite narrowly.[2] For a variety of reasons, most instances of dumping do not clearly fall within this narrow definition, but dumping is nonetheless a predatory practice and a threat to a competitive marketplace.

There may be isolated cases in which dumping is the result of other factors, such as exchange rate changes, long-run declines in marginal costs, and related factors. On the whole, however, repeated dumping is a predatory practice inevitably directly associated with mercantilistic practices such as a sanctuary home market, subsidies, and cartels. In fact, without the existence of one or more of these conditions, repeated dumping is simply impractical.

Absent some sort of intervention, it is impossible to keep prices high in the domestic market and much lower in export markets. Aside from the likely customer complaints this differential pricing would inspire, such a strategy would fail because crafty entrepreneurs would simply ship the lower-cost exported goods back to the home market and undercut the home market price. Further, no company can afford to continually lose money on sales unless the losses can be recouped either through government subsidies or profits in protected markets. Thus, dumping as a long-term strategy is always linked to other market distortions.

As noted, there is a parallel between antidumping law and antitrust law in that both aim at responding to predatory market strategies, but there are also notable differences. In the modern global economy, antidumping laws can be said to be more important in defending a competitive U.S. market. The targets of antitrust laws are normally companies aiming to restrict competition and reap monopoly rents to the detriment of consumers. Although antidumping laws also directly act against companies, their real targets are governments that pursue industrial policies aimed at taking market share, production, and employment from U.S. companies using closed markets, cartelized markets, or subsidies to build production capacity.

From the larger perspective, the targets of antidumping laws are more significant threats to basic fairness and broader U.S. interests than the targets of antitrust laws. Undeniably, the trusts of the late nineteenth century were a major threat to consumer interests, and breaking those trusts did greatly change the shape of the American economy. More recent antitrust actions have, however, responded to lesser threats and thus generated smaller relative benefits.

For their part, antidumping laws continue to counter the efforts of foreign companies, with government support, to wrest dominance from U.S. companies in industries such as semiconductors, supercomputers, bearings, consumer electronics, and steel. Under present conditions, the efforts of these companies to take sales from U.S. companies with attendant U.S. losses in market share, employment in high-wage industries, and investment pose a greater threat to the U.S. national interest than Microsoft's efforts to link its software programs. And yet economists who enthusiastically accept the importance of antitrust laws continue to criticize antidumping laws.

But beyond the comparison with antitrust laws, it offends basic notions of fairness to force U.S. companies and U.S. workers to compete on what can only be called a profoundly unlevel playing field with foreign companies that reap the benefits of protected home markets and state-constructed production capacity. The economic argument that the U.S. economy as a whole benefits from lower prices or that foreign governments with sanctuary markets are only harming themselves is unlikely to provide much solace to workers laid off from bearing plants, steel mills, or semiconductor fabrication facilities because of dumping. These workers and the owners of the closed facilities are likely to find little comfort in the prospect that they can now buy a supercomputer at a bargain-basement price.

The position taken by some classical economists that such an implicit trade-off between employment and lower prices makes good economic sense is profoundly counterintuitive. Even if the economics of this argument could be established (which they cannot), the overwhelming unfairness of allowing dumping to wreak havoc on U.S. companies and workers would nevertheless justify government action to halt dumping. These workers and companies are being denied their basic economic right to reap the benefits of an efficient economic enterprise by a foreign government's industrial policy that may provide some transient consumer benefit. No matter what terms are used to describe such an economic trade-off, it fails the test of basic fairness and is simply not acceptable.

Antidumping laws strive to provide a level playing field for U.S. companies and U.S. workers, and this level playing field has benefits beyond simple fairness. Despite occasional complaints from the United States' trading partners (some of which are justified), most observers would concede that the U.S. market is among the most open in the world. As the WTO concluded after reviewing U.S. trade practices, by and large, in the United States imported products compete head-to-head with domestic production with little government interference.[3] In fact, throughout the postwar period the United States has been the leader in the cause of global free trade.

Much is rightly made of U.S. benevolence in implementing the Marshall Plan to help its defeated World War II adversaries rebuild their shattered countries; it is difficult, if not impossible, to find another example in history of victors exhibiting as much generosity toward their defeated foes.[4] What is often overlooked in assessing the Marshall Plan is that the United States' willingness to open its markets to imports from Japan and Germany had more to do with those countries' economic recovery than did the transfers of aid.

Similarly, the United States has opened its market to far more recent adversaries, such as China, Russia, and now Vietnam. Much of the economic resurgence China has experienced in the last decade can be directly linked to the more than $60 billion in annual exports to the United States that China enjoys; without an open U.S. market the Chinese economic miracle would simply not have been possible.

This willingness to open the domestic market to imports and keep it open, often at considerable cost to domestic interests, is an even more dramatic example of U.S. benevolence than the Marshall Plan. Surely the United States has gained from imports; after all, trade is not the same as aid.

Most countries, however, have been far less willing to open their markets to imports, even if according to economic models it would be in their economic interest to do so.

The United States has been willing and able to keep its markets generally open because of a political consensus in favor of free trade and open markets. This political consensus has allowed both U.S. political parties to endorse the principle of free trade, negotiate agreements to lower trade barriers, and resist domestic interests that sought protection. The consensus was built around the premises that open markets mean opportunities and that competition is good for American companies and American workers.

Sadly, that nearly fifty-year-old political consensus appears to be eroding. Increasingly, Americans have become incensed about competing in a rigged game. The closed Japanese market raised American ire for many years, but support for free trade in general continued. Now the doubts seem more generalized. The recent North American Free Trade Agreement is viewed as bad for the U.S. economy by a large majority of Americans.[5] Candidates from both political parties have had success espousing economic philosophies that turn away from free trade. In 1997, for the first time in twenty years, the Congress did not grant the president's request for negotiating authority to conclude new trade agreements. President Clinton may be able to salvage at least some limited authority to negotiate, but clearly the political balance has changed. There is a broad coalition of groups, including organized labor and environmentalists, fighting against extending President Clinton negotiating authority. At best, the political consensus for free trade is under more stress than at any other time in the postwar era. At worst, it has already dissolved.

One reality that the unconditional supporters of free trade, many of whom are vociferous critics of antidumping laws, have chosen to ignore is that real progress toward free trade is impossible if the American public is not willing to support it. No free-trade agreements will be concluded if Americans feel they are not in their interest. In fact, if they feel it necessary, the American public could easily begin moving away from free trade and undoing many of the trade liberalization accomplishments of the last forty-five years. After all, the condemnation of the WTO or of a NAFTA panel is unlikely to mean much to the average voter.

A resurgence of naked protectionism would be a setback for the world and U.S. economies, and for that reason preserving or rebuilding the political consensus is a critical priority. That consensus, however, is built on a basic concept of fairness. If foreign competition is fair, it can gain political support even if it forces adjustments in the U.S. economy. But if it is unfair, American voters will rightly reject foreign competition. The unfortunate reality is that a considerable amount of foreign competition is unfair. Many foreign companies benefit from protected home markets, cartels, and subsidies; foreign industrial policies aim to and often succeed in subverting market outcomes.

U.S. options for responding to this unfairness are increasingly quite limited. Use of most of the traditional trade policy tools, such as threatening trade sanctions, are constrained by the WTO. Unfortunately, as its recent decision on Japan's photographic film market demonstrates, the WTO presently appears not to be prepared to combat these examples of broader unfairness, such as the operation of foreign cartels.

This leaves antidumping laws as the only viable tool for countering trade unfairness and establishing something approaching a level playing field. As noted elsewhere, antidumping laws are, at most, a partial remedy. Antidumping actions can be costly and time-consuming, and action is possible only after injury has already occurred. Antidumping action also cannot eliminate the core problems, which are often foreign cartels or government-built excess capacity. In spite of all these limitations, however, antidumping laws are an effective response to the most grievous symptom of foreign industrial policy—loss of the U.S. market to dumped imports.

U.S. antidumping laws are also a remedy available to any domestic industry that can prove its complaint. This remedy operates largely free from intervention by foreign agents, foreign embassies, or even the various diplomatic agencies of the U.S. government, which at least at times, argue for placing the interests of dumpers above those of American companies and workers.

Antidumping laws are the only direct assurance that most U.S. companies and workers have of a measure of fairness in competition with imports. As such, they are critical to preserving and nurturing the notion that free trade is fundamentally fair trade and a good thing for the average American. If U.S. antidumping laws were abolished or otherwise constrained, the consensus in favor of free trade would likely weaken further and calls would soon be made to raise general barriers against imports. For this reason alone, any who truly support free trade should rise above the minutiae of best information available and NME antidumping procedures and embrace antidumping laws as the best potential hope for preserving a political consensus for free trade.

By providing an objective set of criteria against which to judge trade complaints of unfairness, antidumping laws promote free trade in another way. Inevitably and universally, when an industry comes under intense international competition there are calls for protection and allegations of unfairness. Some of these claims have merit and some do not. By setting objective criteria to judge whether imports are fairly traded, antidumping laws and countervailing-duty laws provide a test to screen claims with merit from those that do not.

If antidumping laws did not exist, the calls for government intervention and protection would certainly continue, but there would be no fixed criteria for judging claims of fairness and it would probably be left to the Congress, not administrative authorities, to make the decision. The result is likely to be that the Congress would more likely respond when there is a strong political constituency in favor of protection, regardless of the merits. This approach would risk conflict with international agreements, which do not make allowances for occasional congressional action, and result in protection against perceived unfairnesses that do not really exist. Thus, by providing objective, internationally negotiated criteria to judge unfairness, antidumping laws provide for a sound review of claims of unfairness, make it possible to resist claims without merit, and actually contribute to the integrity of the world trading system by providing an essential safety valve.

## Economic Benefits of Antidumping Laws

Often, the debate over antidumping laws seems to be between proponents, who argue primarily from the perspective of fairness, and opponents, who argue the laws are bad economics. This drawing of battle lines probably came about because antidumping laws grew primarily out of concerns over fairness. The economic case for antidumping laws is, however, every bit as strong as the fairness-based case. Using modern economic thinking on international trade, it is possible to build a strong case for antidumping laws without any reference to issues of fairness.

The economics of antidumping laws can be defended from a number of economic perspectives. First, like antitrust laws, antidumping laws seek to battle the establishment of international monopolies and cartels by ensuring that U.S. firms can at least compete within the confines of the U.S. market. The benefits of ensuring a truly competitive market in these instances, including protecting consumers, stimulating innovation, and encouraging other positive market outcomes, are well understood and require little defense.

As critics rightly point out, however, antidumping laws and antitrust laws are different, with different standards for proof and different remedies. Most important, antidumping laws also attack a different set of problems. As explained in detail with reference to numerous examples in this volume, the primary purpose of antidumping laws is to offset the negative effect of foreign trade barriers, subsidies, cartels, and industrial policy both within the U.S. market and, to the extent that they deter the underlying foreign practice, globally. The most important point this volume strives to make in this connection is that dumping should be considered part and parcel of a larger commercial strategy aimed at gaining market share, building industries, retaining employment, and, in the extreme, eliminating competing U.S. industries. In fact, dumping is best understood as a symptom of these trade-distorting commercial strategies. The debate over dumping is not simply an issue of importing cheap products.

Once the connection between dumping and various foreign practices aimed at distorting the market is understood, the economic case in favor of antidumping laws is quite easy to make. Trade barriers, cartels, subsidies, and related practices are almost universally condemned by economists, and few would deny that eliminating the injurious effect of these practices would generate a net improvement in global wealth.

Unfortunately, there is no time-effective remedy available to directly eliminate foreign trade barriers, bust foreign trusts, and end foreign efforts to build production capacity not linked to the market. Some of the negative impacts of these trade distortions, particularly those that impact the consumers and taxpayers in the country that maintains these trade distortions, fall outside the borders of the United States. Antidumping laws do, however, insulate the U.S. domestic economy from the negative effects of these practices.

With antidumping law in place, at least within the U.S. market, prices and production can be determined by the market, not by foreign industrial policies. In other words, the function of the market can be restored, not compromised, by antidumping duties. To the extent that the WTO's new procedures for addressing the impact of dumping in third markets succeed, antidumping duties will become even more effective, particularly if antidumping actions can be pursued in various markets in parallel. If so, antidumping actions would become a more powerful deterrent to dumping in the first place.

Antidumping laws thus have come to be known as a second-best solution. Such solutions, usually in the form of taxes, have frequently been suggested as remedies under conditions of imperfect competition or other market failures. They do not eliminate the primary distortion, but they offset some or all of the distortion it creates and allow the market function to be restored.

Antidumping laws are also useful tools in designing and pursuing a policy based upon what is widely known as strategic trade theory. There is still debate on the proper scope and application of strategic trade theory and the definition of strategic industries. Some have expressed concerns that the concepts may be distorted to justify simple protectionism or other ill-advised policies. Nonetheless, there seems to be an emerging consensus that some of the underlying premises of strategic trade policy are correct. In particular, the concept of strategic industries generating significant positive ripple effects, or externalities that broadly benefit the economy, through R&D investment and their linkages to other industries has gained wide support. (Of course, it has long been accepted that certain industries play a critical role in supporting America's ability to defend itself.) The premise that certain manufacturing industries generate consistently higher wages and thus justify the special attention of policy makers is also widely accepted.

It is far more than happenstance that many of the industries that are generally defined as strategic by trade theorists are the very industries— semiconductors, supercomputers, and so on—that have frequently been ravaged by dumping. Regardless of the theoretical merits of their strategies, it seems that many U.S. trading partners have long been willing to define these industries as strategic and pursue their policy accordingly. As explained above, antidumping duties are one of the few available and effective tools for countering this kind of industry targeting. If it were not for antidumping laws, the United States would be without an effective response to these mercantilistic strategies in key industries, and U.S. companies would likely have been driven completely out of certain industries, including consumer electronics and semiconductors.

More broadly, antidumping duties are perhaps the only available tool for the United States to pursue a policy of its own based upon strategic trade theory. Raising new trade barriers is generally prohibited by international agreements. Subsidies are similarly constrained. In addition, subsidies have proven politically difficult in an era in which such programs are castigated as corporate welfare and constrained by budget concerns. Through use of innovative initiatives such as government-initiated antidumping cases in critical areas and use of critical-circumstances reviews to ensure timely action, antidumping duties are a potential tool of strategic trade theory. In fact, given the obvious limitations on other possible policy tools, those who advocate strategic trade policy should be strong defenders of antidumping laws.

### Systemic Competition

Perhaps the strongest economic reason for the continued U.S. use of antidumping laws stems from the reality of competition among different economic systems in the world. It is popular to suggest that the world is moving toward market economics. This statement is true, but it is simply incorrect to assume that the movement is necessarily toward market economics as practiced in the United States.

The Japanese model of state-directed capitalism has been copied by a number of countries. The recent economic difficulties in Asia probably do point up one of the weaknesses of this strategy, but, at the same time, the WTO has effectively endorsed important aspects of the Japanese system as WTO-consistent. The practitioners of state-driven capitalism seem to concede that the economic crisis in Asia requires some changes in their model, but few have suggested that it warrants abandoning it. The Japanese approach has worked well for decades—at least in the opinion of its practitioners. They are hardly likely to abandon it after having an off year, any more than the United States considers abandoning its version of market economics during a recession. This is particularly true when relatively minor corrections, such as policing bank lending and practicing sound fiscal policy, seem to provide credible solutions to these problems.

Beyond that, Japan is no longer the only standard-bearer for different economic thinking. China is conducting its own effort, so far successful, to marry some of the features of Japanese economics with the command-driven economy created by Mao Zedong. Russia, Vietnam, and a number of other former Communist countries seem to be following a similar path. The merger of Communist and capitalist economics seems even more inclined than the Japanese model to generate government industrial policies emphasizing sanctuary markets and subsidies.

Even Europe, which follows an economic model generally quite similar to that of the U.S. model, differs with the United States on key issues. European politicians are fond of contrasting their policies on caring for the unemployed and pursuing other social objectives through their economic policies with the more purely market-oriented policies of the United States.

The ultimate success or failure of the various economic models remains to be seen. The U.S. model has many virtues, but it is a conceit to assume that the U.S. model will prevail as the only viable model for organizing a market economy; certainly, it is utterly without basis to assume it will prevail quickly. The advocates of other economic approaches believe, some with good reason, that their version of market economics is not only viable but superior to the U.S. approach in important ways and better suited to the unique needs of their countries.

As a result, the world will likely see de facto competition between various versions of market economics continuing for some time. As discussed in detail in Chapter 3, Japanese and European approaches tend to rely heavily upon, respectively, sanctuary markets and government-supported production capacity. Both of these economic policies often result in dumping in foreign markets, and the United States—as the most open and lucrative market—invariably feels the effects. The new NME economies, such as

China and Russia, pursue similar policies and are often starved for hard currency and willing to sell at dumped prices to gain it. Once again, the result is dumping in the U.S. market.

Absent antidumping laws, these strategies would have a devastating impact on the U.S. economy. Other things being equal, without antidumping laws the U.S. economy would become a quite unattractive site in which to invest or operate a manufacturing company, particularly in the attractive high-tech and manufacturing industries in which dumping is common. In these industries, dumping would be a constant threat; in fact, it is still a significant threat even with antidumping laws in place. This would reduce the profitability of these U.S. companies in good times, deepen and lengthen the impact of economic downturns, reduce market share, and reduce employment in these sectors over time. U.S. companies would be forced to invest cautiously in new capacity and perhaps even close existing capacity.

The simulations in Chapter 4 demonstrate that the ultimate result of eliminating antidumping laws is likely to be (and very nearly was) a dramatic downsizing or complete loss of key U.S. industries such as semiconductors and consumer electronics. A similar case could be made in a number of other manufacturing sectors, ranging from supercomputers to steel.

These losses by the United States would be (and in some cases have already been) mirrored by corresponding gains in the dumping countries. Over time, the U.S. economic model is likely to be damaged and discredited by dumping, while other competing models stand to gain significantly. The long-term losses for the citizens of the United States and, indeed, the world could be staggering.

Although far from a perfect remedy, antidumping laws help to insulate the U.S. economy from the negative impacts of dumping, foreign trade barriers, subsidies, and cartels. They allow the United States to maintain a vibrant, freewheeling market economy with limited government intervention domestically and to avoid being victimized by the beggar-thy-neighbor policies of its trading partners. Antidumping laws directly help U.S. companies compete on a level playing field with foreign companies and, in so doing, allow the U.S. model of market economics to compete with other competing models.

## Economic Costs

Much space has already been devoted to answering the specific charges of critics and analyzing the various economic analyses advanced as critiques of antidumping law. They are discussed in detail in Chapter 5. There is no need to rehash these discussions. One point does, however, merit repeating:

Most of the economic estimates that conclude antidumping laws have a significant negative impact on the U.S. economy are quite superficial.

The most frequently discussed study in this category is that done by the ITC in 1995. By the admission of dissenting ITC commissioners, this study is simply a short-term (one-year) analysis of the impact of tariffs.[6] It makes no effort to consider the longer-term competitive impacts of dumping and antidumping laws on the U.S. economy, which are the central focus of this book. As a result, the ITC's report is really little more than a simple restatement of the almost universally accepted point that, at least through a static analysis, tariffs generally have a negative impact on the economy of the country that imposes them.

The ITC's estimate of a $1.59 billion total one-year cost of antidumping and countervailing-duty orders under a static analysis is completely eclipsed by the economic costs of seriously damaging or losing even one high-wage manufacturing industry, such as semiconductor production.[7] Thus, as demonstrated in Chapter 4, even using the ITC's price tag, antidumping law is an excellent investment for the U.S. economy.[8]

### The Uruguay Round and Antidumping Laws

Compelling justifications for antidumping laws can be made from either the perspective of equity and fairness or from a more straightforward economic perspective. These general justifications do not, however, mean that current antidumping laws are perfect and incapable of being improved. Like all programs that require complex administrative actions, particular decisions will always be debatable, and at times mistakes will be made. Inevitably, there must be room for refining and adjusting procedures to improve their operation.

Over the years, critics have made some valid observations regarding problems with certain antidumping procedures. The application of antidumping duties in cases involving very small dumping margins or low levels of imports, the procedures for accounting for forward pricing in start-up companies, and antidumping orders that are no longer required have all been identified as weaknesses in the system.

The Uruguay Round of international trade negotiations undertook a wholesale rewrite of antidumping procedures. The final Uruguay Round agreement essentially created a new, detailed, and internationally accepted antidumping procedure. The Uruguay Round antidumping code was, in fact, so significant that it is included in its entirety in Appendix A. Among the many improvements made by the Uruguay Round are new *de minimis* dumping margins, minimum levels of imports for inclusion in an antidumping order, new standing requirements, new forward pricing provisions, and a new sunset review procedure.

Most of the legitimate concerns about antidumping laws have been addressed by the Uruguay Round, but as conditions change and experience points out new problems, other meritorious changes will be suggested. That is not to say that all proposed changes will be meritorious. A variety of interest groups, including foreign governments and companies, importers, and laissez-faire economists, are tireless critics of antidumping law. As they often admit, the first preference of these groups would be the complete abolition of antidumping laws, but they recognize that abolition is not a politically realistic option.

Given that reality, critics of antidumping laws have proposed a number of changes, including placing a short-supply exception in U.S. antidumping laws, eliminating the special antidumping procedures for NMEs, and implementing sunset provisions in a manner that would eliminate all antidumping orders after five years, regardless of their merits. As explained in detail in the last chapter, these proposed changes are not marginal improvements, but merely thinly veiled attempts to eviscerate antidumping laws. Proposals such as a short-supply exception or a sweeping sunset provision sound reasonable enough, but upon detailed examination they prove to fundamentally compromise the basic principles of antidumping laws; they are wolves in sheep's clothing.

Especially after going through such a large-scale rewrite of antidumping laws, it would seem wise if such subversion could be temporarily put aside to allow the Uruguay Round procedures a chance to prove themselves. After decades of debate, such a major rewrite certainly warrants at least a ten-year test period to evaluate the operation of these procedures. In the meantime, the focus should be on implementing existing antidumping procedures both in the United States and around the world rather than on debating still more changes.

U.S. antidumping laws are carefully and transparently administered, overseen by U.S. courts and now by the WTO. Under such a transparent and rigorously monitored system, there is little chance of abuse. Critics would be wise to focus their attention on the implementation of antidumping law in countries that do not have the same traditions of transparency and judicial oversight as the United States and who have demonstrated a preference for implementing their laws through "black box" procedures that have considerable potential for abuse. (See Appendix B.) If all of these countries adopted U.S. antidumping laws and procedures, the cause for free and open trade would be advanced considerably.

## Concluding Comments

Over close to a century of operation, antidumping laws have established a strong record of performance. There is a compelling historical, legal, moral, and economic case for the continued application of such laws. In recent years, however, antidumping laws have come under such fire from critics that much of this affirmative case has been pushed into the background. The objective of this book is to ensure that the affirmative case for antidumping law is a part of the policy debate on this topic.

In today's international-trade environment, antidumping laws are more essential than ever. The U.S. economy is open to international trade, and formal global barriers to international trade have been considerably reduced. Unfortunately, at the same time, collusion and cartels have created a new wave of private-sector protectionism. Around the world, governments still engage in industrial policies aimed at distorting market outcomes.

Similarly, market economics has won the ideological struggle with nonmarket economics. The open U.S. model for a market economy, however, must compete with a variety of other market models, most originating in Asia. Permutations of these Asian models have gained favor in many countries around the world. One thing these permutations have in common is that they all are likely to spawn dumping, much of which will affect the U.S. market.

As a result of these trends, dumping has become an even more serious threat to the United States than it was in previous decades. Companies from Japan, Korea, Brazil, and other countries continue to dump, but they have been joined by a new generation of dumpers from reforming nonmarket economies, led by China and Russia. Without antidumping laws, the U.S. economy would likely be ravaged by mercantilistic national strategies. U.S. industries, particularly those in manufacturing and high-technology sectors, would be injured by repeated dumping. Over time, investment and capacity in these sectors would shrink and much high-wage employment would be lost.

Dumping is more than just the sale of products at low prices, it is a part of various mercantilistic market strategies aimed at market domination, boosting market share, and increasing employment. Countering these strategies and avoiding their negative impact upon the U.S. economy is a compelling reason to "pay more for imports" or, more precisely, to insist that competition take place on a level playing field. With most other trade policy tools encumbered by international agreements or limited by budgetary concerns, antidumping laws are a critical safeguard against mercantilistic foreign trade strategies. The open U.S. economic system is viable only if it is able to counter these foreign strategies. Thus, antidumping laws are a critical element of U.S. economic and trade policy.

## Notes

1. Jacob Viner, *Dumping: A Problem in International Trade* (Chicago: University of Chicago Press, 1923).

2. Still, there are a number of instances of dumping described in this book involving products, including televisions, semiconductors, and steel, that seem to meet even these narrow definitions.

3. World Trade Organization, *Trade Policy Review: The United States* (Geneva: WTO, 1996).

4. "The Marshall Plan and Its Legacy: Essays," *Foreign Affairs* 76, 3 (May-June 1997): 159–185.

5. Paula L. Green, "Poll: 57 Percent of U.S. Public Against Free Trade Pacts with Latin America," *Journal of Commerce,* November 8, 1996, p. 2A.

6. U.S. International Trade Commission, *The Economic Effects of Antidumping and Countervailing Duty Orders and Suspension Agreements* (Washington, DC: ITC, June 1995), views of Vice Chairman Janet Nuzum and Commissioner David Rohr, pp. vii-ix.

7. Ibid., p. x.

8. The simulation also counters the ITC's assessment of the cost of antidumping duties. The impact of the costs of dumping duties are included in the simulation in Chapter 4.

# Appendix A

**AGREEMENT ON IMPLEMENTATION OF ARTICLE VI
OF THE GENERAL AGREEMENT ON TARIFFS AND TRADE 1994**

*Members* hereby *agree* as follows:

## PART I

### Article 1

### Principles

An anti-dumping measure shall be applied only under the circumstances provided for in Article VI of GATT 1994 and pursuant to investigations initiated[1] and conducted in accordance with the provisions of this Agreement. The following provisions govern the application of Article VI of GATT 1994 in so far as action is taken under anti-dumping legislation or regulations.

### Article 2

### Determination of Dumping

2.1 For the purpose of this Agreement, a product is to be considered as being dumped, i.e. introduced into the commerce of another country at less than its normal value, if the export price of the product exported from one country to another is less than the comparable price, in the ordinary course of trade, for the like product when destined for consumption in the exporting country.

---

[1]The term "initiated" as used in this Agreement means the procedural action by which a Member formally commences an investigation as provided in Article 5.

2.2 When there are no sales of the like product in the ordinary course of trade in the domestic market of the exporting country or when, because of the particular market situation or the low volume of the sales in the domestic market of the exporting country,[2] such sales do not permit a proper comparison, the margin of dumping shall be determined by comparison with a comparable price of the like product when exported to an appropriate third country, provided that this price is representative, or with the cost of production in the country of origin plus a reasonable amount for administrative, selling and general costs and for profits.

2.2.1 Sales of the like product in the domestic market of the exporting country or sales to a third country at prices below per unit (fixed and variable) costs of production plus administrative, selling and general costs may be treated as not being in the ordinary course of trade by reason of price and may be disregarded in determining normal value only if the authorities[3] determine that such sales are made within an extended period of time[4] in substantial quantities[5] and are at prices which do not provide for the recovery of all costs within a reasonable period of time. If prices which are below per unit costs at the time of sale are above weighted average per unit costs for the period of investigation, such prices shall be considered to provide for recovery of costs within a reasonable period of time.

2.2.1.1 For the purpose of paragraph 2, costs shall normally be calculated on the basis of records kept by the exporter or producer under investigation, provided that such records are in accordance with the generally accepted accounting principles of the exporting

---

[2]Sales of the like product destined for consumption in the domestic market of the exporting country shall normally be considered a sufficient quantity for the determination of the normal value if such sales constitute 5 per cent or more of the sales of the product under consideration to the importing Member, provided that a lower ratio should be acceptable where the evidence demonstrates that domestic sales at such lower ratio are nonetheless of sufficient magnitude to provide for a proper comparison.

[3]When in this Agreement the term "authorities" is used, it shall be interpreted as meaning authorities at an appropriate senior level.

[4]The extended period of time should normally be one year but shall in no case be less than six months.

[5]Sales below per unit costs are made in substantial quantities when the authorities establish that the weighted average selling price of the transactions under consideration for the determination of the normal value is below the weighted average per unit costs, or that the volume of sales below per unit costs represents not less than 20 percent of the volume sold in transactions under consideration for the determination of the normal value.

country and reasonably reflect the costs associated with the production and sale of the product under consideration. Authorities shall consider all available evidence on the proper allocation of costs, including that which is made available by the exporter or producer in the course of the investigation provided that such allocations have been historically utilized by the exporter or producer, in particular in relation to establishing appropriate amortization and depreciation periods and allowances for capital expenditures and other development costs. Unless already reflected in the cost allocations under this sub-paragraph, costs shall be adjusted appropriately for those non-recurring items of cost which benefit future and/or current production, or for circumstances in which costs during the period of investigation are affected by start-up operations.[6]

2.2.2 For the purpose of paragraph 2, the amounts for administrative, selling and general costs and for profits shall be based on actual data pertaining to production and sales in the ordinary course of trade of the like product by the exporter or producer under investigation. When such amounts cannot be determined on this basis, the amounts may be determined on the basis of:

(i) the actual amounts incurred and realized by the exporter or producer in question in respect of production and sales in the domestic market of the country of origin of the same general category of products;

(ii) the weighted average of the actual amounts incurred and realized by other exporters or producers subject to investigation in respect of production and sales of the like product in the domestic market of the country of origin;

(iii) any other reasonable method, provided that the amount for profit so established shall not exceed the profit normally realized by other exporters or producers on sales of products of the same general category in the domestic market of the country of origin.

---

[6]The adjustment made for start-up operations shall reflect the costs at the end of the start-up period or, if that period extends beyond the period of investigation, the most recent costs which can reasonably be taken into account by the authorities during the investigation.

2.3 In cases where there is no export price or where it appears to the authorities concerned that the export price is unreliable because of association or a compensatory arrangement between the exporter and the importer or a third party, the export price may be constructed on the basis of the price at which the imported products are first resold to an independent buyer, or if the products are not resold to an independent buyer, or not resold in the condition as imported, on such reasonable basis as the authorities may determine.

2.4 A fair comparison shall be made between the export price and the normal value. This comparison shall be made at the same level of trade, normally at the ex-factory level, and in respect of sales made at as nearly as possible the same time. Due allowance shall be made in each case, on its merits, for differences which affect price comparability, including differences in conditions and terms of sale, taxation, levels of trade, quantities, physical characteristics, and any other differences which are also demonstrated to affect price comparability.[7] In the cases referred to in paragraph 3, allowances for costs, including duties and taxes, incurred between importation and resale, and for profits accruing, should also be made. If in these cases price comparability has been affected, the authorities shall establish the normal value at a level of trade equivalent to the level of trade of the constructed export price, or shall make due allowance as warranted under this paragraph. The authorities shall indicate to the parties in question what information is necessary to ensure a fair comparison and shall not impose an unreasonable burden of proof on those parties.

2.4.1 When the comparison under paragraph 4 requires a conversion of currencies, such conversion should be made using the rate of exchange on the date of sale,[8] provided that when a sale of foreign currency on forward markets is directly linked to the export sale involved, the rate of exchange in the forward sale shall be used. Fluctuations in exchange rates shall be ignored and in an investigation the authorities shall allow exporters at least 60 days to have adjusted their export prices to reflect sustained movements in exchange rates during the period of investigation.

2.4.2 Subject to the provisions governing fair comparison in paragraph 4, the existence of margins of dumping during the investigation phase

---

[7]It is understood that some of the above factors may overlap, and authorities shall ensure that they do not duplicate adjustments that have been already made under this provision.

[8]Normally, the date of sale would be the date of contract, purchase order, order confirmation, or invoice, whichever establishes the material terms of sale.

shall normally be established on the basis of a comparison of a weighted average normal value with a weighted average of prices of all comparable export transactions or by a comparison of normal value and export prices on a transaction-to-transaction basis. A normal value established on a weighted average basis may be compared to prices of individual export transactions if the authorities find a pattern of export prices which differ significantly among different purchasers, regions or time periods, and if an explanation is provided as to why such differences cannot be taken into account appropriately by the use of a weighted average–to–weighted average or transaction-to-transaction comparison.

2.5 In the case where products are not imported directly from the country of origin but are exported to the importing Member from an intermediate country, the price at which the products are sold from the country of export to the importing Member shall normally be compared with the comparable price in the country of export. However, comparison may be made with the price in the country of origin, if, for example, the products are merely transshipped through the country of export, or such products are not produced in the country of export, or there is no comparable price for them in the country of export.

2.6 Throughout this Agreement the term "like product" ("produit similaire") shall be interpreted to mean a product which is identical, i.e. alike in all respects to the product under consideration, or in the absence of such a product, another product which, although not alike in all respects, has characteristics closely resembling those of the product under consideration.

2.7 This Article is without prejudice to the second Supplementary Provision to paragraph 1 of Article VI in Annex I to GATT 1994.

*Article 3*

*Determination of Injury*[9]

3.1 A determination of injury for purposes of Article VI of GATT 1994 shall be based on positive evidence and involve an objective examination of

---

[9]Under this Agreement the term "injury" shall, unless otherwise specified, be taken to mean material injury to a domestic industry, threat of material injury to a domestic industry or material retardation of the establishment of such an industry and shall be interpreted in accordance with the provisions of this Article.

both *(a)* the volume of the dumped imports and the effect of the dumped imports on prices in the domestic market for like products, and *(b)* the consequent impact of these imports on domestic producers of such products.

3.2 With regard to the volume of the dumped imports, the investigating authorities shall consider whether there has been a significant increase in dumped imports, either in absolute terms or relative to production or consumption in the importing Member. With regard to the effect of the dumped imports on prices, the investigating authorities shall consider whether there has been a significant price undercutting by the dumped imports as compared with the price of a like product of the importing Member, or whether the effect of such imports is otherwise to depress prices to a significant degree or prevent price increases, which otherwise would have occurred, to a significant degree. No one or several of these factors can necessarily give decisive guidance.

3.3 Where imports of a product from more than one country are simultaneously subject to anti-dumping investigations, the investigating authorities may cumulatively assess the effects of such imports only if they determine that *(a)* the margin of dumping established in relation to the imports from each country is more than *de minimis* as defined in paragraph 8 of Article 5 and the volume of imports from each country is not negligible and *(b)* a cumulative assessment of the effects of the imports is appropriate in light of the conditions of competition between the imported products and the conditions of competition between the imported products and the like domestic product.

3.4 The examination of the impact of the dumped imports on the domestic industry concerned shall include an evaluation of all relevant economic factors and indices having a bearing on the state of the industry, including actual and potential decline in sales, profits, output, market share, productivity, return on investments, or utilization of capacity; factors affecting domestic prices; the magnitude of the margin of dumping; actual and potential negative effects on cash flow, inventories, employment, wages, growth, ability to raise capital or investments. This list is not exhaustive, nor can one or several of these factors necessarily give decisive guidance.

3.5 It must be demonstrated that the dumped imports are, through the effects of dumping, as set forth in paragraphs 2 and 4, causing injury within the meaning of this Agreement. The demonstration of a causal relationship between the dumped imports and the injury to the domestic industry shall be based on an examination of all relevant evidence before the authorities. The authorities shall also examine any known factors other than the dumped imports which at the same time are injuring the domestic industry, and the injuries caused by these other factors must not be attributed to the dumped imports. Factors which may be relevant in this respect include, *inter alia,* the volume and prices of imports not sold at dumping prices, contraction in demand or changes in the patterns of consumption, trade restrictive practices of and competition between the foreign and domestic producers, developments in technology and the export performance and productivity of the domestic industry.

3.6 The effect of the dumped imports shall be assessed in relation to the domestic production of the like product when available data permit the separate identification of that production on the basis of such criteria as the production process, producers' sales and profits. If such separate identification of that production is not possible, the effects of the dumped imports shall be assessed by the examination of the production of the narrowest group or range of products, which includes the like product, for which the necessary information can be provided.

3.7 A determination of a threat of material injury shall be based on facts and not merely on allegation, conjecture or remote possibility. The change in circumstances which would create a situation in which the dumping would cause injury must be clearly foreseen and imminent.[10] In making a determination regarding the existence of a threat of material injury, the authorities should consider, *inter alia,* such factors as:

(i) a significant rate of increase of dumped imports into the domestic market indicating the likelihood of substantially increased importation;

(ii) sufficient freely disposable, or an imminent, substantial increase in, capacity of the exporter indicating the likelihood of substantially increased dumped exports to the importing Member's market, taking into account the availability of other export markets to absorb any additional exports;

(iii) whether imports are entering at prices that will have a significant

---

[10]One example, though not an exclusive one, is that there is convincing reason to believe that there will be, in the near future, substantially increased importation of the product at dumped prices.

depressing or suppressing effect on domestic prices, and would likely increase demand for further imports; and

(iv) inventories of the product being investigated.

No one of these factors by itself can necessarily give decisive guidance but the totality of the factors considered must lead to the conclusion that further dumped exports are imminent and that, unless protective action is taken, material injury would occur.

3.8 With respect to cases where injury is threatened by dumped imports, the application of anti-dumping measures shall be considered and decided with special care.

## Article 4

### Definition of Domestic Industry

4.1 For the purposes of this Agreement, the term "domestic industry" shall be interpreted as referring to the domestic producers as a whole of the like products or to those of them whose collective output of the products constitutes a major proportion of the total domestic production of those products, except that:

(i) when producers are related[11] to the exporters or importers or are themselves importers of the allegedly dumped product, the term "domestic industry" may be interpreted as referring to the rest of the producers;

(ii) in exceptional circumstances the territory of a Member may, for the production in question, be divided into two or more competitive markets and the producers within each market may be regarded as a separate industry if *(a)* the producers within such market sell all or almost all of their production of the product in question in that market, and *(b)* the

---

[11]For the purpose of this paragraph, producers shall be deemed to be related to exporters or importers only if *(a)* one of them directly or indirectly controls the other; or *(b)* both of them are directly or indirectly controlled by a third person; or *(c)* together they directly or indirectly control a third person, provided that there are grounds for believing or suspecting that the effect of the relationship is such as to cause the producer concerned to behave differently from non-related producers. For the purpose of this paragraph, one shall be deemed to control another when the former is legally or operationally in a position to exercise restraint or direction over the latter.

demand in that market is not to any substantial degree supplied by producers of the product in question located elsewhere in the territory. In such circumstances, injury may be found to exist even where a major portion of the total domestic industry is not injured, provided there is a concentration of dumped imports into such an isolated market and provided further that the dumped imports are causing injury to the producers of all or almost all of the production within such market.

4.2 When the domestic industry has been interpreted as referring to the producers in a certain area, i.e. a market as defined in paragraph l(ii), anti-dumping duties shall be levied[12] only on the products in question consigned for final consumption to that area. When the constitutional law of the importing Member does not permit the levying of anti-dumping duties on such a basis, the importing Member may levy the anti-dumping duties without limitation only if *(a)* the exporters shall have been given an opportunity to cease exporting at dumped prices to the area concerned or otherwise give assurances pursuant to Article 8 and adequate assurances in this regard have not been promptly given, and *(b)* such duties cannot be levied only on products of specific producers which supply the area in question.

4.3 Where two or more countries have reached under the provisions of paragraph 8(a) of Article XXIV of GATT 1994 such a level of integration that they have the characteristics of a single, unified market, the industry in the entire area of integration shall be taken to be the domestic industry referred to in paragraph 1.

4.4 The provisions of paragraph 6 of Article 3 shall be applicable to this Article.

*Article 5*

*Initiation and Subsequent Investigation*

5.1 Except as provided for in paragraph 6, an investigation to determine the existence, degree and effect of any alleged dumping shall be initiated upon a written application by or on behalf of the domestic industry.

5.2 An application under paragraph 1 shall include evidence of *(a)* dumping, *(b)* injury within the meaning of Article VI of GATT 1994 as interpreted by this Agreement and *(c)* a causal link between the dumped imports

---

[12]As used in this Agreement "levy" shall mean the definitive or final legal assessment or collection of a duty or tax.

and the alleged injury. Simple assertion, unsubstantiated by relevant evidence, cannot be considered sufficient to meet the requirements of this paragraph. The application shall contain such information as is reasonably available to the applicant on the following:

(i) the identity of the applicant and a description of the volume and value of the domestic production of the like product by the applicant. Where a written application is made on behalf of the domestic industry, the application shall identify the industry on behalf of which the application is made by a list of all known domestic producers of the like product (or associations of domestic producers of the like product) and, to the extent possible, a description of the volume and value of domestic production of the like product accounted for by such producers;

(ii) a complete description of the allegedly dumped product, the names of the country or countries of origin or export in question, the identity of each known exporter or foreign producer and a list of known persons importing the product in question;

(iii) information on prices at which the product in question is sold when destined for consumption in the domestic markets of the country or countries of origin or export (or, where appropriate, information on the prices at which the product is sold from the country or countries of origin or export to a third country or countries, or on the constructed value of the product) and information on export prices or, where appropriate, on the prices at which the product is first resold to an independent buyer in the territory of the importing Member;

(iv) information on the evolution of the volume of the allegedly dumped imports, the effect of these imports on prices of the like product in the domestic market and the consequent impact of the imports on the domestic industry, as demonstrated by relevant factors and indices having a bearing on the state of the domestic industry, such as those listed in paragraphs 2 and 4 of Article 3.

5.3 The authorities shall examine the accuracy and adequacy of the evidence provided in the application to determine whether there is sufficient evidence to justify the initiation of an investigation.

5.4 An investigation shall not be initiated pursuant to paragraph 1 unless the authorities have determined, on the basis of an examination of the degree of support for, or opposition to, the application expressed[13] by domestic producers of the like product, that the application has been made by or on behalf of the domestic industry.[14] The application shall be considered to have been made "by or on behalf of the domestic industry" if it is supported by those domestic producers whose collective output constitutes more than 50 per cent of the total production of the like product produced by that portion of the domestic industry expressing either support for or opposition to the application. However, no investigation shall be initiated when domestic producers expressly supporting the application account for less than 25 per cent of total production of the like product produced by the domestic industry.

5.5 The authorities shall avoid, unless a decision has been made to initiate an investigation, any publicizing of the application for the initiation of an investigation. However, after receipt of a properly documented application and before proceeding to initiate an investigation, the authorities shall notify the government of the exporting Member concerned.

5.6 If, in special circumstances, the authorities concerned decide to initiate an investigation without having received a written application by or on behalf of a domestic industry for the initiation of such investigation, they shall proceed only if they have sufficient evidence of dumping, injury and a causal link, as described in paragraph 2, to justify the initiation of an investigation.

5.7 The evidence of both dumping and injury shall be considered simultaneously *(a)* in the decision whether or not to initiate an investigation, and *(b)* thereafter, during the course of the investigation, starting on a date not later than the earliest date on which in accordance with the provisions of this Agreement provisional measures may be applied.

5.8 An application under paragraph 1 shall be rejected and an investigation shall be terminated promptly as soon as the authorities concerned are satisfied that there is not sufficient evidence of either dumping or of injury to justify proceeding with the case. There shall be immediate termination in

---

[13]In the case of fragmented industries involving an exceptionally large number of producers, authorities may determine support and opposition by using statistically valid sampling techniques.

[14]Members are aware that in the territory of certain Members employees of domestic producers of the like product or representatives of those employees may make or support an application for an investigation under paragraph 1.

cases where the authorities determine that the margin of dumping is *de minimis*, or that the volume of dumped imports, actual or potential, or the injury, is negligible. The margin of dumping shall be considered to be *de minimis* if this margin is less than 2 per cent, expressed as a percentage of the export price. The volume of dumped imports shall normally be regarded as negligible if the volume of dumped imports from a particular country is found to account for less than 3 per cent of imports of the like product in the importing Member, unless countries which individually account for less than 3 per cent of the imports of the like product in the importing Member collectively account for more than 7 per cent of imports of the like product in the importing Member.

5.9 An anti-dumping proceeding shall not hinder the procedures of customs clearance.

5.10 Investigations shall, except in special circumstances, be concluded within one year, and in no case more than 18 months, after their initiation.

*Article 6*

*Evidence*

6.1 All interested parties in an anti-dumping investigation shall be given notice of the information which the authorities require and ample opportunity to present in writing all evidence which they consider relevant in respect of the investigation in question.

6.1.1 Exporters or foreign producers receiving questionnaires used in an anti-dumping investigation shall be given at least 30 days for reply.[15] Due consideration should be given to any request for an extension of the 30-day period and, upon cause shown, such an extension should be granted whenever practicable.

6.1.2 Subject to the requirement to protect confidential information, evidence presented in writing by one interested party shall be made available promptly to other interested parties participating in the investigation.

---

[15]As a general rule, the time-limit for exporters shall be counted from the date of receipt of the questionnaire, which for this purpose shall be deemed to have been received one week from the date on which it was sent to the respondent or transmitted to the appropriate diplomatic representative of the exporting Member or, in the case of a separate customs territory Member of the WTO, an official representative of the exporting territory.

6.1.3 As soon as an investigation has been initiated, the authorities shall provide the full text of the written application received under paragraph 1 of Article 5 to the known exporters[16] and to the authorities of the exporting Member and shall make it available, upon request, to other interested parties involved. Due regard shall be paid to the requirement for the protection of confidential information, as provided for in paragraph 5.

6.2 Throughout the anti-dumping investigation all interested parties shall have a full opportunity for the defence of their interests. To this end, the authorities shall, on request, provide opportunities for all interested parties to meet those parties with adverse interests, so that opposing views may be presented and rebuttal arguments offered. Provision of such opportunities must take account of the need to preserve confidentiality and of the convenience to the parties. There shall be no obligation on any party to attend a meeting, and failure to do so shall not be prejudicial to that party's case. Interested parties shall also have the right, on justification, to present other information orally.

6.3 Oral information provided under paragraph 2 shall be taken into account by the authorities only in so far as it is subsequently reproduced in writing and made available to other interested parties, as provided for in subparagraph 1.2.

6.4 The authorities shall whenever practicable provide timely opportunities for all interested parties to see all information that is relevant to the presentation of their cases, that is not confidential as defined in paragraph 5, and that is used by the authorities in an anti-dumping investigation, and to prepare presentations on the basis of this information.

6.5 Any information which is by nature confidential (for example, because its disclosure would be of significant competitive advantage to a competitor or because its disclosure would have a significantly adverse effect upon a person supplying the information or upon a person from whom that person acquired the information), or which is provided on a confidential basis by parties to an investigation shall, upon good cause shown, be treated as such by the authorities. Such information shall not be disclosed without specific permission of the party submitting it.[17]

---

[16]It being understood that, where the number of exporters involved is particularly high, the full text of the written application should instead be provided only to the authorities of the exporting Member or to the relevant trade association.

[17]Members are aware that in the territory of certain Members disclosure pursuant to a narrowly-drawn protective order may be required.

6.5.1 The authorities shall require interested parties providing confidential information to furnish non-confidential summaries thereof. These summaries shall be in sufficient detail to permit a reasonable understanding of the substance of the information submitted in confidence. In exceptional circumstances, such parties may indicate that such information is not susceptible of summary. In such exceptional circumstances, a statement of the reasons why summarization is not possible must be provided.

6.5.2 If the authorities find that a request for confidentiality is not warranted and if the supplier of the information is either unwilling to make the information public or to authorize its disclosure in generalized or summary form, the authorities may disregard such information unless it can be demonstrated to their satisfaction from appropriate sources that the information is correct.[18]

6.6 Except in circumstances provided for in paragraph 8, the authorities shall during the course of an investigation satisfy themselves as to the accuracy of the information supplied by interested parties upon which their findings are based.

6.7 In order to verify information provided or to obtain further details, the authorities may carry out investigations in the territory of other Members as required, provided they obtain the agreement of the firms concerned and notify the representatives of the government of the Member in question, and unless that Member objects to the investigation. The procedures described in Annex I shall apply to investigations carried out in the territory of other Members. Subject to the requirement to protect confidential information, the authorities shall make the results of any such investigations available, or shall provide disclosure thereof pursuant to paragraph 9, to the firms to which they pertain and may make such results available to the applicants.

6.8 In cases in which any interested party refuses access to, or otherwise does not provide, necessary information within a reasonable period or significantly impedes the investigation, preliminary and final determinations, affirmative or negative, may be made on the basis of the facts available. The provisions of Annex II shall be observed in the application of this paragraph.

---

[18]Members agree that requests for confidentiality should not be arbitrarily rejected.

6.9 The authorities shall, before a final determination is made, inform all interested parties of the essential facts under consideration which form the basis for the decision whether to apply definitive measures. Such disclosure should take place in sufficient time for the parties to defend their interests.

6.10 The authorities shall, as a rule, determine an individual margin of dumping for each known exporter or producer concerned of the product under investigation. In cases where the number of exporters, producers, importers or types of products involved is so large as to make such a determination impracticable, the authorities may limit their examination either to a reasonable number of interested parties or products by using samples which are statistically valid on the basis of information available to the authorities at the time of the selection, or to the largest percentage of the volume of the exports from the country in question which can reasonably be investigated.

> 6.10.1 Any selection of exporters, producers, importers or types of products made under this paragraph shall preferably be chosen in consultation with and with the consent of the exporters, producers or importers concerned.

> 6.10.2 In cases where the authorities have limited their examination, as provided for in this paragraph, they shall nevertheless determine an individual margin of dumping for any exporter or producer not initially selected who submits the necessary information in time for that information to be considered during the course of the investigation, except where the number of exporters or producers is so large that individual examinations would be unduly burdensome to the authorities and prevent the timely completion of the investigation. Voluntary responses shall not be discouraged.

6.11 For the purposes of this Agreement, "interested parties" shall include:

> (i) an exporter or foreign producer or the importer of a product subject to investigation, or a trade or business association a majority of the members of which are producers, exporters or importers of such product;

> (ii) the government of the exporting Member; and

> (iii) a producer of the like product in the importing Member or a trade

and business association a majority of the members of which produce the like product in the territory of the importing Member.

This list shall not preclude Members from allowing domestic or foreign parties other than those mentioned above to be included as interested parties.

6.12 The authorities shall provide opportunities for industrial users of the product under investigation, and for representative consumer organizations in cases where the product is commonly sold at the retail level, to provide information which is relevant to the investigation regarding dumping, injury and causality.

6.13 The authorities shall take due account of any difficulties experienced by interested parties, in particular small companies, in supplying information requested, and shall provide any assistance practicable.

6.14 The procedures set out above are not intended to prevent the authorities of a Member from proceeding expeditiously with regard to initiating an investigation, reaching preliminary or final determinations, whether affirmative or negative, or from applying provisional or final measures, in accordance with relevant provisions of this Agreement.

*Article 7*

*Provisional Measures*

7.1 Provisional measures may be applied only if:

(i) an investigation has been initiated in accordance with the provisions of Article 5, a public notice has been given to that effect and interested parties have been given adequate opportunities to submit information and make comments;

(ii) a preliminary affirmative determination has been made of dumping and consequent injury to a domestic industry; and

(iii) the authorities concerned judge such measures necessary to prevent injury being caused during the investigation.

7.2 Provisional measures may take the form of a provisional duty or, preferably, a security—by cash deposit or bond—equal to the amount of the anti-dumping duty provisionally estimated, being not greater than the provisionally estimated margin of dumping. Withholding of appraisement is an appropriate provisional measure, provided that the normal duty and the estimated amount of the anti-dumping duty be indicated and as long as the withholding of appraisement is subject to the same conditions as other provisional measures.

7.3 Provisional measures shall not be applied sooner than 60 days from the date of initiation of the investigation.

7.4 The application of provisional measures shall be limited to as short a period as possible, not exceeding four months or, on decision of the authorities concerned, upon request by exporters representing a significant percentage of the trade involved, to a period not exceeding six months. When authorities, in the course of an investigation, examine whether a duty lower than the margin of dumping would be sufficient to remove injury, these periods may be six and nine months, respectively.

7.5 The relevant provisions of Article 9 shall be followed in the application of provisional measures.

## Article 8

### Price Undertakings

8.1 Proceedings may[19] be suspended or terminated without the imposition of provisional measures or anti-dumping duties upon receipt of satisfactory voluntary undertakings from any exporter to revise its prices or to cease exports to the area in question at dumped prices so that the authorities are satisfied that the injurious effect of the dumping is eliminated. Price increases under such undertakings shall not be higher than necessary to eliminate the margin of dumping. It is desirable that the price increases be less than the margin of dumping if such increases would be adequate to remove the injury to the domestic industry.

8.2 Price undertakings shall not be sought or accepted from exporters unless the authorities of the importing Member have made a preliminary affirma-

---

[19]The word "may" shall not be interpreted to allow the simultaneous continuation of proceedings with the implementation of price undertakings except as provided in paragraph 4.

tive determination of dumping and injury caused by such dumping.

8.3 Undertakings offered need not be accepted if the authorities consider their acceptance impractical, for example, if the number of actual or potential exporters is too great, or for other reasons, including reasons of general policy. Should the case arise and where practicable, the authorities shall provide to the exporter the reasons which have led them to consider acceptance of an undertaking as inappropriate, and shall, to the extent possible, give the exporter an opportunity to make comments thereon.

8.4 If an undertaking is accepted, the investigation of dumping and injury shall nevertheless be completed if the exporter so desires or the authorities so decide. In such a case, if a negative determination of dumping or injury is made, the undertaking shall automatically lapse, except in cases where such a determination is due in large part to the existence of a price undertaking. In such cases, the authorities may require that an undertaking be maintained for a reasonable period consistent with the provisions of this Agreement. In the event that an affirmative determination of dumping and injury is made, the undertaking shall continue consistent with its terms and the provisions of this Agreement.

8.5 Price undertakings may be suggested by the authorities of the importing Member, but no exporter shall be forced to enter into such undertakings. The fact that exporters do not offer such undertakings, or do not accept an invitation to do so, shall in no way prejudice the consideration of the case. However, the authorities are free to determine that a threat of injury is more likely to be realized if the dumped imports continue.

8.6 Authorities of an importing Member may require any exporter from whom an undertaking has been accepted to provide periodically information relevant to the fulfilment of such an undertaking and to permit verification of pertinent data. In case of violation of an undertaking, the authorities of the importing Member may take, under this Agreement in conformity with its provisions, expeditious actions which may constitute immediate application of provisional measures using the best information available. In such cases, definitive duties may be levied in accordance with this Agreement on products entered for consumption not more than 90 days before the application of such provisional measures, except that any such retroactive assessment shall not apply to imports entered before the violation of the undertaking.

## Article 9

### Imposition and Collection of Anti-Dumping Duties

9.1 The decision whether or not to impose an anti-dumping duty in cases where all requirements for the imposition have been fulfilled, and the decision whether the amount of the anti-dumping duty to be imposed shall be the full margin of dumping or less, are decisions to be made by the authorities of the importing Member. It is desirable that the imposition be permissive in the territory of all Members, and that the duty be less than the margin if such lesser duty would be adequate to remove the injury to the domestic industry.

9.2 When an anti-dumping duty is imposed in respect of any product, such anti-dumping duty shall be collected in the appropriate amounts in each case, on a non-discriminatory basis on imports of such product from all sources found to be dumped and causing injury, except as to imports from those sources from which price undertakings under the terms of this Agreement have been accepted. The authorities shall name the supplier or suppliers of the product concerned. If, however, several suppliers from the same country are involved, and it is impracticable to name all these suppliers, the authorities may name the supplying country concerned. If several suppliers from more than one country are involved, the authorities may name either all the suppliers involved, or, if this is impracticable, all the supplying countries involved.

9.3 The amount of the anti-dumping duty shall not exceed the margin of dumping as established under Article 2.

9.3.1 When the amount of the anti-dumping duty is assessed on a retrospective basis, the determination of the final liability for payment of anti-dumping duties shall take place as soon as possible, normally within 12 months, and in no case more than 18 months, after the date on which a request for a final assessment of the amount of the anti-dumping duty has been made.[20] Any refund shall be made promptly and normally in not more than 90 days following the determination of final liability made pursuant to this subparagraph. In any case, where a refund is not made within 90 days, the authorities shall provide an explanation if so requested.

---

[20]It is understood that the observance of the time-limits mentioned in this subparagraph and in subparagraph 3.2 may not be possible where the product in question is subject to judicial review proceedings.

9.3.2 When the amount of the anti-dumping duty is assessed on a prospective basis, provision shall be made for a prompt refund, upon request, of any duty paid in excess of the margin of dumping. A refund of any such duty paid in excess of the actual margin of dumping shall normally take place within 12 months, and in no case more than 18 months, after the date on which a request for a refund, duly supported by evidence, has been made by an importer of the product subject to the anti-dumping duty. The refund authorized should normally be made within 90 days of the above-noted decision.

9.3.3 In determining whether and to what extent a reimbursement should be made when the export price is constructed in accordance with paragraph 3 of Article 2, authorities should take account of any change in normal value, any change in costs incurred between importation and resale, and any movement in the resale price which is duly reflected in subsequent selling prices, and should calculate the export price with no deduction for the amount of anti-dumping duties paid when conclusive evidence of the above is provided.

9.4 When the authorities have limited their examination in accordance with the second sentence of paragraph 10 of Article 6, any anti-dumping duty applied to imports from exporters or producers not included in the examination shall not exceed:

(i) the weighted average margin of dumping established with respect to the selected exporters or producers or,

(ii) where the liability for payment of anti-dumping duties is calculated on the basis of a prospective normal value, the difference between the weighted average normal value of the selected exporters or producers and the export prices of exporters or producers not individually examined,

provided that the authorities shall disregard for the purpose of this paragraph any zero and *de minimis* margins and margins established under the circumstances referred to in paragraph 8 of Article 6. The authorities shall apply individual duties or normal values to imports from any exporter or producer not included in the examination who has provided the necessary information during the course of the investigation, as provided for in subparagraph 10.2 of Article 6.

9.5 If a product is subject to anti-dumping duties in an importing Member, the authorities shall promptly carry out a review for the purpose of determining individual margins of dumping for any exporters or producers in the exporting country in question who have not exported the product to the importing Member during the period of investigation, provided that these exporters or producers can show that they are not related to any of the exporters or producers in the exporting country who are subject to the anti-dumping duties on the product. Such a review shall be initiated and carried out on an accelerated basis, compared to normal duty assessment and review proceedings in the importing Member. No anti-dumping duties shall be levied on imports from such exporters or producers while the review is being carried out. The authorities may, however, withhold appraisement and/or request guarantees to ensure that, should such a review result in a determination of dumping in respect of such producers or exporters, anti-dumping duties can be levied retroactively to the date of the initiation of the review.

## Article 10

### Retroactivity

10.1 Provisional measures and anti-dumping duties shall only be applied to products which enter for consumption after the time when the decision taken under paragraph 1 of Article 7 and paragraph 1 of Article 9, respectively, enters into force, subject to the exceptions set out in this Article.

10.2 Where a final determination of injury (but not of a threat thereof or of a material retardation of the establishment of an industry) is made or, in the case of a final determination of a threat of injury, where the effect of the dumped imports would, in the absence of the provisional measures, have led to a determination of injury, anti-dumping duties may be levied retroactively for the period for which provisional measures, if any, have been applied.

10.3 If the definitive anti-dumping duty is higher than the provisional duty paid or payable, or the amount estimated for the purpose of the security, the difference shall not be collected. If the definitive duty is lower than the provisional duty paid or payable, or the amount estimated for the purpose of the security, the difference shall be reimbursed or the duty recalculated, as the case may be.

10.4 Except as provided in paragraph 2, where a determination of threat of injury or material retardation is made (but no injury has yet occurred) a definitive anti-dumping duty may be imposed only from the date of the determination of threat of injury or material retardation, and any cash deposit made during the period of the application of provisional measures shall be refunded and any bonds released in an expeditious manner.

10.5 Where a final determination is negative, any cash deposit made during the period of the application of provisional measures shall be refunded and any bonds released in an expeditious manner.

10.6 A definitive anti-dumping duty may be levied on products which were entered for consumption not more than 90 days prior to the date of application of provisional measures, when the authorities determine for the dumped product in question that:

(i) there is a history of dumping which caused injury or that the importer was, or should have been, aware that the exporter practises dumping and that such dumping would cause injury, and

(ii) the injury is caused by massive dumped imports of a product in a relatively short time which in light of the timing and the volume of the dumped imports and other circumstances (such as a rapid build-up of inventories of the imported product) is likely to seriously undermine the remedial effect of the definitive anti-dumping duty to be applied, provided that the importers concerned have been given an opportunity to comment.

10.7 The authorities may, after initiating an investigation, take such measures as the withholding of appraisement or assessment as may be necessary to collect anti-dumping duties retroactively, as provided for in paragraph 6, once they have sufficient evidence that the conditions set forth in that paragraph are satisfied.

10.8 No duties shall be levied retroactively pursuant to paragraph 6 on products entered for consumption prior to the date of initiation of the investigation.

*Article 11*

*Duration and Review of Anti-Dumping Duties and Price Undertakings*

11.1 An anti-dumping duty shall remain in force only as long as and to the extent necessary to counteract dumping which is causing injury.

11.2 The authorities shall review the need for the continued imposition of the duty, where warranted, on their own initiative or, provided that a reasonable period of time has elapsed since the imposition of the definitive anti-dumping duty, upon request by any interested party which submits positive information substantiating the need for a review.[21] Interested parties shall have the right to request the authorities to examine whether the continued imposition of the duty is necessary to offset dumping, whether the injury would be likely to continue or recur if the duty were removed or varied, or both. If, as a result of the review under this paragraph, the authorities determine that the anti-dumping duty is no longer warranted, it shall be terminated immediately.

11.3 Notwithstanding the provisions of paragraphs 1 and 2, any definitive anti-dumping duty shall be terminated on a date not later than five years from its imposition (or from the date of the most recent review under paragraph 2 if that review has covered both dumping and injury, under this paragraph), unless the authorities determine, in a review initiated before that date on their own initiative or upon a duly substantiated request made by or on behalf of the domestic industry within a reasonable period of time prior to that date, that the expiry of the duty would be likely to lead to continuation or recurrence of dumping and injury.[22] The duty may remain in force pending the outcome of such a review.

11.4 The provisions of Article 6 regarding evidence and procedure shall apply to any review carried out under this Article. Any such review shall be carried out expeditiously and shall normally be concluded within 12 months of the date of initiation of the review.

11.5 The provisions of this Article shall apply *mutatis mutandis* to price undertakings accepted under Article 8.

## Article 12

### Public Notice and Explanation of Determinations

12.1 When the authorities are satisfied that there is sufficient evidence to justify the initiation of an anti-dumping investigation pursuant to Article 5, the Member or Members the products of which are subject to such investi-

---

[21]A determination of final liability for payment of anti-dumping duties, as provided for in paragraph 3 of Article 9, does not by itself constitute a review within the meaning of this article.

[22]When the amount of the anti-dumping duty is assessed on a retrospective basis, a finding in the most recent assessment proceeding under subparagraph 3.1 of Article 9 that no duty is to be levied shall not by itself require authorities to terminate the definitive duty.

gation and other interested parties known to the investigating authorities to have an interest therein shall be notified and a public notice shall be given.

12.1.1 A public notice of the initiation of an investigation shall contain, or otherwise make available through a separate report,[23] adequate information on the following:

(i) the name of the exporting country or countries and the product involved;

(ii) the date of initiation of the investigation;

(iii) the basis on which dumping is alleged in the application;

(iv) a summary of the factors on which the allegation of injury is based;

(v) the address to which representations by interested parties should be directed;

(vi) the time-limits allowed to interested parties for making their views known.

12.2 Public notice shall be given of any preliminary or final determination, whether affirmative or negative, of any decision to accept an undertaking pursuant to Article 8, of the termination of such an undertaking, and of the termination of a definitive anti-dumping duty. Each such notice shall set forth, or otherwise make available through a separate report, in sufficient detail the findings and conclusions reached on all issues of fact and law considered material by the investigating authorities. All such notices and reports shall be forwarded to the Member or Members the products of which are subject to such determination or undertaking and to other interested parties known to have an interest therein.

12.2.1 A public notice of the imposition of provisional measures shall set forth, or otherwise make available through a separate report, sufficiently detailed explanations for the preliminary determinations on

---

[23]When authorities provide information and explanations under the provisions of this Article in a separate report, they shall ensure that such report is readily available to the public.

dumping and injury and shall refer to the matters of fact and law which have led to arguments being accepted or rejected. Such a notice or report shall, due regard being paid to the requirement for the protection of confidential information, contain in particular:

(i) the names of the suppliers, or when this is impracticable, the supplying countries involved;

(ii) a description of the product which is sufficient for customs purposes;

(iii) the margins of dumping established and a full explanation of the reasons for the methodology used in the establishment and comparison of the export price and the normal value under Article 2;

(iv) considerations relevant to the injury determination as set out in Article 3;

(v) the main reasons leading to the determination.

12.2.2 A public notice of conclusion or suspension of an investigation in the case of an affirmative determination providing for the imposition of a definitive duty or the acceptance of a price undertaking shall contain, or otherwise make available through a separate report, all relevant information on the matters of fact and law and reasons which have led to the imposition of final measures or the acceptance of a price undertaking, due regard being paid to the requirement for the protection of confidential information. In particular, the notice or report shall contain the information described in subparagraph 2.1, as well as the reasons for the acceptance or rejection of relevant arguments or claims made by the exporters and importers, and the basis for any decision made under subparagraph 10.2 of Article 6.

12.2.3 A public notice of the termination or suspension of an investigation following the acceptance of an undertaking pursuant to Article 8 shall include, or otherwise make available through a separate report, the non-confidential part of this undertaking.

12.3 The provisions of this Article shall apply *mutatis mutandis* to the initiation and completion of reviews pursuant to Article 11 and to decisions under Article 10 to apply duties retroactively.

## Article 13

## Judicial Review

Each Member whose national legislation contains provisions on anti-dumping measures shall maintain judicial, arbitral or administrative tribunals or procedures for the purpose, *inter alia,* of the prompt review of administrative actions relating to final determinations and reviews of determinations within the meaning of Article 11. Such tribunals or procedures shall be independent of the authorities responsible for the determination or review in question.

## Article 14

## Anti-Dumping Action on Behalf of a Third Country

14.1 An application for anti-dumping action on behalf of a third country shall be made by the authorities of the third country requesting action.

14.2 Such an application shall be supported by price information to show that the imports are being dumped and by detailed information to show that the alleged dumping is causing injury to the domestic industry concerned in the third country. The government of the third country shall afford all assistance to the authorities of the importing country to obtain any further information which the latter may require.

14.3 In considering such an application, the authorities of the importing country shall consider the effects of the alleged dumping on the industry concerned as a whole in the third country; that is to say, the injury shall not be assessed in relation only to the effect of the alleged dumping on the industry's exports to the importing country or even on the industry's total exports.

14.4 The decision whether or not to proceed with a case shall rest with the importing country. If the importing country decides that it is prepared to take action, the initiation of the approach to the Council for Trade in Goods seeking its approval for such action shall rest with the importing country.

*Article 15*

*Developing Country Members*

It is recognized that special regard must be given by developed country Members to the special situation of developing country Members when considering the application of anti-dumping measures under this Agreement. Possibilities of constructive remedies provided for by this Agreement shall be explored before applying anti-dumping duties where they would affect the essential interests of developing country Members.

## PART II

*Article 16*

*Committee on Anti-Dumping Practices*

16.1 There is hereby established a Committee on Anti-Dumping Practices (referred to in this Agreement as the "Committee") composed of representatives from each of the Members. The Committee shall elect its own Chairman and shall meet not less than twice a year and otherwise as envisaged by relevant provisions of this Agreement at the request of any Member. The Committee shall carry out responsibilities as assigned to it under this Agreement or by the Members and it shall afford Members the opportunity of consulting on any matters relating to the operation of the Agreement or the furtherance of its objectives. The WTO Secretariat shall act as the secretariat to the Committee.

16.2 The Committee may set up subsidiary bodies as appropriate.

16.3 In carrying out their functions, the Committee and any subsidiary bodies may consult with and seek information from any source they deem appropriate. However, before the Committee or a subsidiary body seeks such information from a source within the jurisdiction of a Member, it shall inform the Member involved. It shall obtain the consent of the Member and any firm to be consulted.

16.4 Members shall report without delay to the Committee all preliminary or final anti-dumping actions taken. Such reports shall be available in the Secretariat for inspection by other Members. Members shall also submit, on a semi- annual basis, reports of any anti-dumping actions taken within the preceding six months. The semi-annual reports shall be submitted on an agreed standard form.

16.5 Each Member shall notify the Committee *(a)* which of its authorities are competent to initiate and conduct investigations referred to in Article 5 and *(b)* its domestic procedures governing the initiation and conduct of such investigations.

## Article 17

### Consultation and Dispute Settlement

17.1 Except as otherwise provided herein, the Dispute Settlement Understanding is applicable to consultations and the settlement of disputes under this Agreement.

17.2 Each Member shall afford sympathetic consideration to, and shall afford adequate opportunity for consultation regarding, representations made by another Member with respect to any matter affecting the operation of this Agreement.

17.3 If any Member considers that any benefit accruing to it, directly or indirectly, under this Agreement is being nullified or impaired, or that the achievement of any objective is being impeded, by another Member or Members, it may, with a view to reaching a mutually satisfactory resolution of the matter, request in writing consultations with the Member or Members in question. Each Member shall afford sympathetic consideration to any request from another Member for consultation.

17.4 If the Member that requested consultations considers that the consultations pursuant to paragraph 3 have failed to achieve a mutually agreed solution, and if final action has been taken by the administering authorities of the importing Member to levy definitive anti-dumping duties or to accept price undertakings, it may refer the matter to the Dispute Settlement Body ("DSB"). When a provisional measure has a significant impact and the Member that requested consultations considers that the measure was taken contrary to the provisions of paragraph 1 of Article 7, that Member may also refer such matter to the DSB.

17.5 The DSB shall, at the request of the complaining party, establish a panel to examine the matter based upon:

(i) a written statement of the Member making the request indicating how a benefit accruing to it, directly or indirectly, under this Agreement has been nullified or impaired, or that the achieving of the objectives of the Agreement is being impeded, and

(ii) the facts made available in conformity with appropriate domestic procedures to the authorities of the importing Member.

17.6 In examining the matter referred to in paragraph 5:

(i) in its assessment of the facts of the matter, the panel shall determine whether the authorities' establishment of the facts was proper and whether their evaluation of those facts was unbiased and objective. If the establishment of the facts was proper and the evaluation was unbiased and objective, even though the panel might have reached a different conclusion, the evaluation shall not be overturned;

(ii) the panel shall interpret the relevant provisions of the Agreement in accordance with customary rules of interpretation of public international law. Where the panel finds that a relevant provision of the Agreement admits of more than one permissible interpretation, the panel shall find the authorities' measure to be in conformity with the Agreement if it rests upon one of those permissible interpretations.

17.7 Confidential information provided to the panel shall not be disclosed without formal authorization from the person, body or authority providing such information. Where such information is requested from the panel but release of such information by the panel is not authorized, a non-confidential summary of the information, authorized by the person, body or authority providing the information, shall be provided.

## PART III

### Article 18

### Final Provisions

18.1 No specific action against dumping of exports from another Member can be taken except in accordance with the provisions of GATT 1994, as interpreted by this Agreement.[24]

---

[24]This is not intended to preclude action under other relevant provisions of GATT 1994, as appropriate.

18.2 Reservations may not be entered in respect of any of the provisions of this Agreement without the consent of the other Members.

18.3 Subject to subparagraphs 3.1 and 3.2, the provisions of this Agreement shall apply to investigations, and reviews of existing measures, initiated pursuant to applications which have been made on or after the date of entry into force for a Member of the WTO Agreement.

18.3.1 With respect to the calculation of margins of dumping in refund procedures under paragraph 3 of Article 9, the rules used in the most recent determination or review of dumping shall apply.

18.3.2 For the purposes of paragraph 3 of Article 11, existing anti-dumping measures shall be deemed to be imposed on a date not later than the date of entry into force for a Member of the WTO Agreement, except in cases in which the domestic legislation of a Member in force on that date already included a clause of the type provided for in that paragraph.

18.4 Each Member shall take all necessary steps, of a general or particular character, to ensure, not later than the date of entry into force of the WTO Agreement for it, the conformity of its laws, regulations and administrative procedures with the provisions of this Agreement as they may apply for the Member in question.

18.5 Each Member shall inform the Committee of any changes in its laws and regulations relevant to this Agreement and in the administration of such laws and regulations.

18.6 The Committee shall review annually the implementation and operation of this Agreement taking into account the objectives thereof. The Committee shall inform annually the Council for Trade in Goods of developments during the period covered by such reviews.

18.7 The Annexes to this Agreement constitute an integral part thereof.

## ANNEX I

### PROCEDURES FOR ON-THE-SPOT INVESTIGATIONS PURSUANT TO PARAGRAPH 7 OF ARTICLE 6

1. Upon initiation of an investigation, the authorities of the exporting Member and the firms known to be concerned should be informed of the intention to carry out on-the-spot investigations.

2. If in exceptional circumstances it is intended to include non-governmental experts in the investigating team, the firms and the authorities of the exporting Member should be so informed. Such non-governmental experts should be subject to effective sanctions for breach of confidentiality requirements.

3. It should be standard practice to obtain explicit agreement of the firms concerned in the exporting Member before the visit is finally scheduled.

4. As soon as the agreement of the firms concerned has been obtained, the investigating authorities should notify the authorities of the exporting Member of the names and addresses of the firms to be visited and the dates agreed.

5. Sufficient advance notice should be given to the firms in question before the visit is made.

6. Visits to explain the questionnaire should only be made at the request of an exporting firm. Such a visit may only be made if *(a)* the authorities of the importing Member notify the representatives of the Member in question and *(b)* the latter do not object to the visit.

7. As the main purpose of the on-the-spot investigation is to verify information provided or to obtain further details, it should be carried out after the response to the questionnaire has been received unless the firm agrees to the contrary and the government of the exporting Member is informed by the investigating authorities of the anticipated visit and does not object to it; further, it should be standard practice prior to the visit to advise the firms concerned of the general nature of the information to be verified and of any further information which needs to be provided, though this should not preclude requests to be made on the spot for further details to be provided in the light of information obtained.

8. Enquiries or questions put by the authorities or firms of the exporting Members and essential to a successful on-the-spot investigation should, whenever possible, be answered before the visit is made.

## ANNEX II

### BEST INFORMATION AVAILABLE IN TERMS OF PARAGRAPH 8 OF ARTICLE 6

1. As soon as possible after the initiation of the investigation, the investigating authorities should specify in detail the information required from any

interested party, and the manner in which that information should be structured by the interested party in its response. The authorities should also ensure that the party is aware that if information is not supplied within a reasonable time, the authorities will be free to make determinations on the basis of the facts available, including those contained in the application for the initiation of the investigation by the domestic industry.

2. The authorities may also request that an interested party provide its response in a particular medium (e.g. computer tape) or computer language. Where such a request is made, the authorities should consider the reasonable ability of the interested party to respond in the preferred medium or computer language, and should not request the party to use for its response a computer system other than that used by the party. The authority should not maintain a request for a computerized response if the interested party does not maintain computerized accounts and if presenting the response as requested would result in an unreasonable extra burden on the interested party, e.g. it would entail unreasonable additional cost and trouble. The authorities should not maintain a request for a response in a particular medium or computer language if the interested party does not maintain its computerized accounts in such medium or computer language and if presenting the response as requested would result in an unreasonable extra burden on the interested party, e.g. it would entail unreasonable additional cost and trouble.

3. All information which is verifiable, which is appropriately submitted so that it can be used in the investigation without undue difficulties, which is supplied in a timely fashion, and, where applicable, which is supplied in a medium or computer language requested by the authorities, should be taken into account when determinations are made. If a party does not respond in the preferred medium or computer language but the authorities find that the circumstances set out in paragraph 2 have been satisfied, the failure to respond in the preferred medium or computer language should not be considered to significantly impede the investigation.

4. Where the authorities do not have the ability to process information if provided in a particular medium (e.g. computer tape), the information should be supplied in the form of written material or any other form acceptable to the authorities.

5. Even though the information provided may not be ideal in all respects, this should not justify the authorities from disregarding it, provided the interested party has acted to the best of its ability.

6. If evidence or information is not accepted, the supplying party should be informed forthwith of the reasons therefor, and should have an opportunity to provide further explanations within a reasonable period, due account being taken of the time-limits of the investigation. If the explanations are considered by the authorities as not being satisfactory, the reasons for the rejection of such evidence or information should be given in any published determinations.

7. If the authorities have to base their findings, including those with respect to normal value, on information from a secondary source, including the information supplied in the application for the initiation of the investigation, they should do so with special circumspection. In such cases, the authorities should, where practicable, check the information from other independent sources at their disposal, such as published price lists, official import statistics and customs returns, and from the information obtained from other interested parties during the investigation. It is clear, however, that if an interested party does not cooperate and thus relevant information is being withheld from the authorities, this situation could lead to a result which is less favourable to the party than if the party did cooperate.

# Appendix B

# Foreign Antidumping Laws

The United States is certainly not alone in its use of antidumping laws as a means of regulating unfair and potentially damaging foreign trade. As Table B.1 illustrates, the European Union, Canada, and Australia, to name but a few, have all initiated a significant number of antidumping measures in recent years. [1]

It is not only the world's leading economies that are employing antidumping laws, however. As trade begins to play an increasingly important role in emerging economies, they are implementing and employing antidumping procedures of their own. Table B.1 illustrates this new reality. In 1995–1996, three of the top five initiators of dumping actions were smaller, emerging markets. New users of antidumping law are likely to continue to emerge. [2] It seems probable, therefore, that the use of antidumping laws will continue to grow for the foreseeable future.

The Uruguay Round agreement brought antidumping controls firmly under the authority of the WTO. In part, this agreement was a response to the notorious lack of transparency that plagued many antidumping procedures around the world. For the most part, the Uruguay Round agreement simplified this process by enforcing uniformity in such significant areas as the issue of sunset reviews, *de minimis* margins, standards for proof, requirements for transparency, and the standing required to initiate an investigation. [3]

Nevertheless, certain significant differences remain in the way countries apply their antidumping laws. This appendix explores some of these differences by examining the antidumping laws in five representative entities: Canada, the European Union, and Australia, all long-established practitioners of antidumping law, and China and Mexico, two important economies that are just beginning to establish their antidumping procedures.

## Canada

Canada was the first country to adopt an antidumping law. Now Canada runs its antidumping program as a system of prospective enforcement. The

Table B.1

**Top Five Initiators of Antidumping Investigations, 1993–1996**

| 7/1/93–6/30/94 | | 7/1/94–6/30/95 | | 7/1/95–6/30/96 | |
|---|---|---|---|---|---|
| European Union | 47 | European Union | 37 | South Africa | 30 |
| United States | 47 | United States | 30 | Argentina | 27 |
| Australia | 45 | Mexico | 18 | European Union | 23 |
| Brazil | 30 | Brazil | 12 | United States | 21 |
| Mexico | 23 | Canada | 9 | India | 20 |
| | | New Zealand | 9 | | |
| | | Mexico | 9 | | |

*Source:* GATT/WTO.

Antidumping and Countervailing Duties Division of Revenue Canada (which is roughly equivalent to the U.S. Customs Service) establishes undumped export price levels to serve as "prospective normal values." Thus, exporters know the undumped price when they enter the market and can adjust their prices accordingly.[4] This system is relatively straightforward and does indeed reduce the amount of complaints filed and duties levied against exporters. Nevertheless, a significant number of antidumping investigations are launched every year.

Canada allows both individual companies and industry trade associations to submit antidumping complaints under the provisions of the Special Import Measures Act (SIMA). As specified in the WTO, however, at least 50 percent of the industry must agree to support the complaint. An additional national regulation requires that the product involved must represent at least 3 percent of Canada's total imports. Revenue Canada (RC) receives the complaint and initiates an investigation to determine if dumping has taken place.[5] RC's investigators tend to have a substantial amount of industry-specific knowledge and are highly regarded for the thoroughness of their investigations. If no dumping is found to have taken place, the investigation is halted and the complaint can proceed no further. If, however, dumping is determined to have occurred, the investigation is handed over to the Canadian International Trade Tribunal (CITT).

The CITT has three basic criteria that must be determined in an antidumping investigation: (1) Did the dumping result in material injury to Canadian producers of similar goods? (2) What is the level or extent of this material injury, on both a country-wide and individual exporter basis? (3) What is a suitable duty to be imposed upon the exporter? As is the case in most other antidumping statutes, the definition of "material injury" is never specifically codified in the SIMA and remains a subjective determination to be made by the members of the CITT.[6] Canada also applies the *de minimis* level of dumping required for the imposition of duties (which is 2 percent) on a country-wide basis; this means that an exporter who dumps below this level can still be included in an antidumping order as long as the dumping level for the entire exporting country exceeds the *de minimis* level. The United States, conversely, applies *de minimis* on an individual-exporter basis, automatically dismissing complaints against firms that dump at or below this *de minimis* standard.[7]

The CITT holds a hearing at which both sides may present their case. The petitioner, however, is not automatically granted access to the findings of Revenue Canada's investigation. Permission for this access must be specifically requested, and only a lawyer representing the petitioner is ever allowed to actually read the documents acquired. Once both sides have presented their case, a preliminary determination is made. If no material injury is found, or if it is not significant enough to warrant penalties, the investigation is halted. If, conversely, material injury is found, the case moves forward to a final determination under which duties are imposed.

The CITT virtually always applies an antidumping duty as a means of alleviating the material injury being caused by dumped imports. It should be noted that under Canadian law these "taxes" can be penalty-based; in other words, the duty may exceed the actual cost of the harm done by the dumping, although Canada has proved loath to apply such penalties, especially in cases involving important trading partners.[8] Conversely, an exporter can be relieved of these duties through the means of a suspension agreement. Generally, if the importer will agree to suspend dumping, the CITT will agree not to levy the duty, although it retains the right to do so if dumping should reoccur. Canada has had a sunset review period of five years since 1984, and it remains in force under the WTO.[9] After this period, duties are eliminated unless domestic producers can prove that dumping is likely to reoccur.

## European Union

The European Union generally initiates a substantial number of dumping investigations each year, although officials are quick to point out that these investigations only affect about 0.7 percent of their total imports.[10] When a complaint for dumping is brought, the European Commission receives the complaint and has forty-five days to decide if there is sufficient cause to justify launching an investigation. During this period it consults with its member states through the Advisory Committee, which closely monitors all antidumping actions. Once an investigation is launched, the commission must notify all of the parties involved, and then has twelve to fifteen months to complete its work.[11]

Whereas Canada issues a surrogate normal value preemptively in order to prevent dumping, the European Union, like the United States, sets this value only after an investigation has been launched and only for nonmarket economies (NMEs) in which determining actual price is impossible. Otherwise, actual price is determined through a series of questionnaires submitted to all the parties involved in the investigation.[12] From these questionnaires the commission must determine if three essential criteria are met: (1) Did dumping take place? (2) Did dumping cause material injury to the EU industry? (3) Is it in "the community's interest" to impose antidumping measures? If any of these criteria are not met, the investigation is ended. Of course, the question of material injury remains a fundamentally subjective one. The question of community interest grants the EU considerable discretion in implementation and contributes to an overall lack of transparency in this phase of the EU's procedures.[13]

If all three of these criteria are satisfied, however, provisional duties may be applied by the European Commission after consulting with the Advisory Committee. These provisional duties are in effect for six months (although they can be extended for an additional three months if circumstances warrant), cannot exceed the dumping margin, and must in fact be set at a lower level if it would be sufficient to remove injury. Importers must lodge security for the payment of these duties when they import goods in question, and must continue to do so until definitive duties are set.

Although the European Commission may make recommendations for definitive duties (except in the case of steel and coal products, in which it has the power to levy fines), it is the Council of Ministers that must ultimately determine the imposition of these penalties through a majority vote.[14] Antidumping duties may be assessed as either a percentage of the imported product (ad valorem duties) or a fixed amount per unit. As with provisional duties, definitive duties may not exceed the injury caused by dumping, although they may be retroactively applied up to ninety days in the past. Further, the European Union has a provision in its antidumping code termed "duty as cost."[15] If an exporter's prices fail to rise in either the dumped or domestic market, it is assumed that the firm is merely absorbing the duty as a cost of doing business. Therefore, the margin of dumping is increased and a higher duty can be imposed. These and all duties are subject to sunset review after five years, although interim reviews can be initiated during this period if there is evidence that circumstances have changed significantly.

Exporters subject to duties may, and quite often do, propose an undertaking to increase prices to a level which removes injury or stops dumping. Provided that there is an adequate system of monitoring in place, this option is generally seen as an acceptable alternative to the imposition of duties. As a final appeal, an exporter may seek redress from the European Court of First Instance or, if there has been an error on a point of law, from the European Court of Justice.[16]

## Australia

Australia was an early adopter of antidumping legislation and remains one of its most active users. In addition to WTO provisions, antidumping procedures are covered by the Customs Act of 1901 and the Customs Tariff (Anti-Dumping) Act of 1975.[17]

When a petition to initiate an antidumping investigation is received, it is handled by the Anti-Dumping Authority (ADA). The ADA has twenty-five days to decide if sufficient grounds exist for an investigation, and once it has done so it passes this duty on to the Customs Department. The Customs Department must then establish three factors: (1) Did dumping occur? (2) Did material injury occur? (3) Is there a causal link between dumping and the injury?[18] It should be noted that the Customs Department acts only in an investigatory role, compiling information through a series of questionnaires and on-site visits.

Once the investigation is complete, Customs turns the matter back over to the ADA for adjudication. The ADA can choose to end the matter if the three criteria are not met, or issue interim dumping duties if they are.[19] It is only at this point that the "normal price" of a dumped product is officially established, and duties are levied based upon this determination. It should be noted that at present Australia has a system in place that distinguishes between market economies and NMEs, making this aspect of the investigation particularly difficult. Like the EU and the United States, Australia uses a third country whose economic conditions closely resemble that of the NME as a surrogate market for determining normal value; legislation is currently pending that would end the use of these third-country determinations.[20]

Interim duties that are assessed may not exceed the cost of dumping and are in effect for no longer than 120 days. After 120 days, the ADA must issue a final report with recommendations to the Minister for Customs, who will make the final determination and impose the duties required to remove injury. The duties levied by the Minister may not be penalty-based (as in Canada) and must be the lowest amount required to remove the injury. These duties remain in effect until after a five-year sunset review, and generally the ADA does not allow for undertakings or other means that would require the suspension of these duties, although interim reviews are occasionally granted if an exporter can demonstrate that circumstances have changed dramatically.[21]

## China

For most of its history, China maintained a strictly regulated system of imports that made explicit antidumping laws unnecessary. In recent years, however, China has begun to liberalize its trade practices, and this, combined with its intent to enter the World Trade Organization, has led it to adopt antidumping regulations.[22] In April 1997, China promulgated its first antidumping and countervailing-duty legislation after over two years of preparation.

The Chinese antidumping law has proven to be an almost instantaneous source of controversy. The law states in its opening that if "any country or region adopts discriminatory antidumping or antisubsidy measures" against China, it can in turn "adopt corresponding measures against that country or region." This provision, and the retaliatory system implied in the law's language, clearly violates the rules of the World Trade Organization and would almost certainly be overturned on appeal to the WTO.[23] Indeed, lawyers argue that many of the provisions of this new law violate WTO codes and, unless changed, could prevent China from becoming a member of the organization. In December 1997, China brought an antidumping case against newsprint from the United States, Canada, and South Korea.[24] As this book goes to press, the case is still pending, but its outcome will no doubt serve as an important test of China's new antidumping law and its intention to adhere to the regulations laid out in the Uruguay Round agreement.[25]

China's antidumping law, should it stand, promises to create one of the more complex systems for administering complaints. The Ministry of Foreign Trade and Economic Cooperation (MOFTEC) receives applications from industry representatives (there is no provision made for individual companies to petition, although it is not explicitly forbidden) to initiate antidumping investigations, and must decide in conjunction with the State Economic and Trade Commission (SETC) whether or not to follow through on a complaint. It should be noted that while the WTO requires 50 percent of a domestic industry to support such a complaint, China's law has no such provisions.[26] Once an investigation begins, MOFTEC shares responsibilities in this process with the General Administration of Customs to determine if dumping has occurred. While most countries have either accepted the GATT definition of dumping or promulgated very similar definitions, China's conception of the term is never explicitly defined in their antidumping law, nor is the process for establishing the meaning and extent of material injury.[27] There are many aspects of the world's antidumping codes that allow subjective judgments, but considering China's history of closed trade and the retaliatory overtones contained in the law, this vagueness has proved to be particularly disconcerting for those who do business in China.

Once dumping is determined to have taken place, however, it is left to the SETC and related departments of the State Council to administer the imposition of duties. There are no specific limits placed on the amount of either interim or final duties, but the law states that it should "be in line with the extent of dumping." The taxes may be applied retroactively by the SETC, but they expire after five years. There is no provision for judicial review of antidumping orders.[28]

## Mexico

Mexico has become an increasingly frequent user of antidumping procedures over the past five years, but its system has, in many ways, not evolved as its role in world trade has expanded. Mexico passed a Foreign Trade Law in 1993 that established its antidumping code. In the years following this law, Mexico signed several international treaties (NAFTA, the Uruguay Round agreements) containing antidumping provisions that contradicted the procedures provided in the Foreign Trade Law. Under Mexican law, these international regulations have precedence and govern the way the antidumping code is administered, even though the national law remains (at least as this book is going to press) unamended.[29]

The rules of the GATT and the WTO are, therefore, used as the guides in antidumping cases. Complaints are investigated by the Mexican Secretaría de Comercio y Fomento Industrial (SECOFI), the Mexican equivalent of the U.S. Commerce Department. SECOFI has often been criticized for the lack of transparency in its investigations and decisions, but as it has begun to apply the provisions of the WTO to its antidumping investigations this criticism has quieted somewhat.[30] After an investigation has been made and both dumping and material injury have been found to have taken place, the issue is passed to the Foreign Trade Commission.[31] The FTC was created to act as a source of oversight for SECOFI's investigations and is representative of the efforts by the Mexican government to make their antidumping process as impartial as possible. The commission is relatively toothless, however, and can only make nonbinding recommendations about the penalty to be imposed.[32] The matter is now passed back to SECOFI, which makes the final determination of penalty and is ultimately responsible for enforcing it under Mexican law. This penalty generally takes the form of an antidumping duty sufficient enough to remove the injury, although it can exceed this amount. The penalty expires after a sunset review in five years, and interim reviews are possible if circumstances have sufficiently changed to warrant the reopening of the case.

It should be noted that while Mexico has acted in good faith to apply the WTO antidumping code to members of the WTO, non-WTO members are not granted this consideration and are subject to the relatively obscure antidumping process laid out in the Foreign Trade Law. For instance, after a complaint was filed against China, SECOFI instituted a preliminary duty that went into effect after only five days. This meant that a mere five days after the initiation of the investigation, supplemental tariffs ranging from 300 percent to 1,100 percent were imposed against 25 percent of all Chinese imports to Mexico.[33] Such actions would be unlikely to survive WTO scrutiny.

## Notes

1. Tim Cohen, "SA Most Active in Introducing Antidumping Rules," *Business Day,* November 17, 1997, p.1; Simon Henderson, "EU Defends Dumping Measures," *Financial Times Business Reports,* August 15, 1997, pp. 2–3.

2. World Trade Organization, *GATT Activities 1994–1995* (Geneva: WTO, 1996), pp. 77–78.

3. Gilbert R. Winham and Heather A. Grant, "Antidumping and Countervailing Duties in Regional Trade Agreements: Canada-U.S. FTA, NAFTA and Beyond," *Minnesota Journal of Global Trade,* vol. 3 (Spring 1994): 2.

4. Peter Clark, *A Comparison of the Antidumping Systems of Canada and the USA* (Ottawa: International Economic Relations Division, Department of Finance, 1996) p. 1.

5. Ibid., p. 4.

6. Revenue Canada, *Protective Measures for Canadian Products Against Unfair Foreign Competition,* May 30, 1997, at http://www.rc.gc.ca.

7. Clark, *Comparison,* p. 5.

8. This regulation may not be consistent with the rules laid out by the WTO, and has never been tested before one of their review boards.

9. Clark, *Comparison,* pp. 5–7.

10. Patrick Laurent, "Anti-dumping Policies in a Globalising World," remarks before the European Commission, Stockholm, Sweden, November 5, 1996.

11. European Commission, *Protection Against Dumped Imports, Regulation 384/96,* available at http://europa.eu.int.

12. As noted in Chapter 6, in December 1997 China and Russia were removed from the EU's list of NMEs and became eligible for this process for the first time.

13. Samuel M. Witten, "International Decision: European Community Case Note," *The American Journal of International Law,* vol. 87 (April 1993): 299.

14. European Commission, *Protection Against Dumped Imports.*

15. Laurent, "Anti-dumping Policies."

16. European Commission, *Protection Against Dumped Imports.*

17. Gary Banks, "The Anti-Dumping Experience of a GATT-Fearing Country," in *Antidumping: How It Works and Who Gets Hurt,* J. Michael Finger, ed. (Ann Arbor: University of Michigan Press, 1993), pp. 184–185.

18. Australian Parliament, *Customs Tariff (Anti-Dumping) Bill 1997: Bill Digest* (Canberra: Australian Parliamentary Library, 1997–1998).

19. The Hon. Geoff Prosser, MP, "Minister Releases Review of Anti-Dumping System," Press Release of the Minister responsible for Customs, Australian Government, December 13, 1996.

20. Australian Parliament, *Customs Tariff.*

21. Ibid.

22. "China Drafts Remedy Law to Impose as Early as This Year," *Inside U.S. Trade,* July 27, 1995, p. 21.

23. "China Approves Vague Trade Remedy Law Threatening Retaliation," *Inside U.S. Trade,* April 11, 1997, p. 1.

24. "EU Adjusts Antidumping Law for Chinese, Russian Industries," *Inside U.S. Trade,* December 19, 1997, p. 8.

25. "Chinese AD/CVD Regulations," republished in *Inside U.S. Trade,* April 11, 1997.

26. "China Approves Vague Trade Remedy Law Threatening Retaliation."

27. "Chinese AD/CVD Regulations."

28. Ibid.

29. Michael W. Gordon, Harvey Applebaum, Gabriel Castaneda Gallardo, Terence P. Stewart, and John Gero, "Challenges By Competitors and Governments in Response to Foreign Subsidies, Dumping and Import Surges," *United States–Mexico Law Journal,* vol. 4 (1996): 113.

30. Winham and Grant, "Antidumping," p. 105.

31. This is an illustrative example of how the WTO supersedes Mexican law—the Foreign Trade Law made provisions that "injury" must occur for penalties to be enforced. Once the Uruguay Round went into effect, however, Mexican officials began to use the more specifically defined standard of "material injury."

32. Gordon et al., "Challenges," p. 113.

33. Ibid., p. 111.

# Bibliography

Acs, Zoltan, *The Changing Structure of the U.S. Economy: Lessons from the Steel Industry* (New York: Praeger, 1984).

Adams, F. Gerard and Andrew R. Wechsler, *Conditions of Competition and the Business Cycle for Gray Portland Cement,* monograph submitted in connection with ITA consideration of the Mexican cement antidumping case, 1990.

Ahlbrandt, Roger S., *Involvement of the U.S. Government in the Steel Industry,* Global Study of the Steel Industry Working Paper Series (Pittsburgh: University of Pittsburgh and Carnegie-Mellon University, 1992).

Ahlbrandt, Roger S. and Frank Giarrantani, *The European Communities: Responding to the Crises in the Global Steel Industry,* Global Study of the Steel Industry Working Paper Series (Pittsburgh: University of Pittsburgh and Carnegie-Mellon University, 1992).

Akakwam, Philip A., "The Standard of Review in the 1994 Antidumping Code: Circumscribing the Role of GATT Panels in Reviewing National Antidumping Determinations," *Minnesota Journal of Global Trade* (Summer 1996): 277–310.

Arnold, James R., "The Oilseeds Dispute and the Validity of Unilateralism in a Multilateral Context," *Stanford Journal of International Law* 30 (1994): 187.

Artis, M.J. and N. Lee, *The Economics of the European Union* (Oxford: Oxford University Press, 1994).

Auerbach, Stuart, "U.S. Weighs Trade Move Against Japan," *Washington Post,* March 28, 1984, 7.

———, "Trade Panel Backs U.S. on Complaint Against Japan; GATT Unit Rules that Imports of Many Agricultural Products Unfairly Restricted," *Washington Post,* November 5, 1987, E2.

———, "Japan Stalls Response to GATT Finding; Nation Tries to Block Portions of Trade Ruling," *Washington Post,* December 3, 1987, C1.

———. "The Scramble To Stay Clear of 'Super 301'; Foreign Producers Fear U.S. Trade List," *Washington Post,* April 11, 1989, E1.

———, "Hills: Threat of Unfair Trade List Effective; Countries Now More Willing to Negotiate with U.S. on Barriers," *Washington Post,* May 13, 1989, D12.

———, "U.S. Eyes Three Nations for Unfair Trading; Japan, India and Brazil May Be Cited," *Washington Post,* May 20, 1989, D11.

———, "Bush Hears Debate on Japan Trade; Advisors Dispute 'Unfair' Label," *Washington Post,* May 23, 1989, C1.

———, "Global Stakes High as Decision on Japan Trade Nears," *Washington Post,* May 25, 1989, C12.

———, "Japan Cited by Bush as Unfair Trader; Brazil, India on List: Tokyo 'Disappointed,' " *Washington Post,* May 26, 1989, A1.

———, "Hills Defends Aggressive Trade Policy; Better System Is Goal, U.S. Official Says," *Washington Post,* June 9, 1989, F2.

————, "Japan off U.S. Unfair Trader List; India Singled out for Possible Retaliation," *Washington Post,* April 28, 1990, D10.

————, "U.S. Won't Retaliate Against India on Trade," *Washington Post,* June 14, 1990, C1.

————, "Raising a Roar over a Ruling; Trade Pact Imperils Environmental Laws," *Washington Post,* October 1, 1991, D1.

————, "Democrats Seek to Extend Tough Trade Law; Measure Allows Sanctions Against Nations that Don't Drop Barriers," *Washington Post,* November 5, 1991, D1.

Australian Parliament, *Customs Tariff (Anti-Dumping) Bill 1997: Bill Digest,* Australian Parliamentary Library, 1997–98.

Baker, Steven, "Why Steel Is Looking Sexy," *Business Week,* April 4, 1994, 106–108.

Balassa, Ben and Marcus Noland, *Japan in the World Economy* (Washington, DC: Institute for International Economics, 1988).

Baldwin, Richard E. and Paul R. Krugman, "Market Access and International Competition: A Simulation Study of 16K Random Access Memories," in *Empirical Methods for International Trade,* R. Feenstra, ed. (Cambridge, MA: MIT Press, 1988).

Banks, Gary, "The Anti-dumping Experience of a GATT-fearing Country," in *Anti-dumping: How It Works and Who Gets Hurt,* J. Michael Finger, ed. (Ann Arbor: University of Michigan Press, 1993).

Barfield, Claude E., "Brother of Gephardt," *Washington Post,* March 9, 1988, A25.

————, "Dumping Know-Nothingism," *Journal of Commerce,* March 18, 1993.

Barnard, Bruce, "Brittan Says His Proposal Won't Copy U.S. Trade Act," *Journal of Commerce,* December 1, 1994, 3A.

Barnett, Donald F. and Robert W. Crandall, *Up from the Ashes: The Rise of the Steel Minimill in the United States* (Washington, DC: Brookings Institution, 1986).

Barnett, Donald F. and Louis Schorsch, *Steel: Upheaval in a Basic Industry* (Cambridge, MA: Ballinger, 1983).

Barnette, Curtis H., "CEO Interview: Bethlehem Steel Corp.," *The Wall Street Transcript* 70, no. 11 (June 14, 1993).

————, Excerpt from speech, "Comments on International Trade," *The Wall Street Transcript* 71, no. 1 (July 5, 1993).

Baron, D.P., "Integrated Strategy, Trade Policy, and Global Competition," *California Management Review* 39, no. 2 (September 30, 1997): 145–161.

Bayard, Thomas O. and Kimberly Ann Elliot, *Reciprocity and Retaliation in U.S. Trade Policy* (Washington, DC: Institute for International Economics, 1994).

Beachy, Debra, "Local Firm Says Mexicans Dumped Steel; Executive Says Actions Have Decimated a Good Market for Texas Companies," *Houston Chronicle,* April 6, 1995, 1.

Beals, Vaughn L., "Harley-Davidson's Key Argument for Tariff Protection," *New York Times,* April 20, 1983.

Beeson, Patty and Frank Giarrantani, *Competitive Adjustment in the U.S. Steel Industry: Some Spatial Aspects of Capacity Change by Integrated Producers,* Global Study of the Steel Industry Working Paper Series (Pittsburgh: University of Pittsburgh and Carnegie-Mellon University, 1993).

Behr, Peter, "12 Nations Are Cited on Steel Exports; Preliminary U.S. Ruling Calls Practices Unfair," *Washington Post,* December 1, 1992, B1.

————, "19 Countries Are Cited for Steel Dumping," *Washington Post,* January 28, 1993, D11.

————, "Steel Firms Gain a Split Decision in Imports Case," *The Washington Post,* July 28, 1993, D1.

———,"Environmentalists Find NAFTA Is No Easy Call; National Groups Remain Sharply Divided," *Washington Post,* August 24, 1993, C2.

———, "Clinton Aims a Warning Shot on Trade—Away from Japan," *Washington Post,* March 4, 1994, B1.

———, "As Trade Triumphs Fade, Clinton Faces Series of Tough Fights," *Washington Post,* May 14, 1994, C1.

———, "White House Seeks Change in Antidumping Penalties," *Washington Post,* June 25, 1994, B1.

Bello, Judith H. et al., "Searching for 'Bubbles of Capitalism': Application of the U.S. Antidumping and Countervailing Duty Laws to Reforming Nonmarket Economies," *George Washington Journal of International Law and Economics* 21 (1992): 665–673.

Bello, Judith H. and Alan Holmer, "GATT Dispute Settlement Agreement: Internationalization or Elimination of Section 301," *International Lawyer* 26 (Fall 1990).

———, *Guide to the U.S.-Canada Free Trade Agreement* (Englewood Cliffs, NJ: Prentice Hall Law and Business, 1990).

Bhagwati, Jagdish and Hugh T. Patrick, *Aggressive Unilateralism* (Ann Arbor: University of Michigan Press, 1990).

Bhala, Raj, "Rethinking Antidumping Law," *George Washington Journal of International Law and Economics* (1995): 70–141.

Blecker, Robert A., Thea M. Lee and Robert E. Scott, *Trade Protection and Industrial Revitalization: American Steel in the 1980s* (Washington, DC: Economic Policy Institute, 1993).

Borrus, Michael and Jeffrey A. Hart, "Display's the Thing: The Real Stakes in the Conflict over High-resolution Displays," *Journal of Policy Analysis and Management* 13, no. 1 (1994).

Bounds, Wendy, "Fuji Photo Film Signs Accord on U.S. Pricing, Japanese Firm Will Raise Charges on Color Paper; Kodak, Konica Benefit," *Wall Street Journal,* August 22, 1994, A4.

Bovard, James, "Commerce's Latest Fair Trade Fraud," *Wall Street Journal,* January 28, 1993.

Bradsher, Keith, "Canada Beer Dispute Flares on Eve of Trade Talks," *New York Times,* July 25, 1992, 35.

Brander, James and Barbara Spencer, "Export Subsidies and International Market Share Rivalry," *Journal of International Economics* (February 1985).

Burnham, James B., *Changes and Challenges: The Transformation of the U.S. Steel Industry,* Policy Study 115 (St. Louis: Washington University, 1993).

Buzbee, Bill, Testimony before the International Trade Commission, August 27, 1997, at http://www.scd.ucar.edu./info/itc.html.

Cadbaw, R. Michael, "Intellectual Property and International Trade: Merger or Marriage of Convenience?" *Vanderbilt Journal of Transnational Law* 22 (Spring 1989).

Calvani, Terry and Gilde Breidenbach, "An Introduction to the Robinson-Patman Act and Its Enforcement by the Government," *Antitrust Law Journal* (Fall 1990): 765–775.

Cartland, Michael, "Antidumping and Competition Policy," *Law and Policy in International Business* 28 (1994): 289.

Chimerine, Lawrence, Alan Tonelson, Karl von Schriltz and Gregory Stanko, *Can the Phoenix Survive? The Fall and Rise of the American Steel Industry* (Washington, DC: Economic Strategy Institute, 1994).

"China Approves Vague Trade Remedy Law Threatening Retaliation," *Inside U.S. Trade,* April 11, 1997, 1.

"China Drafts Remedy Law to Impose as Early as This Year," *Inside U.S. Trade,* July 27, 1995, 21.

"Chinese AD/CVD Regulations," *Inside U.S. Trade*, April 11, 1997.

Choate, Pat, *Agents of Influence: How Japan Manipulates America's Political and Economic System* (New York: Simon and Schuster, 1990).

Chow, Tai-Hwa, *Industrial Policy of Japan: The Steel Industry (1950–1990)*, Global Study of the Steel Industry Working Paper Series (Pittsburgh: University of Pittsburgh and Carnegie-Mellon University, 1993).

Chung, Michael Y., "U.S. Antidumping Laws: A Look at the New Legislation," *North Carolina Journal of International Law & Commercial Regulation* 20 (Summer 1995).

Clark, Gordon L., *Corporate Restructuring in the U.S. Steel Industry: Adjustment Strategies and Local Labor Relations*, working paper (Pittsburgh: Carnegie-Mellon University, 1987).

Clark, Peter, *A Comparison of the Antidumping Systems of Canada and the USA* (Ottawa: International Economic Relations Division, Department of Finance, 1996).

Coalition for Open Trade, *Addressing Private Restraints of Trade: Industries and Governments Search for Answers Regarding Trade-and-Competition Policy* (Washington, DC: COT, 1997).

Codevilla, David A., "Discouraging the Practice of What We Preach: Saarstahl I, Inland Steel and the Implementation of the Uruguay Round of GATT 1994," *George Mason Independent Law Review* (Summer 1995): 435.

Cohen, Tim, "SA Most Active in Introducing Antidumping Rules," *Business Day*, November 17, 1997, 1.

Cohn, Lynne M., "Benedict Set to Tackle Dumping of Metal by Developing Nations," *American Metal Market*, August 24, 1994, 6.

Cole, Jeff, "Boeing Contests Loan Request for Russian Jets—Plane Maker Sees Danger in Backing for Engines from Pratt and Whitney," *Wall Street Journal*, March 6, 1995, A2.

Congressional Budget Office, *A Review of U.S. Antidumping and Countervailing-Duty Law and Policy* (Washington, DC: CBO, 1994).

———, *U.S. Antidumping and Countervailing Duty Law: A Policy Untethered from Its Rationale* (Washington, DC: CBO, 1994).

Corden, Max, "Monopoly, Tariffs and Subsidies," *Economica* 34 (1967): 50–58.

Cordray, Monique L., "GATT v. WIPO," *Journal of the Patent and Trademark Office Society* 70 (February 1994).

Correnti, John D., Excerpt from speech, "Correnti Credits Culture for Success," *American Metal Market*, August 4, 1993, 14.

Crandall, Robert W., *The U.S. Steel Industry in Recurrent Crises: Policy Options in a Competitive World* (Washington, DC: Brookings Institution, 1981).

Cronk, Jack, Excerpt from speech, "Let's Ask Our Customers What's Expected," *American Metal Market*, September 21, 1993, 14.

Crutsinger, Martin, "U.S., Japan Reach Deals, Heading off Trade War," *Commercial Appeal* (Memphis), October 2, 1994.

Culbertson, William Smith, *Commercial Policy in War Time and After* (New York and London: D. Appleton, 1924).

Danforth, John C., "Trade Accord Should Be Renegotiated," *St. Louis Post-Dispatch*, February 13, 1994, 3B.

Darlin, Damon, "Japan's Farm Lobby Fighting Reforms by Exploiting National Distrust of U.S.," *Wall Street Journal*, July 7, 1988.

———, "Closing Door: South Korea Regresses on Opening Markets, Trade Partners Say," *Wall Street Journal*, June 12, 1990, A1.

Darnall, Robert J., Excerpt from speech, "On Steel Technology," *The Wall Street Transcript* 71, no. 1 (July 5, 1993).

Davis, Bob, "Economy: Japanese and U.S. Business Groups Propose Plan to Resolve Trade Tensions," *Wall Street Journal,* June 24, 1994, A2.

De Hercalito Lima, Jose Guilherme, *Restructuring the U.S. Steel Industry: Semi-Finished Steel Imports, International Integration, and U.S. Adoption* (Boulder, CO: Westview Press, 1991).

Department of Commerce, *U.S. Foreign Trade Highlights* (Washington, DC: DOC, 1990).

Dewey, Ballantine, Bushby, and Wood, *Privatizing Protection: Japanese Market Barriers in Consumer Photographic Film and Consumer Photographic Paper,* report prepared for Eastman Kodak Company, May 1995.

Dewey, Ballantine, Bushby, and Wood, *Japanese Barriers on Imported Photographic Film and Paper* (Washington, DC: Dewey Ballantine, 1997).

Dick, Andrew, "Learning-by-doing and Dumping in the Semiconductor Industry," *Journal of Law and Economics* 34 (1991): 133–159.

Dickens, William and Kevin Lang, "Why It Matters What We Make: A Case for Active Trade Policy," in *The Dynamics of Trade and Employment,* William Dickens, Laura D'Andrea Tyson, and John Zysman, eds. (Cambridge, MA: Ballinger Press, 1988).

Dryden, Steven, *Trade Warriors* (New York: Oxford University Press, 1995).

Du Bois, Martin, "EC Ministers Clear Aid Plan for Steelmakers: Six State-Owned Companies to Receive $7.66 Billion In Bid to Revive Industry," *Wall Street Journal,* December 20, 1993, A9.

Dumler, Christopher M., *Anti-dumping Laws Trash Supercomputer Competition,* CATO Briefing Paper no. 32 (Washington, DC: CATO Institute, 1997).

Dunne, Nancy, "U.S. Threatens WTO Complaint Against Japan," *Financial Times,* March 29, 1995, 6.

*EC Commission Decision of July 18, 1990,* Official Journal No. L 220/28, August 15, 1990.

Eches, Alfred E., Excerpt from speech, "Import Restraints Can Fuel Growth," *American Metal Market,* July 5, 1993.

Economist Intelligence Unit, "USA Trade: Polls Find Public Indifferent to NAFTA," *EIU ViewsWire,* December 19, 1997.

Ehrenhaft, Peter D., Brian Vernon Hindley, Constantine Michalopoulos and L. Alan Winters, *Policies on Imports from Economies in Transition: Two Case Studies,* World Bank Studies of Economies in Transition Series (Washington, DC: World Bank, 1997).

"EU Adjusts Antidumping Law for Chinese, Russian Industries," *Inside U.S. Trade,* December 19, 1997, 8.

European Commission, *Protection Against Dumped Imports, Regulation 384/96,* available at http://europa.eu.int.

*Federal Register,* "Antidumping and Countervailing Duty Procedures," vol. 62, no. 96 (May 19, 1997): 27383–27405.

Federal Trade Commission, Bureau of Economics, *Effects of Unfair Imports on Domestic Industries: U.S. Antidumping and Countervailing Duty Cases, 1980 to 1988,* by Morris E. Morkre and Kenneth H. Kelly (Washington, DC: FTC, 1994).

Fenton, Frank, "World Steel Trade: New Directions in the Americas and Pacific Basin," remarks at the national convention of the American Institute for International Steel, New Orleans, March 19, 1994.

Ferdinand, Pamela, "Six Flat-Roll Makers Fined for Running Illegal Cartel," *American Metal Market,* July 20, 1990.

*Final Texts of the GATT Uruguay Round Agreements,* "Agreement on Subsidies and Countervailing Measures," published by the GATT, October 1994.

————, "Agreement on Implementation of Article VI of the General Agreement on Tariffs and Trade," published by the GATT, October 1994.

————, "Agreement on Agriculture," published by the GATT, October 1994.

Finger, J. Michael, ed., *Antidumping: How It Works and Who Gets Hurt* (Ann Arbor: University of Michigan Press, 1993).

Finger, J. Michael, *The Origins and Evolution of Antidumping Regulation,* Trade Policy Working Paper (Washington, DC: World Bank, October 1991).

Flamm, Kenneth, *Mismanaged Trade? Strategic Policy and the Semiconductor Industry* (Washington, DC: Brookings Institution, 1996).

Flat Panel Display Task Force, *Building U.S. Capabilities in Flat Panel Displays, Final Report* (Washington, DC: DOD, 1994).

Fletcher, Jeremy, "Structural Changes in the Stainless Steel Industry," speech at *Metal Bulletin*'s convention "Stainless Steel and Its Raw Materials," Marbella, Spain, June 12–15, 1990.

Fors, Gunnar, "Stainless Steel in Sweden: Antidumping Attacks Responsible International Citizenship," in *Antidumping: How It Works and Who Gets Hurt,* J. Michael Finger, ed. (Ann Arbor: University of Michigan Press, 1993).

Friedberg, Aaron L., *The Weary Titan: Britain and the Experience of Relative Decline, 1895–1905* (Princeton: Princeton University Press, 1988).

"Frozen Pipes," *The Economist,* April 6, 1991, 69.

"Fuji Statement on Signing Suspension Agreement with Department of Commerce," *Business Wire,* August 9, 1994.

Garten, Jeffrey, *A Cold Peace: America, Japan, Germany, and the Struggle for Supremacy* (New York: Twentieth Century Fund, 1992).

Garvey, Robert, Excerpt from speech, "The Role of Materials Recycling in Solid Waste Solutions for the 21st Century," *The Wall Street Transcript* 71, no. 1 (July 5, 1993).

Gellman Research Associates, Inc., *An Economic and Financial Review of Airbus Industrie* (Jenkintown, PA: U.S. Department of Commerce, 1990).

General Accounting Office, *International Trade: The Health of the U.S. Steel Industry* (Washington, DC: GAO, 1989).

"German Exchange Rate Scheme Found to be Export Subsidy for Airbus Parts," *Inside U.S. Trade,* January 24, 1992, 1.

Gordon, Greg, "Trade Ruling Favors Cray in Rift with Japan Firms; NEC, Others Found Guilty of 'Dumping,' " *Minneapolis Star Tribune,* September 27, 1997, 1D.

Gordon, Michael W., Harvey Appelbaum, Gabriel Castaneda Gallardo, Terence P. Stewart and John Gero, "Challenges by Competitors and Governments in Response to Foreign Subsidies, Dumping and Import Surges," *United States–Mexico Law Journal,* 1996, 107–123.

Gould, David M. and William C. Gruben, "Will Fair Trade Diminish Free Trade?" *Business Economics* 32, no. 2 (April 1997): 7.

Grant, John H., *Steel Industry Trends in U.S.A.—1993,* working paper (Pittsburgh: University of Pittsburgh, 1993).

Grant, John H., Roger S. Ahlbrandt, Frank Giarrantani and John E. Prescott, *Restructuring for Competitiveness in the Global Steel Industry,* Global Study of the Steel Industry Working Paper Series (Pittsburgh: University of Pittsburgh and Carnegie-Mellon University, 1993).

Green, Paula L., "Poll: 57 Percent of US Public Against Free-trade Pacts with Latin America," *Journal of Commerce,* November 8, 1996, 2A.

Griliches, Zvi, *The Search for R&D Spillovers* (Cambridge, MA: Harvard University Press, 1990).

Grossman, Gene M., ed., *Imperfect Competition and International Trade* (Cambridge, MA: MIT Press, 1994).

Grossman, Gene M. and Elhanan Helpman, *Innovation and Growth in the Global Economy* (Cambridge, MA: MIT Press, 1991).

Gruber, Harold, *Learning and Strategic Product Innovation Theory and Evidence for the Semiconductor Industry* (Amsterdam: North Holland, 1994).

Haflich, Frank, "Nucor Corp. Assesses German Thin-Slab Casting Technology," *American Metal Market,* December 2, 1993.

Hamel, Gary and C.K. Prahalad, "Do You Really Have a Global Strategy," *Harvard Business Review,* July-August 1985: 139.

Hamilton, Alexander, *Report on Manufactures,* 1791.

Hardie, Crista, "Two Korean Memory Makers Challenge Anti-Dump Order," *Electronic News,* May 26, 1997, 13.

Harding, James, "China: EU Gesture over Dumping Rules Welcomed," *Financial Times,* December 18, 1997.

Heaton, Robert E., "Specialty Steel and the Exciting Challenges of the 90s," speech at the Association of Iron and Steel Engineers, Pittsburgh, PA, April 9, 1990.

———, "Globalization of Specialty Steel," speech at the Steel Service Center Institute's First Specialty Metals Division Conference, Tampa, FL, March 2, 1991.

———, "Mill View of the Supplier Chain," speech at the Steel Service Center Institute Specialty Metals Division Conference, Tampa, FL, March 4, 1994.

———, "Imports, GATT, MSA and NAFTA: International Trade and Specialty Steel," speech at the Steel Service Center Institute Specialty Metals Division Conference, Tampa, FL, March 5, 1994.

Henderson, Simon, "EU Defends Dumping Measures," *Financial Times Business Reports* 17, no. 17 (August 15, 1997): 2.

Hindley, Brian and Patrick A. Messerlin, *Antidumping Industrial Policy: Legalized Protection in the WTO and What to Do About It* (Washington, DC: AEI Publication, 1997).

Hoag, David H., Excerpt from speech, "Steel's Growing Success in the Marketplace," *The Wall Street Transcript* 71, no. 1 (July 5, 1993).

Hogan, William T., S.J., *Global Steel in the 1990s: Growth or Decline* (Lexington, MA: Lexington Books, 1991).

———, *Capital Investment in Steel: A World Plan for the 1990s* (New York: Lexington Books, 1992).

———, *Minimills and Integrated Mills: A Comparison of Steelmaking in the United States* (Lexington, MA: Lexington Books, 1987).

Holman, Richard A., Clay L. Hoes and Robert J. Shenosky, "Roundtable Discussion: Steel Industry," *The Wall Street Transcript* 73, no. 11 (March 14, 1994).

Holschuh, Lenhard J., Excerpt from speech, "Meeting Challenges to Steel's Image," *The Wall Street Transcript* 71, no. 1 (July 5, 1993).

Howell, Thomas R., "Dumping: Still a Problem in International Trade," in *International Friction and Cooperation in High-Technology Development and Trade,* papers and proceedings of a conference held by the National Research Council's Board on Science, Technology, and Economic Policy, Charles W. Wessner, ed. (Washington, DC: National Academy Press, 1997).

Howell, Thomas R., Jeffrey D. Neuchterlein and Susan B. Hester, *Semiconductors in China: Defining American Interests* (Washington, DC: Semiconductor Industry Association and Dewey Ballantine, 1995).

Howell, Thomas R., William A. Noellert, Jesse G. Kreier and Allan Wm. Wolff, *Steel and the State: Government Intervention and Steel's Structural Crisis* (Boulder, CO: Westview Press, 1988).

Hudson, Ray and David Sadler, *The International Steel Industry: Restructuring, State Policies and Localities* (New York: Routledge, 1989).

Hufbauer, Gary and Shelton Erb, *Subsidies in International Trade* (Washington, DC: Institute for International Economics, 1984).

Hurabiell, Marie Louise, "Protectionism Versus Free Trade: Implementing the GATT Antidumping Agreement in the United States," *Journal of International Business Law* (Fall 1995): 567–613.

"Industry Still Has Anti-Import Tricks up Its Sleeve," *Journal of Commerce,* June 23, 1987.

Iverson, F. Kenneth, "CEO Interview: Nucor Corp.," *The Wall Street Transcript* 70, no. 10 (June 7, 1993).

Jackson, John, *The World Trading System: Law and Policy of International Economic Relations* (Cambridge: MIT Press, 1994).

———, *World Trade and the Law of GATT* (Charlottesville, VA: Mitchie, 1969).

Jacobson, John E., "Future Winners in World Steel: Minimills, Dofasco, China," *New Steel,* January 1994, 28.

———, "Stainless Steel: Promotional Efforts May Recast Industry," *American Metal Market,* August 18, 1993.

———, "Steelmaking Savvy in the 90s," *American Metal Market,* November 12, 1992.

Joelson, Mark, "In the New Europe, A Shift in the Gears of Trade," *Legal Times,* June 20, 1994, 20.

Johnson, Chalmers, *Japan: Who Governs? The Rise of the Developmental State* (New York: W.W. Norton, 1995).

Karr, Albert R., "U.S. to Take Over Five Pension Plans of Sharon Steel," *Wall Street Journal,* October 22, 1993, A6.

Katrak, Homi, "Multinational Monopolies and Commercial Policy," *Oxford Economic Papers,* vol. 29, 1977, pp. 283–291.

Katz, Lawrence F. and Lawrence H. Summers, "Industry Rents: Evidence and Implications," *Brookings Papers on Economic Activity: Microeconomics,* 1989.

Keatley, Robert, "International-World Economy: Steel Ruling Shows How Dumping Laws Ignore New Realities of World Trade," *Wall Street Journal,* August 13, 1993, A4.

Kelly, Nancy, "The New Antidumping Regulations from Commerce," *New Steel* 13, no. 6 (June 1997): 105.

Kierzkowski, Harry K., ed. *Monopolistic Competition in International Trade* (Oxford: Clarendon Press, 1984).

Krugman, Paul R., *Peddling Prosperity,* (New York: W.W. Norton Press, 1994).

Krugman, Paul R. and Maurice Obstfeld, *International Economics: Theory and Policy* (New York: HarperCollins, 1994).

Labor/Industry Coalition for International Trade, *Keeping Trade Free and Fair* (Washington, DC: LICIT, 1995).

Lantz, Robert H., "The Search for Consistency: Treatment of Nonmarket Economies in Transition Under United States Antidumping and Countervailing Duty Laws," *The American University Journal of International Law and Policy* (Spring 1995): 993–1073.

Laurent, Patrick, "Anti-dumping Policies in a Globalising World," remarks before the European Commission, Stockholm, Sweden, November 5, 1996.

Law and Economics Consulting Group, "Pleadings Before the U.S./International Trade Commission in the Matter of Certain Flat-rolled Carbon Steel Products: Pre-hearing Brief on Behalf of Petitioners," Washington, DC, 1993.

Lim, Benjamin Kang, "Socialism Right Choice for China–Premier Li Peng," *Reuters World Service,* July 29, 1996.

Lipstein, Robert A., review of *Anti-Dumping and Anti-Trust Issues in Free Trade Areas,* by Gabrielle Marceau, *The American Journal of International Law,* October 1995, 866–868.

Litan, Robert and Richard Boltuck, eds., *Down in the Dumps* (Washington, DC: Brookings Institution, 1991).

Long, William R., "Brazil's President Moving Swiftly to Stimulate, Transform Country—Latin America: Bold Steps of the Last Six Months Are Stirring Excitement and Uncertainty," *Los Angeles Times,* September 29, 1990, 16.

Maggs, John, "White House Abruptly Seeks Major Dump Law Changes," *Journal of Commerce,* June 24, 1994, 1A.

Marcus, Peter F. and Karlis M. Kirsis, Excerpt from speech, "Diversity to Decide Minimill Success," *American Metal Market,* June 27, 1993, 14.

Marley, Michael, "Minimills Cook up New Melt Mix Recipes," *American Metal Market,* February 24, 1994, 4Af.

"The Marshall Plan and Its Legacy," *Foreign Affairs* (May–June 1997): 159–185.

Mastel, Greg, *Trading with the Middle Kingdom* (Washington, DC: Economic Strategy Institute, 1995).

———, *American Trade Laws After the Uruguay Round* (Armonk, NY: M.E. Sharpe, 1996).

———, *The Rise of the Chinese Economy* (Armonk, NY: M.E. Sharpe, 1997).

Mastel, Greg and Rachel Hines, *Section 301: A Catalyst for Free Trade* (Washington, DC: Economic Strategy Institute, 1995).

Mastel, Greg and Andrew Szamosszegi, *U.S. Export Programs: Business Necessity or Corporate Welfare?* (Washington, DC: Economic Strategy Institute, 1995).

Mazzaferro, Aldo J., "Research Analyst Interview: Steel Stocks," *The Wall Street Transcript* 72, no. 1 (October 4, 1993).

McManus, George J., "Improved Performance by Both DC and AC Electrics," *Iron Age, New Steel,* February 1994, 28f.

Melvin, James R. and Robert D. Warne, "Monopoly and the Theory of International Trade," *Journal of International Economics* 3 (1973): 117–134.

Meszaros, James A., "Application of the United States' Law of Countervailing Duties to Nonmarket Imports: Effects of the Recent Foreign Reforms," *ILSA Journal of International and Comparative Law* (Winter 1996): 463–492.

"Midnight Oil Burns to Save EC's Steel; Plans by Germany, Italy Thrown Out," *American Metal Market,* November 11, 1993, 1.

Milbank, Dana, "Strategy Shift with Minimill: USX Corp. Unit Responds to Recent Threat Posed by Low-Cost, Lean Mills," *Wall Street Journal,* August 5, 1992, A3.

———, "British Steel's Great Pain Turns to Profit: Despite Woes, Other EC Steelmakers Resist Cutbacks," *Wall Street Journal,* December 28, 1993, A4.

Mintz, John, "Betting It All on 777; Making a New Jet on Which Its Future Rests, Boeing Remade Itself Too," *Washington Post,* March 26, 1995, H1.

Miranda, Jorge, "Should Antidumping Laws Be Dumped?" *Law and Policy in International Business* 28 (1996): 255–288.

Mirow, K.R. and H. Maurer, *Webs of Power: International Cartels and the World Economy* (Boston: Houghton Mifflin, 1982).

Moran, Theodore, "The Globalization of America's Defense Industries: Managing the Threat of Foreign Dependence," *International Security* 15 (Summer 1990): 57–100.

Morkre, Morris and Kenneth H. Kelly, *Effects of Unfair Imports on Domestic Industries: U.S. Dumping and Countervailing Duty Cases,* FTC Bureau of Economics Staff Report, 1994.

Moskow, Michael, "Steel Industry Now Poised to Compete," *American Metal Market,* June 8, 1992.

Munford, Christopher, "Newest Technologies Praised for an Ability to Better Operations," *American Metal Market,* October 7, 1993, 6.

Murray, Tracy, "Administration of the Antidumping Duty Law," in *Down in the Dumps,* Robert Litan and Richard Boltuck, eds. (Washington, DC: Brookings Institution, 1991).

Murray, Tracy and Donald J. Rousslang, "A Method for Estimating Injury Caused by Unfair Trade Practices," *International Review of Law and Economics* 9, 2 (December 1989): 149–164.

National Advisory Committee on Semiconductors, *Attaining Preeminence in Semiconductors* (Washington, DC: U.S. GPO, 1992).

National Research Council, *Conflict and Cooperation in National Competition for High-Technology Industry* (Washington, DC: National Academy Press, 1996).

*New York Times* (editorial), December 10, 1997, A34.

Norman, John T., "U.S. Study Ordered of Japanese Curb on Orange Imports," *Wall Street Journal,* May 26, 1988.

Norton, Erle and Martin Du Bois, "Foiled Competition: Don't Call It a Cartel, but World Aluminum Has Forged New Order," *Wall Street Journal,* June 9, 1994, 1.

Office of the U.S. Trade Representative, *1997 National Trade Estimate Report on Foreign Trade Barriers* (Washington, DC: GPO, 1997).

Organization for Economic Cooperation and Development, *Arrangement on Guidelines for Officially Supported Export Credits* (Washington, DC: OECD, 1982).

Paarlberg, Robert L., *Fixing Farm Trade: Policy Options for the United States* (Cambridge, MA: Ballinger, 1988).

Palmeter, N. David, "The Antidumping Law: A Legal and Administrative Nontariff Barrier," in *Down in the Dumps,* Robert Litan and Richard Boltuck, eds. (Washington, DC: The Brookings Institution, 1991).

Pare, Terence P., "The Big Threat to Big Steel's Future: Major Steel Producers Face Competition from Domestic Mills," *Fortune,* July 15, 1991, 106.

Porter, Michael, *The Competitive Advantage of Nations* (New York: Free Press, 1990).

Pendleton, Scott, "Florida Growers Say Time Is Ripe to Stem Mexican Tomato Flow," *Christian Science Monitor,* April 12, 1995, 3.

Preston, Richard, *American Steel: Hot Metal Men and the Resurrection of the Rust Belt* (New York: Prentice Hall, 1991).

Prestowitz, Clyde Jr., *Trading Places: How We Allowed Japan to Take the Lead* (New York: Basic Books, 1988).

Prestowitz, Clyde, Naotaka Matsukata and Andrew Szamosszegi, *Prospects for U.S.-Japanese Semiconductor Trade in the 21st Century* (Washington, DC: Economic Strategy Institute, 1996).

Prosser, Hon. Geoff (MP), "Minister Releases Review of Anti-dumping System," Press Release of the Minister Responsible for Customs, Australian Government, December 13, 1996.

Putnam, Hayes and Bartlett, Inc., *Economic Effects of Extending Steel VRAs* (New York: Putnam, Hayes and Bartlett, 1989).

Ragosta, John A., Brent Bartlett, Michael R. Geroe and John R. Magnus, *CVD Law from the General to the Specific: Some of the Significant Issues and Developments* (Washington, DC: Georgetown University, 1994).

Regan, Bob, "Beer Can War Not Bottled Up; Washington Spews Hints of New Action," *American Metal Market,* June 17, 1993, 1.

"The Remaking, Shaping and Treating of U.S. Steel," *Metal Producing* 33 (June 1985): 49–72.

*Report of the Tariff Commission,* vol. 1 (London: P.S. King, 1904).

"Rethinking the 1916 Antidumping Act," *Harvard Law Review* 110 (May 1997): 1555–1572.

Revenue Canada, *Protective Measures for Canadian Products Against Unfair Foreign Competition,* May 30, 1997, available at http://www.rc.gc.ca.

Robertson, Jack, Jennifer Baljko and Mark LaPedus, "Taiwan SRAM Makers Face Severe Dumping Penalties," *Electronic Buyer's News,* September 29, 1997.

Roth, Senator William and C. Fred Bergsten, "The Silver Lining of Asia's Economic Crisis," *Washington Post,* December 27, 1997, C8.

Rowen, Hobart, "Hills Optimistic About Japanese Cooperation; Paris OECD Talks to Begin Amid Uncertainty on Trade Issue," *Washington Post,* May 31, 1989, F4.

———, "'Gephardt II's' Meat Ax Approach to Trade," *Washington Post,* September 15, 1991, A10.

Sandholtz, Wayne, Michael Borrus and John Zysman, eds., *The Highest Stakes: The Economic Foundations of the Next Security System* (London and New York: Oxford University Press, 1992).

Saxenson, Annalee, *Regional Advantage: Culture and Competition in Silicon Valley and Rte. 28* (Cambridge, MA: Harvard University Press, 1994).

Scheuerman, William, *The Steel Crises: The Economics and Politics of a Declining Industry* (New York: Praeger, 1986).

Schlebusch, Walter, Excerpt from speech, "Steel's Success Requires Efficiency," *American Metal Market,* October 4, 1993, 21.

Schmitt, Bill, "Metals Industry Will Help Shape New Trade Law," *American Metal Market,* January 19, 1995, 12.

Schorsch, Louis L., Excerpt from speech, "Strategic Options to Consider," *American Metal Market,* August 25, 1993, 13.

Scolieri, Peter, "U.S. Steel Keeps Minimill in Mind; but Usher Says Target 'High End,'" *American Metal Market,* October 6, 1993, 6.

———, "New Mini-Mill Entrants May Mean a Hot Time in the Ol' SBQ Bar Market," *American Metal Market,* November 8, 1993, 15.

Scott, Allen J. and D.P. Angel, "The U.S. Semiconductor Industry: A Locational Analysis," *Environment and Planning* 19, no. 7 (July 1987): 875–912.

Simmons, Richard P., "Innovation in Steel: Perspectives," speech at Steel Service Center Institute's 81st Annual Meeting, Washington, DC, May 13–16, 1990.

Simon, Denis Fred, ed., *The Emerging Technological Trajectory of the Pacific Rim* (Armonk, NY: M.E. Sharpe, 1995).

Smith, Adam, *The Wealth of Nations* (New York: Random House, 1994).

Specialty Steel Industry of the United States and American Federation of Labor–Congress of Industrial Organizations, *Import Surges Again Imperil Specialty Steel Industry and Workers' Jobs: History Repeating Itself* (Washington, DC: Specialty Steel Industry of the United States and AFL-CIO, 1993).

Specialty Steel Industry of the United States, "Flood of Specialty Steel Imports Continues" (Washington, DC: Specialty Steel Industry of the United States, 1994).

———, *GATT Implementing Legislation Priorities* (Washington, DC: Specialty Steel Industry of the United States, 1994).

———, *The Case for Expansion of the National Steel Policy* (Washington, DC: Specialty Steel Industry of the United States, 1989).

Stewart, Terence P., *Antidumping and Countervailing Duty Laws: Their Use and Misuse* (University of Georgia and the Institute of Social Science, University of Tokyo: Dean Rusk Center for International and Comparative Law, 1997).

Stokes, Bruce, "A Parley without a Point?" *The National Journal* 21, no. 42 (October 18, 1997): 2098.

Szamosszegi, Andrew and Clyde V. Prestowitz Jr., *Korea's Economic Dilemma* (Washington, DC: Economic Strategy Institute, 1997).

Tae-soo, Sohn, "Seoul to Bring U.S. to WTO; Accuses U.S. of Failure to Drop Dumping Duties on Chips," *The Korea Herald,* July 19, 1997.

Tae-soo, Sohn, "Korea, U.S. to Resume Trade Battle; Head-on Clash Unlikely Between Seoul, Washington Soon," *The Korea Herald,* November 6, 1997.

Thurow, Lester, *Head to Head: The Coming Economic Battle Among Japan, Europe, and America* (New York: Morrow, 1992).

Tiffany, Paul A., *The Decline of American Steel: How Management, Labor, and Government Went Wrong* (New York: Oxford University Press, 1988).

Tilton, Mark, *Restrained Trade: Cartels in Japan's Basic Materials Industries* (Ithaca, NY: Cornell University Press, 1997).

Toot, Joseph F. Jr., Excerpt from executive speech at AISI 101st General Meeting, New York, *The Wall Street Transcript* 71, no. 1 (July 5, 1993).

Truell, Peter, "U.S. Won't Name More 'Unfair Traders,' Sparking Some Criticism from Congress," *Wall Street Journal,* April 30, 1990, A3.

Tyson, Laura D'Andrea, *Who's Bashing Whom? Trade Conflict in High-Technology Industries* (Washington, DC: Institute for International Economics, 1992).

U.S. Department of Commerce, "Commerce Department Initials Agreements Suspending the Antidumping Investigations on Carbon Steel Plate from the Russian Federation, Ukraine, and the People's Republic of China," press release, September 25, 1997.

U.S. International Trade Commission, *The Year in Trade, 1993, Operations of the Trade Agreements Program* (Washington, DC: ITC, 1993).

———, "Prehearing Brief in the Matter of *Color Negative Photographic Paper from Japan and the Netherlands* Before the U.S. International Trade Commission," Investigation #731–TA-661, 662, August 17, 1994.

———. *The Economic Effects of Antidumping and Countervailing Duty Orders and Suspension Agreements* (Washington, DC: ITC, 1995).

U.S. Tariff Commission, *Information Concerning Dumping and Unfair Foreign Competition in the United States and Canada's Anti-Dumping Law,* House Ways and Means Committee Print, 66th Congress, 1st Session, 1919.

U.S. Trade Promotion Coordinating Committee, *National Export Strategy* (Washington, DC: GPO, 1994), 108.

Usher, Thomas J., Excerpt from speech, "Remarks," *The Wall Street Transcript* 71, no. 1 (July 5, 1993).

Valentine, Paul W., "Panasonic to Repay $16 Million to Settle Lawsuit," *Washington Post,* January 19, 1989, F1.

Vayle, Eric, "Collision Course in Commercial Aircraft," Harvard Business School case study, 1991.

Vega-Canovas, Gustavo, "Disciplining Anti-dumping in North America: Is NAFTA Chapter Nineteen Serving Its Purpose?" *Arizona Journal of International and Comparative Law* (Spring 1997): 479–510.

Viani, Laura, "Underfunded Pensions Listed; Ravenswood, LTV Top List with Nine More," *American Metal Market,* November 24, 1993, 2.

Viner, Jacob, *Dumping: A Problem in International Trade* (Chicago: University of Chicago Press, 1923).

Wang, Sanghan, "U.S. Trade Laws Concerning Nonmarket Economies Revisited for Fairness and Consistency," *Emory International Law Review* (Winter 1996): 593–655.

Warshofsky, Fred, *The Chip War: The Battle for the World of Tomorrow* (New York: Charles Scribner, 1989).

Wessner, Charles W., ed., *International Friction and Cooperation in High-Technology Development and Trade,* papers and proceedings of a conference held by the National Research Council's Board on Science, Technology, and Economic Policy (Washington, DC: National Academy Press, 1997).

Winham, Gilbert R. and Heather A. Grant, "Antidumping and Countervailing Duties in Regional Trade Agreements: Canada–U.S. FTA, NAFTA and Beyond," *Minnesota Journal of Global Trade* (Spring 1994): 2–33.

Witten, Samuel M., "International Decision: European Community Case Note," *American Journal of International Law* (April 1993): 298–305.

World Bank, *Bureaucrats in Business: The Economics and Politics of Government Ownership* (Oxford: Oxford University Press, 1995).

———, *China: Foreign Trade Reform,* World Bank Country Study (Washington, DC: World Bank, 1994).

The World Trade Organization, *GATT Activities 1994–1995* (Geneva: WTO, 1996).

———, *Trade Policy Review: The United States* (Geneva: WTO, 1996).

WuDunn, Sheryl, "U.S. Companies Slip on Way to Winter Olympics," *New York Times,* March 20, 1995, A4.

Yamamura, Kozo and Jan Van Den Berg, "Japan's Rapid-Growth Policy on Trial: The Television Case," in *Law and Trade Issues of the Japanese Economy,* K. Yamamura and G. Saxonhouse, eds. (Seattle: University of Washington Press, 1986).

Yu, Seongjae, "Korea's High Technology Strategy," in *The Emerging Technological Trajectory of the Pacific Rim,* Denis Fred Simon, ed. (Armonk, NY: M.E. Sharpe, 1995).

# Index

# About the Author

Dr. Mastel is Director of Studies and Vice President at the Economic Strategy Institute (ESI). He joined ESI in October 1994. Previously, he worked in the U.S. Senate for eight years at various posts, including chief international trade adviser to the chairman of the Senate Finance Committee's International Trade Subcommittee. While working in the Senate, Dr. Mastel was an official congressional adviser to U.S. trade negotiators and worked on issues including extension of fast track trade negotiating authority, the Uruguay Round trade agreement, MFN status for China, Super 301, and the North American Free Trade Agreement.

Dr. Mastel holds a Ph.D. in International Economics and an MBA. He is a member of a number of economic and trade advisory boards. Dr. Mastel frequently writes and provides analysis for the *Washington Post,* the *Los Angeles Times,* the *Washington Times,* the *Wall Street Journal,* and many other publications. He has authored articles for numerous scholarly journals, including *Foreign Policy,* the *Washington Quarterly,* and the *International Economy,* and has appeared on CNN, CBS, NBC, ABC, the *NewsHour with Jim Lehrer,* and the *Nightly Business Report.* Dr. Mastel is also the author of *American Trade Laws after the Uruguay Round* (M.E. Sharpe, 1996) and *The Rise of the Chinese Economy* (M.E. Sharpe, 1997).